WAR AND PEACE IN TWENTIETH-CENTURY BRITAIN

Studies in Memory of Paul Addison

EDITED BY ANTOINE CAPET

STONE TOWER PRESS

War and Peace in Twentieth-Century Britain:
Studies in Memory of Paul Addison

Stone Tower Press
7 Ellen Rd.
Middletown, RI 02842
stonetowerpress.com

Paperback ISBN: 979-8-9852553-6-2

Formatting and cover design by Amy Cole, JPL Design Solutions

The cover image: A Royal Observer Corps spotter scans the skies of London. Battle of Britain air observer keeping watch over London. Alamy image ER405A

These articles first appeared in *Cercles, An Interdisciplinary Journal of English Studies*, No. 37, 2020 and *Finest Hour*. They are presented here with permission of the contributors and sources from which they are derived.

Printed in the United States of America

CONTENTS

INTRODUCTION

Antoine Capet 1

MEMORIALS AND ESSAYS

1 Paul Addison—A Tribute
Gordon Brown 5

2 Paul Addison, 1943–2020: What Matters Is the Truth
Richard M. Langworth 9

3 Winston Churchill and the Drink Question
Roland Quinault 13

4 Baldwin's Bulldog: Churchill's 1925 Fight Against Tariffs
David Freeman 33

5 Citizens and Statesmen in Churchill's *Thoughts and Adventures*
James W. Muller 53

6 The People's Convention, 1940–1941: A Soviet Stalking Horse?
Richard Overy 69

7 Per ABCA ad Attlee? The Origins and Early Reception of Paul Addison's *The Road to 1945*
Richard Toye 99

8 Paul Addison: War, Peace and Social Change
John Campbell 135

9 The Road From 1945
Kenneth O. Morgan 145

10 Paul Addison: Publications 1971–2020
Antoine Capet 169

SELECTED BOOK REVIEWS BY PAUL ADDISON

1 *In Command of History: Churchill Fighting and Writing the Second World War*
David Reynolds 193

2 *The Good Fight Battle of Britain Propaganda and the Few*
Garry Campion 201

3 *Churchill: Le Dictionnaire*
Antoine Capet 207

4 *The End is Nigh: British Politics, Power, and the Road to the Second World War*
Robert Crowcroft 213

5 *Churchill, The Life: An Authorised Pictorial Biography*
Max Arthur 219

NOTES ON CONTRIBUTORS 221

INTRODUCTION

ANTOINE CAPET
Université de Rouen

A collection of essays in memory of a deceased colleague and friend (as he was to all the contributors to this volume) is a very peculiar genre in that it owes its existence to his death—a sad event, of course—but at the same time revives fond memories of past encounters in which intensely serious academic sessions were often preceded or followed by more down-to-earth activities, with lively conversation on less arduous topics often round a table of *bon viveurs*—and no doubt Paul was one.

The accepted French word for such a collection is (or was, since the practice seems to be declining) *Mélanges ('Mélanges offerts à X…')*: technically, an inappropriate word if one wants to pay tribute to a respected colleague, with its overtones of 'mixed bag' or 'hotchpotch'. When preparing the present volume, however, I came to realise how fitting it was as a description of the different angles from which it was possible to evoke the interests and intellectual evolution of the person, and above all how Paul had provided inspiration, not for unquestioning imitation, but for further lines of research in the considerable span of his publications, extending from 1971 to 2020—exactly fifty years.

I recalled in fact the long title of a book of *Mélanges offerts à Churchill*, as detailed as *Winston Spencer Churchill: Servant of Crown and Commonwealth: A Tribute by Various Hands presented to him on his Eightieth Birthday.*[1] 'Some "Various Hands"!', Churchill must have thought, since they included no less than a Prince, four Viscounts, four Knights, three former, current or future Prime Ministers, a Dame of the British Empire, an Admiral, the Director of the Tate Gallery and the former President of the British Academy (with only one University Professor).

We cannot quite match this—though we have a Baron and a former Prime Minister: we are one up however on the diversity of nationalities and generations among the contributors. What unites them, beyond their durably pleasant experience of friendly contacts with Paul Addison, is their interest in Churchill and British political history, and especially the strong impression which both *The Road to 1945* and *Churchill on the Home Front* made on them, above all his other fine works, which are all listed at the end of this collection. If I may be allowed an intrusion into my personal experience, I will never forget the revelation—there is no other word—brought about by Paul's image in *The Road to 1945* of Churchill assimilated to an island surrounded by an irresistibly mounting tide, that of claims for social reform, when I was preparing my *Thèse d'État* on 'Les classes dirigeantes britanniques et la réforme sociale, 1931-1951' (long ago—it was submitted in 1987). No doubt all the contributors—who immediately agreed to join the undertaking—would have similar personal memories to cite (and some allude to them, in fact).

Why should this tribute appear in a journal published by a team from the University of Rouen, it may be asked? The answer is that Paul Addison was a regular speaker, chairman or attendee to the series of conferences on Twentieth-Century British History which it regularly organised in the late 20th and early 21st centuries. The most memorable is probably the Annual Conference of the Social History Society, which was hosted by the University in January 2004. Two of the present contributors, Lord Morgan and Roland Quinault, were present, as well as the late John Ramsden. Ben Pimlott was on the list of speakers—but we learnt at the last minute that he would not come, since he was suddenly affected by the terminal illness which was to take him away only a few weeks later. No doubt these two deceased colleagues would have enthusiastically contributed to the present collection if the Old Man, as Churchill sometimes called his Creator, had decided otherwise.

Rather than ending on this sad note, however, we must rejoice that so many of Paul's colleagues and friends have survived to honour his memory.

ENDNOTES

1 Edited by Sir James Marchant K.B.E. London: Cassell, 1954.

MEMORIALS AND ESSAYS

CHAPTER 1

PAUL ADDISON—A TRIBUTE

GORDON BROWN

Paul Addison, who died in January 2020 after a long illness bravely endured, was not only one of the finest historians of his generation, but a humanitarian whose great personal humility was matched by a personal warmth, an endearing geniality and an unimpeachable decency that made him admired and respected by all who knew him. I am one of many who feel privileged to have benefited from his teaching and his wisdom, and to have been able to count him as a friend.

His best-known works—*The Road to 1945* (1975), *Churchill on the Home Front* (1992) and *Churchill: The Unexpected Hero* (2005)—are the result of more than fifty years of historical research since he graduated from Oxford in 1964, and all will stand the test of time. His last book, *The Spirit of the Blitz*, co-edited with Professor Jeremy Crang, published posthumously, and which recounts the inside story of Mass Information, the unit that secretly monitored the state of popular morale during the Second World War, will reinforce his already considerable reputation.

Paul's other great attribute—his personal kindness—will also never be forgotten. When I visited him a few days before he died, he was honest about how much weaker he was than he had wanted his friends to know, and he was realistic—not angry or bitter—about the fate that had befallen him. Indeed, he had lost none of his interest in the world around him, debating that very day whether he should do an interview sought by the former Labour leader Ed Miliband for his *Reasons to be Cheerful* podcast about the relevance of 1945 to the present day. 'Now my batteries are flat and I do not expect to keep body and soul together for much longer', he said in his last email to me. But moving on to write of the good that many people whom he knew were doing, he ended with the words, 'there is hope'.

I first came across Paul more than 50 years ago. I had just completed several weeks in hospital and then in recuperation after a sports injury had damaged my eyesight; so I arrived at Edinburgh University months after term had started and I must have appeared quite lost when I turned up at his history tutorial. Paul had just started as a lecturer and was, I suspect, almost as nervous as me; but quickly he communicated a love of history and a touching concern for all his students that made him popular among all who were taught by him. Like his own tutor, A.J.P. Taylor, Paul wanted history to reach a large popular audience—and not because it had been dumbed down, but through the exciting insights that came from good research and through the brilliance of its exposition. And Paul used to the full his gift for conveying his thoughts in cogent prose and with judgements that were always unprejudiced and balanced. So, two years later, he was the lecturer to go to when I was editor of the University newspaper, *Student*, and was looking for a historian who was also in touch with the contemporary world to review the 1960s in a special edition to commemorate the end of the decade.

Paul was always ready to give frank advice, but was never anything other than fair. Having marked down an essay in which I had too rigidly adhered to the literal text of the question, he gave me advice which I never forgot: to use questions as a springboard for your ideas and arguments, and never allow them to be a straightjacket that imprisoned you. I took his advice again in 2009. Just after the financial crisis broke, I received a letter from Paul, who advised me to pay for the recovery plan by putting up the top rate of tax. Mindful, from his study of the Second World War, of the importance of shared sacrifice, he argued we should act quickly to avoid the accusation that the least well off would suffer disproportionately from the unemployment and hardship that the crisis would bring.

Paul never talked about his family background, until the moment he handed me the family history that he had completed a few months before his death. In it he painstakingly tracked his mother Pauline's family back centuries, but also revealed the financial and other pressures she faced as she brought Paul up. From that experience, however, flowed Paul's well-known compassion for others and his commendable sensitivity to the feelings of the people he met, all of which was enhanced by his wonderful marriage to Rosy, who shared his interests in history, art and culture, and so lovingly cared for him as his cancer spread

A few years ago, just before Sir Martin Gilbert suffered the stroke from which he never recovered, Paul and Rosy, Martin and his wife Esther and Sarah and I enjoyed a wonderful few hours, at my home in Fife on what was a beautiful warm summer evening; unusual because the Scottish weather was so good that we were able to sit outside until late in the evening. That night I learnt again at the feet of Paul and Martin as they dissected our country's history: a discussion I remember so clearly that it makes me even more aware of the great loss to us all, now that their voices are silent. At that time, Martin was embarking on an additional project he never completed—to write the story of my time in government—but that night I became more aware of the importance of history and good historical research. For while history never repeats itself, we can learn enough from it to avoid many of the mistakes made in the past. While Paul was too modest to say so, his work provided memorable insights that achieved that. And by us learning of what went right as well as what went wrong, we can—as Paul said in that last letter to me—genuinely say that 'there is hope'.

CHAPTER 2

PAUL ADDISON, 1943–2020: WHAT MATTERS IS THE TRUTH[1]

RICHARD M. LANGWORTH
Churchill Project, Hillsdale College

29 OCTOBER 1994

A fond and funny memory of Paul Addison is one which few know about. It came during a Washington symposium on 'Churchill as Peacemaker', later published as an outstanding book. During a break, we walked over to the White House, which Paul wanted to see. We stood at the iron fence, gazing at the seat of power across the lawn. As we chatted, Paul remarked on how close we were to the building itself. 'The security seems pretty light', he said. 'It's not hard to visualise some stray lunatic standing here and spraying the walls with bullets'. That same afternoon, a fellow named Francisco Duran did exactly that with a semi-automatic rifle. Paul Addison heard the news white-faced. We all jibed him that microphones were planted on the fence. And now the Secret Service had arrived and was asking to interview him... Paul was not amused!

I have lost count of how often I have dined out on that one. And even more on the Addison maxim: 'I have always thought that, paradoxically, it diminishes Churchill to treat him as superhuman'. Paul was a scrupulous historian. He realised, above all, that what matters is the truth. Tell the truth about your subject, he would say. If your subject is worthy, it needs no enhancement. Primarily, his wife Rosy remembers, he aimed 'to make making history accessible, understandable and comprehensible to his fellow human beings'.

A CORPUS OF EXCELLENCE

We met in mid-1994, when my wife Barbara and I hosted our seventh Churchill Tour. Our second in Scotland, it was a notable adventure, taking us all the way to Scapa Flow in the Orkneys. There we saw, on full-color sonar, the shape of HMS *Royal Oak* on the bottom—torpedoed by *U-47* in 1939. It was an eerie image, like that of USS *Arizona* at Pearl Harbor. Our tour began with a vast exhibit of Churchill in political cartoons, organised for us at Edinburgh University by Paul, and David Stafford, his longtime colleague. From then on, I paid attention, and read every book of theirs I could lay my hands on.

Paul Addison wrote and edited ten Churchill works, listed at the end of this collection. His classic, still a 'standard work', was *Churchill on the Home Front* (1992). Atypically for most Churchill writers then, Paul took the approach of studying the domestic side of Churchill's politics. Until this book, the prevailing impression was that Churchill was bored with domestic issues. Methodically Paul showed how completely wrong that was, weighing the evidence with grace and understanding.

'HIGH SENSE OF THE BRITISH MOMENT'

Paul understood the statesman's greatness, warts and all. 'Which warts', William Buckley said, 'do not deface Churchill because of the nobility of his cause, and his high sense of the British moment'. Nothing will ever surpass 1940—but Churchill accomplished much else. Paul limned the peaks, and the valleys. Churchill's faults like his virtues were on a grand scale, he would say. But there is no doubt that the latter heavily outweighed the former.

Here is an example: Churchill's youthful fling with eugenics, and the idea of sterilising the mentally incompetent. There was quite an uproar about this recently when it was 'discovered'. (Read: someone finally found it in the public records.) Churchill's Eugenics was a fling because he abandoned it quickly, along with most intelligent people. But some readers were outraged. 'I can never think good things of him again', one said. 'No truly educated intelligent person could adopt such views'. (Well... a lot of educated intelligent persons happily adopted Nazism and Bolshevism.) Dr. Addison showed us the balanced way to look at this issue. Churchill's intentions were benign, he wrote, 'but he was blundering into sensitive areas of civil liberty'. Then he drew a deeper lesson no one else had contemplated:

Yet it is rare to discover reflections of a politician on the nature of man. Churchill's belief in the innate virtue of the great majority of human beings was part and parcel of an optimism he often expressed before the First World War.

This was perceptive, broadminded and fair. And Paul also explained why Churchill was unique. Few politicians reflect on 'the nature of man'. Fewer still believe 'in the innate virtue of human beings'. Such understanding is a rare thing among writers of history.

HIS WORK ABIDES

Another Addison triumph was, conversely, one of his shortest: his Churchill entry for the *Oxford Dictionary of National Biography.* Writing for the *DNB* is not easy. One must be deft, economical, balanced and accurate. Paul's Churchill piece is a model of incisive wisdom. It appears in book form in the Oxford VIP series. Everyone should read it: all that matters about Winston Churchill in only 138 pages. And here is another Addison classic: *Churchill: The Unexpected Hero.* The same clear exposition, expanded to 320 pages. Many reviewers call it the best 'brief life' of Churchill ever published.

In August 2018, Paul Addison was diagnosed with lung cancer. He fought it for eighteen months. Last June, we had planned a lunch with Paul and Rosy and a mutual friend, the historian Gordon Barclay, when the Hillsdale College Cruise stopped in Edinburgh. Alas, gales in the Firth of Forth prevented our anchoring. By then Paul had told me of his situation. Around the New Year I asked his friend David Stafford for news. It was not good. On January 21st he left us.

Our grief and loss are deeply felt. Paul was a gentleman scholar: a man of strong convictions, who never let them interfere with his historical judgment. Hagiography is fatal. Truth matters. That was his cardinal lesson. Above all, he left a corpus of excellence from which young people will always learn things worth knowing. His work abides, and as Churchill said, a man never dies as long as he is remembered. All who love history will forever remember Paul Addison.

ENDNOTES

1 First published on the Churchill Project, Hillsdale College site on 26 January 2020.

CHAPTER 3

WINSTON CHURCHILL AND THE DRINK QUESTION

ROLAND QUINAULT
University of London

Paul Addison is best remembered for his studies of Britain in the era of the Second World War, when Churchill dominated the political agenda as the wartime Prime Minister. However, as Paul pointed out, the focus on Churchill's war leadership led to a relative neglect of his domestic policy. Paul rectified that bias with his 1992 book, *Churchill on the Home Front 1900–1955*, which was an insightful and wide-ranging survey. It did not, however, examine all the details of Churchill's domestic policies due to the large amount of relevant material. In particular, Churchill's views on the drink question—the licensing, taxation and regulation of intoxicating liquor—were largely neglected save for a brief reference to his attitude to the 1908 Licensing Bill [*Churchill on the Home Front:* 83–84]. Yet the drink question was an important and controversial political issue during the first half of Churchill's life and one on which he had decided views.

Churchill's interest in the drink question has been obscured by his well-publicised fondness for alcoholic drinks [STELZER, *Dinner with Churchill, passim*]. For much of his adult life, he drank champagne and brandy both at lunch and dinner. He also sipped whisky, diluted with soda, through the day—a habit he acquired while campaigning on the North-West Frontier in the mid 1890s [CHURCHILL, *My Early Life* (1943 Reissue): 140–142]. The high consumption of wine and spirits by Churchill and his household was made possible by generous credit from various wine merchants, which he was slow to repay [LOUGH, *No More Champagne: Churchill and His Money* (2015)]. In the 1930s his spending on alcohol was more than his salary as an MP. In 1935 he refused Lord Rothermere's offer of £2,000 if he turned teetotal for the next year, on the grounds that life would not be worth living. He did, however, accept Rothermere's other offer of £600 if he abstained from brandy and spirits [Winston to Clementine, 30 December 1935, *Speaking for Themselves*: 404–405; CLARKE, *Mr Churchill's Profession:* 135–137].

Churchill's capacity for alcohol has led one eminent geneticist to suggest that he possessed an exceptional gene that protected him from the harmful effects of alcohol [*The Times*, 19 February 1992: 1]. That might explain why Churchill, when Prime Minister during the Second World War, was never apparently the worse for drink [WHEELER-BENNETT: 182–183]. It is more likely, however, that his intake of alcohol was diluted with water and somewhat less than he appeared to drink [JAMES (1973): 389]. In 1952, at a dinner on the yacht of the U.S. President, Churchill declared that he had drunk, on average, a quart of wine or spirits every day for sixty years. He then asked his scientific advisor, Lord Cherwell—a teetotaller—to calculate the level to which all that alcohol would have reached in the room where they were dining. He was disappointed to learn that it would only have reached up to their knees.[1]

Despite Churchill's reputation, in later life, as a heavy drinker, he had been brought up to have the utmost contempt for people who got drunk. His paternal family supported the growing temperance movement in the later Victorian period. Winston's grandfather, the seventh Duke of Marlborough, was a member of the Oxford branch of the Church of England Temperance Society [*Jackson's Oxford Journal*, 13 November 1880]. In 1878 the duke, then Lord Lieutenant of Ireland, supported the Irish Sunday Closing Bill, which was passed despite much opposition [*The Times*, 5 February 1878]. His wife, Frances, regarded intemperance as the curse of England [Frances, Duchess of Marlborough to Winston Churchill, 27 February 1890. *The Churchill Documents* 1: 200]. She had personal experience in that regard for the drunken behaviour of her younger son, Randolph, while an undergraduate at Oxford, was criticised by the United Kingdom Alliance, which campaigned for the suppression of the liquor trade [Harrison, *Drink and the Victorians,* citing *Alliance News*, 2 April 1870: 204]. Yet eight years later, Randolph, by then the Conservative MP for Woodstock, chaired a local meeting of the Alliance [Shiman, *Crusade Against Drink in Victorian England*, citing *Alliance News*, 9 February 1878: 191].

As Conservatives, however, the Churchill family supported a party that had close links with the producers and distributors of alcohol. They opposed the Liberal government's 1872 Licensing Act, which imposed limited restrictions on public houses. They then helped to defeat the Liberal government at the 1874 general election, which Gladstone attributed to 'a torrent of gin and beer' [See Clarke, *Lancashire and the New Liberalism* and Blewett, *The Peers, the Parties and the People*].

At the 1880 general election, Lord Randolph opposed temperance legislation on the grounds that it would unfairly discriminate against workingmen and could not, on its own, make people sober [*Jackson's Oxford Journal*, 20 & 27 March 1880]. He was aware, however, of the growing political weight of the temperance movement and in 1883 he called on the Conservatives to adopt temperance measures as part of a social reform agenda [Churchill, *Lord Randolph Churchill*: 202]. In 1884 he praised the temperance movement as the most important popular reform effort since the days of Wesley, although he wanted to avoid a 'perhaps unwarranted' attack on the drink interest [Randolph Churchill to H.L. Pratt, 7 February 1884, RCHL II/295]. He remained opposed to further burdens and restrictions on publicans and their working-class customers.

Lord Randolph's strong opposition to Irish Home Rule increased his concern with the drink issue. After the 1886 general election, the

Conservatives depended for their parliamentary majority on the Liberal-Unionists, many of whom supported licensing reform. It was claimed that the Liberal-Unionist temperance vote was a critical factor in by-elections [Hamer, *The Politics of Electoral Pressure:* 241–243 & 256–259]. Consequently Randolph sought a compromise settlement of the drink question in order to keep the Liberal-Unionists attached to their alliance with the Conservatives. In 1886, as Chancellor of the Exchequer in Lord Salisbury's second ministry, Randolph supported the principle of Local Option—allowing popularly elected local authorities to decide licensing policy [Randolph Churchill's speech at Dartford. *The Times*, 4 October 1886].

Although Randolph resigned from Salisbury's government at the end of 1886, he continued to urge the need for licensing reform. He supported the 1888 County Councils Bill on the grounds that it provided licensed victuallers with compensation if their licences were removed, while it established the principle of Local Option [Randolph Churchill's speech at Birmingham. *The Times*, 10 April 1888]. He also claimed that alcohol was the parent of more than half the crime and two-thirds of the poverty, misery and disease in the nation [Randolph Churchill's speech at Paddington. *The Times*, 18 November 1888]. His parliamentary lieutenant, Louis Jennings, hoped that Randolph would demolish the old 'alliance between Toryism and the gin palace' [Jennings to Churchill, 18 November 1888, RCHL 1/23/2983]. James Whyte, of the United Kingdom Alliance, urged Randolph to lead the Tory temperance movement [Whyte to Churchill, 27 November 1888, RCHL 1/23/2996]. He replied that the drink question was inseparable from the housing question—as long as much of the population lived in miserable conditions then 'the warmth and false cheerfulness of the public house will be largely sought after' [Churchill to Whyte, 29 November 1888, RCHL 1/23/2997].

In a speech at Walsall, in 1889, Randolph criticised the influence of the large brewers, who controlled nine out of ten of the public houses and had a political organisation ready for action at any moment—'almost like a Prussian army' [*The Times*, 30 July 1889]. His comments led Conservatives at Rotherhithe—a working class constituency—to decline Randolph's offer to speak there on the grounds that they could not afford to offend the brewers and publicans [C.E. Hamilton to Churchill, 6 August 1889, RCHL 1/24/3239]. Nevertheless he believed that the time was ripe for a non-partisan attempt to solve the licensing question [Churchill to Wilfrid Lawson, 7 December 1889, RCHL 1/25/3345].

In 1890 Randolph introduced his own private member's Licensing Bill, in a speech that his son later described as his last great speech in the House of Commons [*Lord Randolph Churchill*: 775]. Randolph claimed that his Bill was 'the first attempt at a final and comprehensive licensing law since the days of Mr Bruce in 1872'. The Bill proposed to give elected local authorities control over licensing and even the power to prohibit the sale of alcohol in certain cases. It also provided for compensation to publicans for the withdrawal of a licence in certain cases [*Parliamentary Debates* (April 1890); Randolph Churchill to Harcourt, 24 January 1890 (Bodleian Library)]. Wilfrid Lawson, of the UK Alliance, largely welcomed Randolph's Bill but not the proposal for compensation. Randolph hoped that the Bill would receive cross-party support but Salisbury's Conservative Government declined to support it. Consequently Randolph withdrew the Bill although he continued to harbour hopes for its re-introduction until his death in 1895.

Randolph's Licensing Bill aroused the interest of his son, Winston, who was then a sixteen year-old schoolboy at Harrow. He wrote to his father:

> When does your Bill come on again? It will be sure to go up for a second reading. Everybody down here is excited about it one way or another. 'I zay zir, yor feyther goin to shut up the Pubs, tip us a drink sir while we can get it' and on the other hand I hear the respectable tradesmen say that they hope it will pass especially those who live near the Public Houses. [Winston to Lord Randolph, ?1 June 1890. *The Churchill Documents* 1: 203]

When Winston embarked on his own political career he followed his father's example with respect to the drink question. In his first election campaign, as a Tory candidate at Oldham, in 1899, he favoured voluntary temperance but opposed 'compulsory abstinence' and the removal of licences without full and fair compensation [Election address, 26 June 1899. *Complete Speeches* I: 36]. After his election to Parliament, in 1900, Winston pointed out that since the Tories now depended on the working classes for their electoral predominance, they needed to resolve social problems, including the liquor question [Birmingham, 6 June 1901. *Complete Speeches* I: 86]. In 1903 Winston observed that for more than fifty years the temperance question had made little progress because it has been mixed up with party politics. He pointed out that although nine out of ten Conservative MPs had ties with the liquor interest, his father had been the first to shape and embody in a bill the principle of the local veto. He then declared: 'I share to the full the sentiments and views which my father held and worked for in connection with temperance' [Kidlington, 2 June 1903. *Complete Speeches* I: 183].

Winston's conversion to Liberalism, in 1904, was facilitated by what were called his 'advanced views' on temperance [W. Finnemore to Herbert Gladstone, 25 January 1904. *The Churchill Documents* 3: 307–308]. When he was adopted as the Liberal candidate for North-West Manchester he declared:

> I have long felt a great desire to have a freer hand in regard to the traffic in strong drink than is permitted to a Conservative member. The liquor interest is highly organized . . . almost as highly as the German army ... and in many constituencies its influence on an election is decisive. [Manchester, 29 April 1904. *Complete Speeches* I: 281]

Winston's description of the drink interest as organised like the German army repeated an analogy that his father had used at Walsall in 1889.

Churchill was strongly opposed to the Conservative Government's 1904 Licensing Bill. That measure was a response to pressure from the licensed trade, which was alarmed by recent developments: a fall in beer consumption, higher excise duty and a sharp increase in the number of licensing applications that were rejected. The 1904 Bill provided compensation, from a tax on licences, for the withdrawal of a licence if it was made on grounds of public policy rather than misconduct. It also ruled that magistrates could only suppress licences if sufficient compensation was available [Nicholls, *The Politics of Alcohol:* 146–147]. Winston was not opposed to reasonable compensation being paid to the publican providing there was no charge upon public funds [Churchill to Samuel Lamb, 26 March 1904. *The Churchill Documents* 3: 324]. But he opposed compensation for the brewers—as his father had in 1889. Winston also pointed out that a reduction in public houses would not necessarily lead to a reduction in consumption [*Parliamentary Debates* (27 June, 1904)]. When the committee stage of the Licensing Bill was limited to just six days, Winston complained that the drink lobby 'pulled the coat tails of Ministers'. He alleged that the Prime Minister, Arthur Balfour, was returned to Parliament by the votes of liquor sellers in his Manchester constituency [*Parliamentary Debates* (1904)].

In the autumn of 1904 Churchill denounced the Licensing Bill in speeches at Caernarfon, where he spoke with Lloyd George, and at Newcastle, where he shared the platform with Sir Wilfrid Lawson of the UK Alliance [*The Times*, 19 October & 6 December 1904]. At a Manchester meeting he denounced the Licensing Act and claimed that only 'a real movement toward true temperance' would alleviate the misery of the working classes [Churchill's speech at Cheetham Town Hall. *The Times*, 29 November 1904: 10]. He was amazed that his Tory opponent, Joynson-Hicks—a temperance advocate and total abstainer—supported a measure that was opposed by men such as the Archbishop of Canterbury, Randall Davidson, and by all sections of temperance opinion [Churchill to the Editor of the *Manchester Guardian*, 9 December 1904. *The Churchill Documents* 3: 382]. During the 1906 general election campaign, Churchill ridiculed Joynson-Hicks as a temperance advocate who was soliciting the vote of every brewer and publican in the constituency [Manchester, 11 January 1906. *Complete Speeches* I: 551]. However

Winston's election success was part of the general Liberal landslide and primarily a victory for Free Trade, rather than temperance.

Although Winston joined the new Liberal government, as Under-Secretary of State for the Colonies, he still linked his support for temperance to the example of his Tory father:

> The cause of temperance is one of the most vital elements in the work of social regeneration ... I have always felt bound to take a sentimental interest in the cause, for I remember that my father, Lord Randolph Churchill, spoke without hesitation or qualification in favour of the course which you all have at heart ... I remember that at a great meeting in Scotland he said—it is strong language to use—'This damnable traffic is the cause of half the crime in Scotland'. He described it as a 'devilish and destructive traffic'. I feel a hereditary interest, a continuity, in much of the work which he did. [Speech to the United Temperance Police Court Mission Bazaar, Manchester, 22 October 1906. *Complete Speeches* I: 686]

In his life of his father, published in 1906, Winston included a long extract from Randolph's Walsall speech and brief details of his 1890 Licensing Bill. He observed, however, that licensing reform was one of a number of issues that trenched 'too closely upon current politics to be conveniently examined here' [*Lord Randolph Churchill*: 775].

Winston's engagement with the licensing question peaked in 1908 for legislative and electoral reasons. The Liberal Government reintroduced a Licensing Bill, deferred from the previous year, as its priority for the parliamentary session. The Bill provided for a graduated reduction in the number of public houses, by about one third, over a period of fourteen years, during which compensation, provided by a levy on the trade, was to be paid for the licences that were extinguished. At the end of that period compensation would cease and local communities would decide future licensing policy. Opponents of the Licensing Bill claimed that it endangered the rights of all property owners and undermined the savings of those who had invested in brewery shares, including widows and orphans.

In a speech at the Peckham by-election, in March 1908, Churchill rejected the notion that the State had no right to deal with the drink traffic. His declaration that the moral forces of the country were strong enough to bear down 'beer-fomented froth and rhetoric' occasioned loud cheers from the audience. He was proud that the government was prepared to deal with the issue even though it was possibly politically disastrous [Peckham, 17 March 1908. *Complete Speeches* I: 909–910]. That proved to be the case at Peckham, where the licensed trade mounted a strong opposition to the Bill, assisted by the Women's Freedom League, which was angered by the failure of the Liberal government to introduce female suffrage [Dundee, 8 May 1908. *Complete Speeches* I: 1047]. The Tory candidate there was returned by a large majority of votes but Churchill declared that 'the noble cause of temperance' was well worth losing by-elections for [Liverpool, 2 April 1908. *Complete Speeches* I: 929].

In April 1908 Asquith became Prime Minister and promoted Churchill to the Cabinet, as President of the Board of Trade. Consequently he had to resign his seat and fight a by-election at North-West Manchester. In his election address, he described the current Licensing Bill as 'a great forward heave in the temperance movement', which he hoped would attract support from many Anglicans [12 April 1908. *The Times*, 13 April 1908]. He also championed Free Trade but declared that he was against Free Trade in liquor [Manchester, 21 April 1908. *Complete Speeches* I: 996]. Churchill was again opposed by Joynson-Hicks, who denounced the Licensing Bill as 'pure Socialism', which could only be passed by muzzling the House of Lords [W. Joynson-Hicks's election address, 13 April 1908. *The Churchill Documents* 4: 775–776]. Countess Markievicz, who later achieved fame as a Sinn Fein supporter and the first woman elected to the House of Commons, drove a coach round North-West Manchester on behalf of the Barmaids' Political Defence League. The barmaids were angered by a clause in the Licensing Bill that barred women from working in pubs [TAYLOR, *Jix*: 89]. At the poll, Joynson-Hicks was returned with a majority of 429 votes. The main reasons for Churchill's defeat were a trade recession and the defection of the Irish vote but the opposition of the drink interest was also a significant factor. Nevertheless Churchill hoped that the Licensing Bill would be enacted and that the political power of the liquor trade would be reduced [Churchill to Sir Edward Donner, 29 April 1908. *The Churchill Documents* 4: 788].

Immediately after his defeat, Churchill accepted an invitation to stand for a vacated seat in the double member constituency of Dundee. The city, a seaport and the centre of jute manufacturing, had a reputation for both drunkenness and temperance. Dundee had many breweries and hundreds of licensed houses. In Scotland generally, the consumption of spirits and the number of licensed premises had declined somewhat from Victorian levels but there had been an increase in convictions for drunkenness and in alcohol-related deaths [Smout, Table 6: Drink in Scotland 1830–1939: 135]. Winston's defence of the Liberal Licensing Bill, during his Dundee election campaign, attracted great cheers [Kinnaird Hall, 4 May 1908. *Complete Speeches* I: 1031]. But while he favoured local option, he opposed a ban on alcohol sales:

> I hesitate to adopt the policy of the prohibitionists. When I am asked that Parliament should now pass a bill saying that not a drop of liquor shall be manufactured or sold I say you may get that when you get to heaven, but I am only thinking of being elected to the House of Commons. [Dundee, 2 May 1908. *Complete Speeches* I: 1024]

That was a riposte to the prohibitionist candidate, Edwin Scrymgeour. He was a Dundee councillor, who had founded the Scottish Prohibition Party in 1901. Scrymgeour had links with the Scottish Labour movement, which was overwhelmingly 'dry'. At the poll Scrymgeour gained only a few hundred votes and Churchill was elected with a large majority. He described his election as a victory for Free Trade, Temperance and Ireland [Dundee, 9 May 1908. *Complete Speeches* I: 1042]. Unlike at Manchester, he was supported by most of the 2,000 or so Roman Catholics of Irish extraction [*Dundee Catholic Herald*, 9 May 1908]. He also benefited from an unofficial alliance with the Labour candidate for the other seat.

In the summer of 1908 Churchill actively campaigned for the Licensing Bill. In a speech in South Wales, where Methodist teetotalism was strong, he declared that the Licensing Bill was 'the sort of thing that makes Liberalism immortal'. He admitted that there were various ways to secure temperance, including shorter hours of labour, healthy working conditions and greater opportunities for leisure and education, but he claimed that the best way was by diminishing temptation. He cited his father's observation that an Act of Parliament could give the people the power to make themselves sober and declared that was the central principle of the Licensing Bill [Pontypool, 9 July 1908. *Complete Speeches* I: 1068–1069].

Winston also spoke at a Hyde Park rally in support of the Licensing Bill, which attracted tens of thousands of demonstrators. He defended the Bill as a determined attempt to make the will of the House of Commons prevail over that of the House of Lords and as a blow 'in favour of democratic reform as opposed to capitalistic monopoly' [*The Times*, 27 July 1908]. His speech led Marie Corelli, the bestselling novelist, to offer herself as 'a humble worker on your side … fighting for the sobriety of the nation' [Marie Corelli to Churchill, 27 July 1908. *The Churchill Documents* 4: 833].

In October 1908 Churchill chaired the annual general meeting of the United Kingdom Alliance, in the Free Trade Hall at Manchester. He described the Licensing Bill as 'the indispensable forerunner of every important reform of social conditions'. When he told the delegates: 'this is not a time to talk of compromise … this is a time to talk of war', they rose and waved their hats [Manchester, 13 October 1908. *Complete Speeches* I: 1100–1105]. Yet when the Bill came before the Lords, Churchill tried to persuade Asquith to make concessions to the Tories. The premier, however, thought that no satisfactory deal was possible [*A Liberal Chronicle, Journals and Papers of J.A. Pease*, entry for 27 November 1908: 92]. The peers rejected the Bill by 272 votes to 96, which occasioned an indignant response from Churchill as Lucy Masterman recorded:

> C. was perfectly furious at the rejection of the Licensing Bill by the Lords, stabbed at his bread, would hardly speak; murmured perorations about 'the heart of every Band of Hope in this country sinking with them. 'We shall send them up a Budget in June as shall terrify them, they have started the class war, they had better be careful' [Lucy Masterman's diary entry, 26 November 1908, in *C.F.G. Masterman*: 114].

Churchill, however, privately admitted that the Licensing Bill was unpopular throughout the English constituencies and that the Lords had gained strength with the electorate by rejecting it [Churchill to H.W. Massingham, 22 January 1909. *The Churchill Documents* 4: 872]. Nevertheless he remained committed to the temperance cause. As President of the Board of Trade, one of his main concerns was the rise in unemployment, which he claimed could be reduced by increased temperance [*Parliamentary Debates* (1909)].

After the rejection of the Licensing Bill he Liberal Government sought to limit alcohol consumption by fiscal means. Lloyd George, in his controversial 1909 Budget, greatly increased the duties on breweries, public houses and spirits. In November the Lords rejected the proposed new duties along with the rest of the Budget. That action, Churchill claimed, had 'sent a message of despair to every social worker, to every philanthropic body, to every Christian minister, and to every little Sunday school throughout the land' [*The People's Rights:* 31].

After the January 1910 general election, Churchill became Home Secretary with responsibility for penal policy. He took the view that a fine was a better punishment for drunkenness than committal to prison because the end of a short sentence was often celebrated by heavy drinking, whereas a heavy fine enforced 'a period of temperance and saving' [*Parliamentary Debates* (1910)]. His support for temperance was again evident when he became First Lord of the Admiralty in 1911. In the Royal Navy it was the practice to issue a daily rum ration to all sailors who did not specifically apply for the money compensation of a halfpenny in lieu. Churchill reversed the process so that all men drew the halfpenny in lieu of the rum ration unless they were marked with the letter 'G' for 'Grog'. He believed that the change would considerably reduce the consumption of liquor on His Majesty's ships [*Parliamentary Debates* (1913)].

During the First World War, it was excessive drinking in the shipyards, rather than at sea, which threatened the efficiency of the Royal Navy. In 1915 Lloyd George alleged that 'drink is doing more damage in the War than all the German submarines put together'. The Shipbuilding Employers Federation, supported by officials at the Admiralty, called for the prohibition of alcohol in areas where munitions were produced. Churchill, however, believed that the naval officials and the shipyard employers exaggerated the weaknesses they noticed in workingmen. He advised Lloyd George not to dissipate his energies on a prohibition campaign but to favour 'small practical measures which would deal with local evils', such as a reduction of the alcohol content in drinks. He pointed out that the French were still drinking their wines and the Germans their beer [Churchill to Lloyd George, 7 April 1915. *The Churchill Documents* 6: 775–776].

When George V made 'the King's pledge'—to abstain from alcohol during the war—Churchill told Lloyd George that he thought the whole thing absurd [Frances Stevenson's diary, 8 April 1915. *The Churchill Documents* 6: 776]. Six months later, after resigning from Asquith's coalition government, Churchill went on active service with the Grenadiers, on the Western Front. There he chose to mess, not at battalion headquarters, which was strictly 'dry', but in the line where alcohol was permitted. He strongly believed in what he described as 'the moderate and regular use of alcohol, especially under conditions of winter war' ['With the Grenadiers': 86–87].

In July 1917 Churchill returned to the Cabinet as Minister of Munitions in Lloyd George's coalition government and was consequently obliged to seek re-election at Dundee. Scrymgeour was his only opponent, which prompted one Dundonian to declare that the issue before the electors was 'shells versus booze'. Churchill alleged that Scrymgeour wanted 'peace with Germany in order to suppress the liquor traffic in Scotland'. Nevertheless Winston also made it clear that he supported temperance:

> It would be a pity if any voting down of the pacifist candidate seemed to indicate that we are not making any effort to eradicate the shocking evils of the misuse of strong drink. The vote which Dundee will give would not only be a vote for the continuance of the war but also a vote for the cause of temperance.

He promised that the government would not interfere with the powers given to localities to hold Local Option polls by the 1913 Scottish Temperance Act. But he viewed drink regulation from the point of view of winning the war and he did not commit himself to proposals for State purchase of the drink trade [Lochee, Dundee, 27 July 1917. *Complete Speeches* III: 2565]. His re-election, by a majority of over 5,000 votes, reflected his pro-war stance rather than his support for temperance.

At the 1918 general election, Scrymgeour stood again, which pleased Churchill who thought that he would take votes from the second Labour candidate [Winston to Clementine Churchill, 27 November 1918. *The Churchill Documents* 8: 428]. In the event, Churchill was easily re-elected, along with Wilkie, the sitting Labour MP. He was helped both by Wilkie's endorsement and the absence of a Conservative candidate due to the 'coupon' arrangement by which Liberal supporters of the coalition were not opposed.

Lloyd George's post-war coalition government promoted temperance by taxation. When Dundee Liberals criticised the 1919 Budget, Churchill pointed out that the only increase in taxation was on alcohol and death duties [Churchill to Sir G. Ritchie, 9 May 1919. *The Churchill Documents* 8: 647–648]. The duty per barrel on beer rose from 50/- to 70/- and was further increased to 100/- in the 1920 Budget. In that year, in Scotland, hundreds of local polls took place under the terms of the 1913 Scottish Temperance Act. Only a few middle class areas, however, voted in favour of prohibition or further licensing restrictions [Smout: 146–147].

At the 1922 general election Scrymgeour again stood for Dundee as a Prohibitionist and Labour candidate [*The Times*, 7 November 1922]. Churchill admired Scrymgeour's persistency and fidelity to his principles but claimed that a vote given to him would have no direct bearing upon the great issues being fought out in Dundee [Churchill's speech at Caird Hall, 11 November 1922. Paterson: 248]. Yet the issue that concerned most Dundonians was their poor living conditions, which had been made worse by the current economic recession. Clementine Churchill, who campaigned in Dundee for Winston, while he was recuperating from an operation, informed him that 'the misery here is appalling. Some of the people look absolutely starving' [Clementine to Winston, 9 November 1922. *Speaking for Themselves:* 265]. Churchill's recent role in combating the Republican insurgency in Ireland meant he was unpopular with the many electors of Irish extraction, whilst his anti- Bolshevik policy was blamed for the stoppage of jute exports to Russia. He had previously always headed the poll but in 1922 he came fourth out of the six candidates for the two Dundee seats. He lost the support that he had previously enjoyed from many Liberal, Labour and Conservative voters. By contrast, Scrymgeour, who had campaigned on various issues, not just prohibition, headed the poll [Walker, 'Dundee's Disenchantment with Churchill']. It has been claimed that critical support for Scrymgeour came from the newly enfranchised working class women [Smout: 147]. Yet many of those women had also voted at the 1918 general election, when Churchill had easily beaten Scrymgeour. The difference in 1922 was that Scrymgeour jointly campaigned with the Labour candidate, Morel, and that the Dundee Jute and Flax Workers Union endorsed both men. Nearly two-thirds of Scrymgeour's support came from joint votes with Morel [Dick, 'Dundee']. As in earlier contests, his support for prohibition had limited electoral appeal. Churchill displayed no bitterness at the victory of his old opponent:

> In Mr Scrymgeour's victory they saw the victory of a man who stood for endurance, and also for moral orderly conceptions of democratic reform and action. They would find he ... would have a useful part

> to play in representing Dundee, where there was such fearful misery and distress and such awful contrast between one class and another. He did not in the least grudge Mr Scrymgeour his victory. [Churchill at the Dundee Liberal Club, 16 November 1922. Paterson, 283]

In 1924 Churchill returned to the Conservative Party as Chancellor of the Exchequer in Baldwin's second ministry. He thus became responsible for the taxation of alcohol. In his 1925 Budget, he imposed a small duty on imported hops and beer to countervail the tax on home-produced ale [*Parliamentary Debates* (1925)]. In 1927 he imposed a higher duty on port on the dubious grounds that it was a more alcoholic drink than whisky, 'our national product', which was usually diluted with water or soda [*Parliamentary Debates*, vol. 205 cc.804–806 (1927)]. More importantly, however, Churchill kept the excise duty on beer at the high rate of 100/- per barrel to which it had been raised in 1920. That reflected the government's need to raise revenue to pay off the vast war debt rather than a desire to induce temperance by fiscal means.

In 1927 Churchill conceded that there was a case for reducing the licence duty paid by publicans because licensing hours had been reduced during and after the war [*Parliamentary Debates*, vol. 209 (1927)]. In 1928, with the prospect of a general election next year, he wished to know if the Cabinet wanted to reduce the publicans' licence duty on electioneering grounds. As that would entail a loss to the revenue of about one million pounds, he was reluctant to do so unless it was 'absolutely necessary for our party interests' [Churchill to Stanley Baldwin, 12 April 1928. *The Churchill Documents* 11: 1258]. He informed King George V that although Labour and Lady Astor would criticise any remission of the duty, it was justified on grounds of fair play [Churchill to George V, 22 April 1928: 1268–1269]. On the next day, however, Churchill told the King that he had decided to postpone the remission of the duty until 1929 on the grounds that it would undermine the '*national* and non-party' nature of his Budget [Churchill to George V, 23 April 1928: 1271]. He held to that line in the Commons [*Parliamentary Debates*, vol. 219 (1928)]. In his 1929 Budget, Churchill honoured his earlier promise and reduced the duty payable by on-licence holders by 25 per cent. At the same time, however, he repealed the tea duty and increased the betting tax. He hoped that would enable the Tories to retain the support of the publicans, while posing as the friends of the sober poor and anti-gambling groups such as the Methodists. In the event, however, the Conservatives were defeated at the 1929 general election, which led to the resignation of Baldwin's ministry.

By the 1930s, the drink issue had greatly declined as a political question, which Churchill attributed to the decay of the Liberal Party and the rise of Labour [Churchill at the Allied Brewery Traders Association dinner, London, 17 March 1930. *Complete Speeches* V: 4726]. But, more importantly, there had been a dramatic drop in alcohol sales. Between 1920 and 1932 there was a 50% reduction in beer consumption per capita in Britain [Gourvish & Wilson: 340]. As Churchill noted, high taxation and regulation had led to an immense decrease of drunkenness and the crimes and disease that it led to [*Parliamentary Debates*, vol. 214 (1928)]. But other developments, including economic recession, unemployment and the rising popularity of the cinema also played a part in reducing consumption.

In the United States, unlike in Britain, the drink question remained highly controversial due to the federal adoption of prohibition in 1920. Churchill always opposed outright prohibition—once again following the example of his father. In 1887 Lord Randolph had argued that total prohibition would have evil consequences [Sunderland, 20 Oct. 1887. Jennings, *Speeches* II: 231]. In 1926 Winston claimed that prohibition inevitably led to evasion and corruption on a vast scale, a general contempt for the law and an infringement of individual liberty. By comparison, he argued, in a speech to the brewers association, that the British policy of highly taxing alcohol fostered respect for the law, while providing revenue for the State and advancing sobriety [Allied Brewery Traders Association dinner, London, 15 March 1926. *Complete Speeches* IV: 3871]. During his Budget speech in 1927, Churchill told Lady Astor: 'I do not think we are likely to learn much from the liquor legislation of the United States' [*Parliamentary Debates*, vol. 205 c.74 (1927)].

After leaving office, in 1929, Churchill toured the United States, an experience that reinforced his opposition to prohibition. His son, Randolph, who accompanied him, carried medicine bottles filled with whisky and brandy so that Winston never went without alcohol. They were served beer in a hotel despite the presence of the local prohibition officer who explained that the government was concerned not with the consumer but only with the bootlegger. Randolph concluded that 'prohibition is a complete farce' [Randolph Churchill's diary, 7–10 September 1929. *Twenty-One Years*: 78–80]. Winston, after his return from the States, denounced what he called 'the folly of intolerant idealism', which led to evasion, subterfuge and hypocrisy ['What I saw in America of Prohibition'. *Daily Telegraph* (2 December 1929): 10].

Churchill's opposition to State policing of private morals had a long pedigree. In the mid-1890s, while a cadet at Sandhurst, he had opposed Mrs Ormiston Chant's campaign to close the bars at the Empire Theatre, in the West End of London, in order to combat prostitution and intemperance. He then drafted a speech—his first but undelivered—on 'the dangers of State intervention with the social habits of law-abiding persons'. Such a warning, he claimed in 1930, might have saved the United States from prohibition! [*My Early Life*: 66, 70].

In 1932, on his return to the U.S., Winston declared that Britain had been more successful in dealing with intemperance because 'we treated the problem as a disease rather than as a moral issue' [Brooklyn Academy of Music, 28 January 1932. *Complete Speeches* V: 5130]. In a newspaper article he pointed out that Britons now consumed only half the beer and less than a quarter of the spirits that they had drunk in 1900, when the population was smaller and poorer. He also noted that convictions for drunkenness in 1930 were less than a third of what they had been in 1913. He attributed the increase in temperance to the 300–400% rise in the cost of licensed alcohol ['Prohibition'. *Sunday Chronicle* (14 August 1932)].

As Prime Minister, during the Second World War, Churchill praised the benefits of moderate drinking. In 1940 he told the Minister of Food:

'The way to lose this war is to try to force the British public into a diet of milk, oatmeal, potatoes etc., washed down on gala occasions with a little lime juice' [Churchill to Lord Woolton, 14 July 1940. *The Churchill Documents* 15: 514]. In 1944 he minuted that the beer ration should go to the troops at the front before those in the rear got a drop [The Prime Minister to the Secretary of State for War, 20 November 1944. *The Churchill Documents* 20: 1969]. In 1945 he insisted that whisky production should be maintained as it was not only an invaluable export and dollar earner but also a 'characteristic British element of ascendancy' [Churchill to the Minister of Food, 3 April 1945. *The Churchill Documents* 21: 842].

During the war, however, alcohol consumption in Britain was reduced in various ways. Although beer was not rationed it was often unavailable or diluted in strength, while its price rose rapidly due to a more than five-fold increase in duty. Consequently excessive drinking posed less of a threat to war production than had been the case during the First World War. Not for the first time, Churchill's personal advocacy of the benefits of alcohol conflicted with the temperance-inducing policies of the government to which he belonged.

Churchill's long involvement with the drink question mirrored the trajectory of that issue in British politics. In the Edwardian period, his advocacy of temperance and licensing reform reflected the prominence of that issue in Liberal politics in that era. It also illustrated his support for social reform and the filial nature of his early politics. During and between the First and Second World Wars Churchill focused on regulation of alcoholic drink consumption by price rather than by licensing. That policy was facilitated by the national need for both additional revenue and sobriety.

The drink question was a controversial issue in all of Winston's parliamentary election campaigns between 1906 and 1922. Six of those contests were at Dundee where the prohibitionist candidate, Scrymgeour, stood against him at every election and finally defeated him in 1922. Nevertheless the electoral importance of the drink question was limited and it was never the predominant electoral issue. After 1922, moreover, the temperance movement rapidly declined as an electoral force, whereas the drink lobby continued to be an important electoral aid to the Conservative Party. Even so, Churchill, first as Baldwin's Chancellor, and then as wartime Premier, maintained high rates of taxation on alcohol, which largely ensured a dramatic reduction in consumption that lasted until the end of his career.

Churchill managed, over his career, to get the best of both worlds on the drink question. As a successful journalist and author he was able to indulge his large appetite for alcoholic drinks. As a government minister, however, he played a significant role in reducing the national consumption of alcohol and thus helped to fulfil his father's desire for greater temperance. The contrast between his personal and his political behaviour in that respect illustrates the truth of Paul Addison's observation that Churchill, in his time, played many parts [*Churchill on the Home Front*: 1; 'The three careers of Winston Churchill'].

ENDNOTES

1 Recollection by the U.S. Secretary of State, Dean Acheson. GILBERT, *'Never Despair', 1945–1965*: 675.

CHAPTER 4

BALDWIN'S BULLDOG: CHURCHILL'S 1925 FIGHT AGAINST TARIFFS

DAVID FREEMAN
California State University, Fullerton

Winston 'Churchill's principal achievement at the Treasury', Paul Addison wrote in *Churchill on the Home Front*, 'was to hold the line in defence of Free Trade' [250]. As Chancellor of the Exchequer from 1924 to 1929, Churchill did allow for the creation of some modest tariffs—especially if they generated revenue on non-essential goods—and some 'safeguarding' of minor industries, but he held firm against anything that would have had a major effect on the British economy. And that was just the way Prime Minister Stanley Baldwin wanted it.

During his tenure at No. 11 Downing Street, Churchill introduced five consecutive budgets, a streak not matched again until Nigel Lawson in the 1980s. The only office that Churchill ever held longer than that of Chancellor was Prime Minister. Yet most historians, even Addison, have focused primarily on just two aspects of Churchill's time as Britain's chief finance minister: the decision to return to the Gold Standard in 1925 and his actions during the General Strike in the following year. There was more to Churchill's five years at the Treasury than just that, and holding the line on Free Trade consumed much of his energy.

In May 1925, after the return to gold had been declared, the iron and steel industry applied to the government for protection under the Safeguarding of Industries Act. Churchill immediately objected. 'He urged the government should refuse a public inquiry', Addison explained, 'and won his case'. 'After this', Addison concluded, 'the protectionist campaign lost momentum, and Churchill was left once more in possession of the heartland of Free Trade' [251]. In a book that surveyed Churchill's political record on domestic matters over more than half a century, Addison tells this story in brief. The full story is long and complicated. And that is the story that follows here.

PRESENT AT THE CREATION

The struggle over protection in the second Baldwin government goes back more than twenty years before the general election of 1924 that brought it into office. The key players in the story are Churchill and Leo Amery. The two men first met when they were schoolboys together at Harrow in the 1880s. They saw little of each other at that time. Amery was older by a year and a star pupil destined for Oxford and All Souls. Churchill, no great scholar, would have to settle for Sandhurst. Both men, however, aspired to a career in politics at the highest level.

Churchill got the jump on Amery, literally. Both men were serving as war correspondents in South Africa in 1899. One morning in November, they were sharing a tent together in the field when Churchill woke Amery well before dawn (not something that became a habit of Churchill's) to ask if his fellow journalist wanted to join him on an excursion being made by British soldiers via armoured train into Boer country. Amery preferred to sleep. Subsequently, the train was ambushed and Churchill taken prisoner for a month until his dramatic escape made him, briefly, a national hero that catapulted him into parliament 'ten years before you!' he later teased Amery [Amery, *My Political Life*:

I, 117]. Churchill was first elected as the Conservative MP for Oldham in 1900. Within four years, he crossed the floor to join the Liberals. The deciding factor had been tariffs.

In 1903, Joseph Chamberlain, then the Colonial Secretary, announced his support for a programme of Imperial Preference. The scheme involved the United Kingdom and the self-governing colonies—as the Dominions were then known—which would grant preferential tariff rates to one another. The primary objective of the plan was not fiscal, but to keep the British Empire close politically through economic interdependence as more colonies became self-governing. Supporters of Chamberlain's vision, who became known as 'whole hoggers', believed that the scheme would be the best way to preserve Britain in the front rank of the world's nations as Germany and the United States continued to develop into dominant commercial powers. No one believed more passionately in this idea than Leo Amery. It sustained him all his life. Churchill, however, once confided to Amery that 'he had tried hard in 1903 to convince himself Joe was right, but the more he read the more he was converted the other way' [*The Churchill Documents* 12: 35].

Chamberlain has the unique distinction of breaking two major political parties. As a Liberal MP, he had opposed Home Rule for Ireland. He led fellow-minded 'Liberal Unionists' to join forces with the Conservatives (the combination becoming known for a generation as the 'Unionists') to prevent self-government for Ireland in the late Victorian era. Chamberlain's call for Imperial Preference had an equally devastating impact on the Unionists. Since the repeal of the Corn Laws in 1846, the United Kingdom had been a nation largely without import tariffs. The only way to implement Chamberlain's plan would be to create new tariffs, which could then be reduced to provide preferential rates for the Dominions. The inescapable problem with this grand dream, however, was that Canada was the largest and most important of the Dominions, and the only tariff at the time that would be beneficial to Canadian producers would be one on wheat. In a sense, a new Corn Law would have to be introduced in Britain. That struck many as political suicide, but, without Canada, Imperial Preference would be still born. Opponents of Chamberlain's plan immediately labelled it as a tax on food and became known as 'little piggers'. Tariffs on grain imports from the United States and other nations outside the Empire would necessarily increase the price of bread. Amery believed that this would eventually be offset by increased consumption of Empire-grown wheat and, with it, a fall in the price as wheat production in the Empire inevitably rose. Such was the theory.

Chamberlain's vision found favour with some traditional Tory supporters in agriculture and industry, few of whom cared about the unity of the Empire as much as they did about the idea of eliminating foreign competition. The urban middle classes, however, along with all sectors of the working classes, could see only an immediate rise in their cost of living. Nevertheless, Free Trade Unionists like Churchill found themselves marginalised within their party. Convinced that the Tories had left the path of reason, Churchill joined the ranks of the adamantly Free Trade Liberal Party in 1904. He chose the perfect time.

After Chamberlain raised the protectionist banner, Prime Minister Arthur Balfour struggled unsuccessfully to hold together the opposing factions within his ruling party. At the end of 1905, he gambled that the Opposition could do no better and resigned to allow Sir Henry Campbell-Bannerman and the Liberals to form a minority government. A general election followed at the start of 1906. Fighting a campaign on their issue of choice, the whole hoggers could not overcome the simple cry of 'dear food'. The Unionists suffered their worst defeat since the formal organisation of the Conservative Party in 1830. They won 157 seats compared with 400 for the Liberals.

The general election of 1906 should have killed the Chamberlain plan stone dead. The new Liberal government quickly passed a resolution 'declaring that the recent election had demonstrated the decisive rejection of tariff reform by the electorate' [SYKES, *Tariff Reform:* 114]. The whole hoggers, nevertheless, convinced themselves that they had successfully purged their ranks of little piggers and could begin the process of educating the electorate on the great advantages of their programme, which had just been so thoroughly rejected by voters. Amery, working as a leader writer for *The Times*, went about this task with gusto. He joined or helped to organise many different groups for this purpose, while continuing to seek his own seat in parliament. He had been among the losers in 1906. Churchill, meanwhile, received his first government appointment from Campbell-Bannerman, beginning what would become the lengthiest ministerial career in twentieth-century Britain.

RETURN OF THE TARIFF REFORMERS

After four unsuccessful attempts, Amery was finally elected to parliament, unopposed, in a 1911 by-election for South Birmingham (later known as Sparkbrook). He owed it all to the patronage of Joseph Chamberlain, but it was Neville Chamberlain, younger son of 'Radical Joe', who performed the necessary political fixing. By this time, Balfour had given way as Unionist leader to Andrew Bonar Law, a nominal protectionist. Joseph Chamberlain, however, perceived that Bonar Law did not share his vision of Imperial unity but merely viewed tariffs as a fiscal policy with which to challenge the Liberals and the socialism of the emerging Labour Party. In any case, events continually worked against the tariff reformers. Reactions to David Lloyd George's 'People's Budget' in 1909, the Parliament Act of 1911, and the debate over Irish Home caused the Unionists to set aside tariffs one way or another, to the continual frustration of the true-believing Amery.

Amery's own path into government was opened due to the support he received from his other great political mentor, Alfred Milner. The protean Milner was an arch-imperialist. His popularity within the Unionist ranks, combined with his enormous capabilities as an administrator, made him one of the key members of the government when Lloyd George formed his coalition during the First World War. Milner secured a position for Amery as an assistant secretary to the War Cabinet and, when Milner became Colonial Secretary after the war, brought along Amery as his under secretary.

Amery fancied that those who joined him in the 'Undersecretaries' Revolt' that brought down the Lloyd George coalition in 1922 did so in order to bring Imperial Preference into being at long last. In his monomania, Amery could be delusional that way. Eighteen years after their devastating loss in 1906, however, the Conservatives (as they were once again known) were back to having many free traders within their ranks. The new Prime Minister, Bonar Law, faced the same danger as Balfour had of risking a party split if he now called for tariff reform. Much to the relief of his colleagues, therefore, Amery, who had become First Lord of the Admiralty, volunteered that the coming general election should be run on the single issue of the change in government. He requested only that Bonar Law 'keep the door open' on the question of fiscal policy, and to this the Prime Minister agreed [*Amery Diaries*, 20 October 1922: 307]. The agreement did not last. In the heat of the campaign, Bonar Law suddenly announced 'that this [forthcoming] Parliament would not make any fundamental change in the fiscal system of this country' [*Baldwin*: 126]. There could be no tariff reform following the coming election. That could only happen if the Tories fought still another election specifically on the issue of tariffs, as they had done in 1906. Amery fumed.

WINSTON IS BACK!

'S.B. is mad!' So Austen Chamberlain told his wife after learning that Prime Minister Stanley Baldwin had appointed Churchill to be his new Chancellor of the Exchequer in 1924 [*Official Biography* V: 60]. Others reacted similarly, and *The Times* joined the chorus in believing that Baldwin had made a mistake. The Conservative Party had just been returned to power after a brief absence of one year. Additionally, for the first time in several years, the party appeared to be restored to unity, since Baldwin's previous government, which had lasted only a few months in 1923, did not include leading Tories like Chamberlain himself and Lord Birkenhead, both of whom had been prominent office holders in the Lloyd George coalition.

Much had happened by the time Baldwin became Prime Minister for the second time in 1924 and shocked Britain's political world with the announcement that Churchill would be his chief financial minister. Churchill had also been a leading member of the Lloyd George coalition but as a Liberal MP. Churchill had lost his seat in 1922, however, and his loathing for socialism led to his gradual migration back to the Conservative fold. Baldwin himself came from the protectionist wing of the Conservative Party, but his support for tariffs became tempered by the embarrassing defeat he suffered in 1923. In the spring of that year, Baldwin had taken over as Prime Minister from the terminally ill Bonar Law and considered himself bound by the election pledge his predecessor had given in 1922 that there would be no tariff reform in that parliament. With the post-war economy fast deteriorating, however, Baldwin convinced himself—with no prodding from Amery—that only the introduction of a tariff system would help reduce unemployment. This meant calling a general election only one year after the last one. Naturally, Amery wholeheartedly supported Baldwin's decision and worked hard to get across the message during the election of 1923. The Conservatives actually increased their vote total from the previous year but lost their overall majority. Although the Tories had the largest number of MPs, Baldwin gave way to Ramsay MacDonald and the first Labour government, which took office with the support of the Liberals at the start of 1924.

Churchill, an arch opponent of socialism, abhorred the new alliance. He was now prepared to rejoin the Conservatives, who had failed once again to make any headway on protection and were not likely to give that wing of the party much room to operate in the future. And so it was as a 'Constitutionalist' candidate with official support from the Conservative Party that he returned to parliament in the general election of 1924 after the Lab/Lib alliance broke apart. Given Churchill's twenty-year absence from the Conservatives, no one expected that he would be appointed to the second most important office in the government. But S. B. had not gone mad. He knew just what he was doing.

In building a new cabinet, Baldwin intended to build one to last. There were several political factors that he kept in mind. Apart from the understandable desire to keep himself in Downing Street for more than just a few months this time, he very much wanted to keep Lloyd George out. Baldwin himself had served in the Lloyd George coalition but had developed a strong distaste for what he regarded as the sharp practice of the Welsh wizard. Churchill, however, had been the principal *protégé* of Lloyd George. By bringing Churchill in as Chancellor while appointing Austen Chamberlain as Foreign Secretary and giving Birkenhead the India Office—light but respectable duty that guaranteed 'F.E.' plenty of time for golf—Baldwin denied Lloyd George the three leading figures that had supported him as Prime Minister. With the troika firmly in his own tent, where he could keep close eye on them, Baldwin knew there would be little chance of a new Conservative-Liberal coalition forming to turn him out and restore Lloyd George to power.

There was a further advantage. Baldwin remained pledged to the idea of tariffs in principle, but he needed to keep Amery and the protectionist wing of the party in check. Fortunate to have returned to No. 10 after his 1923 blunder, Baldwin had no intention of allowing Amery to push him too hard on tariffs a second time. Paul Addison identified the Prime Minister's sound political reasoning for this: 'Nearly three million people, or 17.6 per cent of the electorate, voted Liberal in 1924'. 'Baldwin and MacDonald', Addison concluded, 'saw themselves as competing for the middle ground of Liberal opinion' [*Churchill on the Home Front*: 233]. And Liberal voters remained solidly in the Free Trade camp.

For Baldwin, attracting Liberal support while maintaining that of the protectionists within his own party, meant having nothing more than a modest and preferably non-controversial tariff programme. For his part, Churchill remained at heart an apostle of Free Trade, but like the Prime Minister, he too was willing to allow for some tariffs as a financial and political expedient. At the Exchequer, the immensely capable Churchill would hold the full-throated tariff reformers at bay.

'Of one thing Churchill was certain', Addison wrote: 'He had not become Chancellor of the Exchequer in order to preside over the liquidation of Free Trade' [243].

Baldwin appointed Amery to be Colonial Secretary. Amery happily accepted on the condition that the office be divided into two ministries: one for the colonies and one for the Dominions. Churchill, determined to be a thrifty Chancellor, acceded to this request on the condition that Amery held both offices. Amery initially responded to Churchill's own appointment with caution. If Churchill 'means to play the game about Empire development and Preference, no one could be better', Amery reflected in his diary, but 'if he doesn't, he may make my position very difficult' [*Amery Diaries*, 7 November 1924: 390]. Difficult did not begin to describe what followed. Amery believed that the election manifesto of the Conservatives, which he himself had carefully drafted, left the government 'perfectly free to do all that was needed [to restore protection], so long as the case of each industry was separately investigated' [*My Political Life*: II, 296]. 'That as a convinced Free Trader', Amery later concluded, 'Churchill was likely to throw all the weight of his key position and dominating personality against the policy which Baldwin had put in the forefront of his election address probably never occurred to the Prime Minister's curiously inconsequential mind' [299]. Not for the first or last time, however, Amery had misread the situation. Baldwin's biographers, John Barnes and Keith Middlemass, have identified the truth:

> The Party's Manifesto was not an unlimited opening to protection taken industry by industry; Amery might read it so, [...] but Baldwin's speeches gave the interpretation no such warrant. All that had to be conceded was for Churchill to agree to the safeguarding of a limited number of industries within the lifetime of one parliament, an agreement which Baldwin exacted. Churchill retained his freedom to interpret the Manifesto; only the keenness of Amery's disappointment could suggest that Baldwin failed to see the consequence of the appointment. [*Baldwin*: 282].

The battle lines stood drawn. Amery would have to fight for every tariff he could get while an industrious and supremely capable Churchill opposed him at every turn.

THE BATTLE BEGINS

The new government confronted the issue of Imperial Preference almost immediately. The Imperial Economic Conference of 1923 had proposed the creation of preferences on a variety of commodities. As in the past, the establishment of preferential rates would have to begin by raising duties on equivalent non-Imperial goods. The plan was subsequently scrapped by the MacDonald government. During the 1924 election, however, the Conservatives had pledged to reintroduce it. Having been voted in, the Tories should have been free to do just that. Not for the first time, though, the tariff reformers in the government found themselves hampered by some casual campaign remarks made by their leader. Speaking at Gravesend during the election, Baldwin promised that there would be no net increase on food taxation. This left the protectionists in a quandary. It appeared that new duties could only be introduced if they were offset by reducing pre-existing rates on other foodstuffs, a zero-sum game. Hoping to break free of this constraint, Amery pleaded without success that the Government's fiscal policy in difficult economic times should not be held to ambiguous remarks made in the heat of an election. Churchill, for his part, opposed new food duties in the abstract but was willing to go along with them having himself carefully avoided during the election 'saying anything inconsistent with carrying out the whole of the [Imperial Economic] Conference proposals [...] on the ground that a promise is a promise and that this is an act of high Imperial diplomacy' [Churchill to Baldwin, 4 December 1924. *The Churchill Documents* 11: 290]. Philip Cunliffe-Lister, a protectionist and President of the Board of Trade, offered a solution to the imbroglio. With Churchill's support, the Government dropped the matter of new tariffs and pledged instead to restore only pre-existing duties abandoned by the Labour government. As compensation to the supporters of Imperial Preference, the Government authorised the Treasury to appropriate £1,000,000 towards the creation of a fund intended to improve the marketing of Imperial produce. Lord Derby, a former cabinet minister and a leader of the Free Trade wing of the Conservative Party, wrote to Churchill: 'I strongly approve of your policy. The pledge is kept—and yet here is a chance of some real Imperial Preference, but don't let Amery have too much to do with the spending of the £1,000,000. I distrust him very much' [Derby to Churchill, 18 December 1924. *The Churchill Documents* 11: 311]. Despite Derby's wishes, Amery, as Dominions Secretary, became chairman of the Empire Marketing Board established to implement the spending plan.[1]

At the State Opening of Parliament on 9 December 1924, the King's Speech included an announcement of the Government's intention to introduce a bill for safeguarding employment in 'efficient industries'. During the subsequent debate, 'Baldwin chose to announce that he stood by his [election] pledge not to introduce protection in this Parliament nor to use safeguarding as a wedge to ease the way' [*Baldwin*: 288]. Left unclear, however, was how the Government intended to distinguish between safeguarding and protection or what would be the definition of an 'efficient' industry. The Opposition benches led by Lloyd George pounced on these ambiguities. Baldwin skilfully fended off the attacks with the aid of a paper prepared by Amery. Churchill then supported the Prime Minister with a humorous speech in which he criticised his Labour predecessor, Philip Snowden, for the paradoxical act of having suspended the McKenna Duties—tariffs that had been imposed on some luxury items during the First World War. It nevertheless remained an open question as to what exactly Baldwin would do about tariffs.

The Cabinet had to decide, and on 21 January 1925, it agreed to establish a committee for formulating the procedure by which the Government might implement safeguarding. The committee, chaired by Cunliffe-Lister, included Churchill but not Amery [21 January 1925, CAB 23/49: 174]. The Cabinet Committee on the Safeguarding of Industries reported to the full Cabinet on 3 February [3 February 1925,

CAB 23/49: 206]. Naturally, Amery found the recommendations to be 'unnecessarily restrictive' [*My Political Life*: II, 479]. The White Paper published that same day outlined the procedure to be followed by an industry applying for government protection. Leaders who believed their industry to be suffering from unfair foreign competition were to make a complaint to the Board of Trade, which then determined if sufficient evidence existed to warrant referral to a Committee of Inquiry. The Board office would make its own determination on the matter of 'efficiency'. After considering such matters as an industry's employment figures, revenue generation and 'national importance', the Committee reported to the Board, which in turn made a recommendation to the Cabinet as to whether or not legislation should be enacted through a Finance Bill to establish a protective tariff. Amery would have to involve himself in the minutiae of this bureaucratic process in order to shepherd any tariffs into being—and the process was well outside of his two portfolios.

Churchill introduced his first Budget on 28 April 1925. Amery found himself 'reasonably contented' from an Imperial perspective with the Chancellor's proposals [480]. The McKenna Duties were re-imposed. Preferential rates for Imperial sugar, wines and tobacco were increased, and a new duty on silk was introduced. Churchill guaranteed the new rates for ten years and took care to represent most of the goods being taxed as luxury items, which implied no abandonment of his own Free Trade principles or Baldwin's pledges. The Budget's central feature, a return to the Gold Standard at the pre-war rate of $4.86 per pound sterling, received near universal approval.

With the Budget in place, Amery began to get a feel for the kind of opposition to additional protection that he would get from Churchill. At the Cabinet of 6 May, the Chancellor attempted unsuccessfully to block a proposed inquiry for a duty on lace 'on the ground that one of the White Paper conditions was not literally fulfilled in view of the Safeguarding Committee' [*Amery Diaries*, 6 May 1925: 410]. Churchill feared that a consequence of the Government's safeguarding policy would be a flood of applications from every conceivable industry as

British business owners sought to eliminate foreign competition. 'It was suggested,' at one Cabinet meeting, 'that if a very large number of applications were granted, the effect would be tantamount to the piecemeal imposition of a general tariff and might even amount to a violation of the Prime Minister's pledge' [13 October 1925, CAB 23/51: 23]. However much this would have suited Amery, the Government had to keep close to Baldwin's stated policy. And Churchill's fears were not without merit. Many business owners did see safeguarding as a preferable alternative to capital reinvestment out of their own pockets in order to remain competitive. Requests would have to be screened carefully if there were indeed to be an efficiency standard. By August the Cabinet had turned down applications from industries as disparate as glassware, chrome-tanned upper leather, amorphous carbon electrodes and even metal fittings for coffins. The Cabinet did agree to set up committees to consider the cases made by producers of jewelry, aluminium and enamel hollow-ware, brooms and brushes, as well as packing and wrapping paper. In two cases, gas mantles and cotton gloves, the Cabinet did agree to impose new import duties [5 August 1925, CAB 23/50: 306]. The arguments waged over these fairly trivial items, however, paled in contrast with what became the defining case in the debate over industrial safeguarding.

THE STEEL LINE

In June, Britain's beleaguered iron and steel industry applied for an official safeguarding inquiry. To Amery's dismay, Churchill—who sensed a major change in policy—wished to dismiss the application outright. Baldwin, however, felt that on *prima facie* evidence (the criteria of the White Paper on Safeguarding) an inquiry could not be refused. The Cabinet delayed making an immediate decision. Churchill sent the Prime Minister a lengthy letter on 12 June outlining his concerns about extending protection to include iron and steel. Up to that time, Churchill wrote, the safeguarding procedure had 'only touched articles of small consequence to the general trade of the country, and those have been of finished or luxury class'. Steel, however, was 'one of the fundamental basic raw materials of national industry' affecting 'one way or another all the greatest trades in the country'. Given the widespread affect an increase in the cost of steel would have on British industry in general, Churchill concluded that 'a decision to protect Steel' could not 'be taken apart from the question of a general tariff on foreign imports'. Such a result, the Chancellor insisted, contradicted Baldwin's election pledge against a general tariff. 'I ought not at this very early stage', Churchill's letter continued with a thinly veiled threat of resignation, 'to leave you in any doubt of the serious view which I personally should take of such a proposal' [Churchill to Baldwin, 12 June 1925. *The Churchill Documents* 12: 490–492]. Churchill, of course, was right about what the impact of iron and steel protection would be, which was precisely why Amery supported it.

The Prime Minister found himself in a quandary. Fortunately for Baldwin, circumstances worked to place him in the middle of an almost equally divided Cabinet. The Baldwin family fortune came from the iron industry. The Prime Minister could speak to the issue with greater authority than any of his ministers. Additionally, Baldwin sincerely considered himself a man of his word. He had called the 1923 election because he did not believe he could be released from commitment to the Bonar Law pledge without a mandate from the electorate. He now found himself facing a similar situation after he himself had vowed in the 1924 election not to introduce a general tariff. Churchill's arguments suggested that import duties for iron and steel would constitute a breach of promise. Baldwin had no intention of making the same mistake twice. After three general elections in as many years, he was not about to call a fourth, especially on an issue that continually proved to be unpopular with voters. Yet the issue did remain popular with many proprietors of industry, a key source of funding for the Conservative Party.

With a leadership style that naturally inclined away from snap decisions, Baldwin saw a lengthy investigation into the matter as a way of buying time. To avoid the appearance that the Government might be prepared to violate his election pledge, the inquiry would not take place under the provisions of the White Paper on Safeguarding. Something different was needed. Churchill suggested a Royal Commission, which would enable the Government to accept all, some or none of the resulting recommendations without, in theory, violating any pledges. Cunliffe-Lister had a better idea. He proposed creating a new government committee for economic matters analogous to that already existing for Imperial Defence. Such a committee, chaired and controlled by the Prime Minister, could be more discreet and far-reaching in its inquiries. Accordingly, on 26 June, the Cabinet created the Civil Research Committee (CRC) and charged it with the task of searching for alternatives to protection in assisting the iron and steel industry. The CRC met fifteen times over the second half of the year with Churchill and Amery both serving as members. The record of this long forgotten inquiry illustrates how the two men fought their corners.

CRC INVESTIGATION

On 12 October, the CRC interviewed two past presidents of the National Federation of Iron and Steel Manufacturers. Churchill grilled the men for an hour forcing them to concede that British-made sheet bars cost on average thirty shillings more per ton than foreign-made equivalents. Near the end, Amery intervened with a short series of questions intended to demonstrate that, allowing for transportation expenses on imports and with an effective protective duty in place, the necessary increase in British production, coupled with the concomitant decrease of production in European-made steel, would eliminate the price difference owing to the economies of scale in production. The witnesses eagerly concurred with Amery's off-the-cuff arithmetic. No one mentioned American-made steel [CRC, 12 October 1925, CAB 58: 12].

On 20 October, Amery recorded in his diary that, at the CRC hearing meeting that day, 'a miserable fellow called Scarf [President of the Steel Re-Rollers Association] spent an hour or more explaining to Winston's great satisfaction that anything done for iron and steel would destroy the re-rolling industry' [*Amery Diaries*, 20 October 1925: 423]. The witness agreed with Amery's economies-of-scale argument in principle but countered that closing less efficient plants in favour of more efficient ones would 'make a much bigger reduction in the cost of production than by distributing production over a number of works, some of them less efficient' [CRC Minutes, 20 October 1925, CAB 58: 9]. Logical economic arguments leading to employment reductions held no appeal for Amery. Mr. Scarf gave way to Mr. Whitehead, President of Whitehead Iron and Steel Company Limited, and a witness much more welcome by the Colonial Secretary. 'Whitehead came and dismissed Scarf as entirely unrepresentative of anything but the least efficient employers', Amery happily recorded, 'and definitely expressed his belief in the necessity of iron and steel being safeguarded' [*Amery Diaries*, 20 October 1925: 423].

Ten days later, on 30 October, Churchill and Amery clashed again. Both men pressed for ending the committee's activities with regard to iron and steel, but for different reasons. For his part, Churchill, while considering the evidence presented to the committee to have been one-sided in character, asserted that what he had heard so far led him to believe that the cause of distress in heavy industries was due to two facts. In the first place, existing plant capacity greatly exceeded demand, as a legacy of wartime expansion. Demand naturally had fallen after the war. To remedy the problem, Churchill recommended that the industry should follow the example of Germany and concentrate existing production upon the most efficient and profitable plants, thus allowing economic forces to eliminate those firms that could not pay their way. In the second place, Churchill was convinced that there were many shortcomings within the industry itself and many ways by which, through the introduction of improved methods, economies could be achieved. Conversely, Amery argued that the CRC had concluded that the only alternatives to protection for iron and steel lay between doing nothing and providing a direct subsidy, a complex and objectionable proposal. He therefore argued that a committee of safeguarding inquiry under the guidelines of the White Paper be allowed to go forward. Baldwin, however, postponed a decision to conclude the CRC investigation, citing the absence of three key members [30 October 1925, CAB 58: 13].

Churchill correctly viewed the stream of witnesses appearing before the CRC as one-sided, since most clamoured for protection. Behind the scenes, however, it was Amery who was losing ground. At the 30 October meeting, Churchill circulated a document showing 'that roughly 60% of all British steel was exported and therefore any measures to aid home production must not injure the export trade (which was worth four or five times the total of imports)' [*Baldwin*: 314, footnote]. Churchill also reiterated his argument that British steel cost more than that made on the Continent because of inefficient production methods. A paper produced by the professional staff of the CRC under the direction of Cabinet Secretary Sir Maurice Hankey reinforced the Chancellor's position. Although convoluted compared with the lucid prose of Churchill, this second paper proved valuable to the Free Trade position, because it denied the claim that the iron and steel industry was necessary for stabilisation of defence production.

On 1 November, Churchill sent Baldwin a letter claiming that, so long as the Government stuck to the platform of the 1924 General Election, all would be well. In classic Churchillian prose, the Chancellor warned the Prime Minister that 'if Amery—who publicly repudiated y[ou]r declarations of fiscal policy before the election—is allowed to rush the Conservative Party on to the slippery slope of Protection, then friends will be divided & enemies united & all the vultures will gather for the prey' [Churchill to Baldwin, 1 November 1925. *The Churchill Documents* 12: 567]. Once again Churchill impressed upon Baldwin that a tariff on iron and steel amounted to an incremental general tariff. The Prime Minister, however, had already informed economist W.A.S. Hewins that he disagreed with this view: 'he held that he could safeguard any industry which made out its case'. [Hewins diary, 28 October 1925: 563]. The cause of protection had life in it yet.

At the next meeting of the CRC, however, even the witnesses proved less than helpful to the protectionist cause. Sir Frederick Lewis, Chairman of the shipping concern Lewis, Whitby and Company, testified that German shipyards had given him bids for new ship construction substantially lower than those made by British shipyards. Even if the price of British steel declined with the imposition of a tariff on imported steel, the difference in price would not be enough to make British yards competitive with their German rivals. Churchill asked Lewis if he thought British shipbuilders would agree 'that a protective duty on steel material for shipbuilding would injure their trade', to which Lewis replied 'I should think so' [12 November 1925, CAB 58: 25]. This statement directly contradicted the previous witness, Clarence Smith, who readily agreed with Amery's suggestion that 'the transfer of steel production to this country [as the result of protection] would add considerably to the volume of British shipping', thereby indirectly helping the shipping industry, 'because it would create more freights' [16]. Smith, however, was Chairman of the Consett Iron Industry and not someone like Sir Frederick, whose job actually involved commissioning new ships. The ship of protection was now sinking fast.

The CRC wound up its investigation into the iron and steel industry on 19 November. Speaking first, Churchill pointed out that 'the White Paper setting out the procedure to be followed in the Safeguarding of Industries Act gave the Government full power, even if a *prima facie* case had been established, to refuse to grant an inquiry on the ground of the probable repercussions on other industries of a Safeguarding duty'. Since a duty on iron and steel would obviously have a widespread affect on other industries, as the shipbuilding example demonstrated, Churchill argued that the Government should 'refuse the Steel Industry's application for a Safeguarding inquiry on the ground of repercussion'. Once more the Chancellor expressed his view that the real problem lay in manufacturers' inefficiency, and that the 'proper way to assist the industry was to lead them along the path of further concentration'. To this end, Churchill himself offered to assist in 'preparing a scheme of amalgamation to increase efficiency of the [iron and steel] trade'. If, however, after the application for protection 'were refused the industry were to sulk and refuse to consider the question of further concentration, the Government could only await the working of economic forces' [19 November 1925, CAB 58: 4–5]. Amery responded to this by arguing:

> that nothing had appeared in the evidence in regard to the question of the possible repercussions of a duty that would justify the Government in refusing to grant a Safeguarding inquiry. [...] He recommended therefore that the Committee should report to the Cabinet –
>
> (1.) That they had failed to discover any alternative method of assisting the steel industry in its present difficulties. [and]
>
> (2.) That they saw no economic grounds for refusing the application put forward by the industry for a safeguarding inquiry. [5]

BALDWIN'S TRIUMPH

Baldwin agreed, as he later frankly admitted to the House, that the case for granting a safeguarding inquiry to the iron and steel industry had indeed been made out in the abstract. Churchill's warnings, however, that this would effectively result in an incremental general tariff that violated the 1924 election pledge carried greater weight with the Prime Minister. As Baldwin's biographers point out, 'every argument, from the unity of the Government to his [Baldwin's] avowed aim of peace and social reform, lay against provoking an almost inevitable general election'. [*Baldwin*: 316]. Enough time and committee activity had passed since June that the Prime Minister could honestly tell the protectionists that the request for safeguarding had been thoroughly explored and determined to be politically impossible. On 18 December, the Cabinet agreed that 'in these circumstances, the Prime Minister should announce in the House of Commons that the Government had decided not to grant the application of the Iron and Steel Industry for an Inquiry under the Safeguarding of Industries Procedure'. Moreover, the President of the Board of Trade was directed to refuse applications from any individual sector connected with iron and steel production. The Cabinet did authorise the CRC 'to keep the iron and steel trade under review', which in fact it did for three more years [18 December 1925, CAB 23/51: 191]. The CRC was supposed to promote the well-being of the industry by stimulating orders for railways, securing the scrapping of old merchant ships, and by encouraging amalgamation of steel mills. None of these alternative policies ever amounted to much. The British iron and steel industry remained depressed throughout the decade that followed.

Any chance for the introduction of widespread protection during the second Baldwin government had ended. For his defeat, Amery naturally blamed Churchill. Indirectly, he blamed Baldwin, who, in an effort to block Lloyd George from returning to power, 'had given the key position in the Cabinet to an avowed and determined opponent of the whole policy in which he [Baldwin] professed to believe, and, indeed, thought he believed' [AMERY: II, 479]. Amery was correct in his analysis, but he obviously failed to understand Baldwin. The Prime Minister did not share the Colonial Secretary's Imperial vision. For Baldwin, tariffs were never more than a domestic fiscal policy. Since that policy had been twice rejected by voters and never won support outside of just one segment of the Conservative Party, Baldwin saw no sound reason to make tariff reform the main thrust of his domestic policy when he became Prime Minister again in 1924. There would be some introduction of tariffs, but no more. The major legislation of the Government would be the reforms prepared by Health Secretary Neville Chamberlain with Churchill's full support. Churchill also served as Baldwin's bulldog by successfully marginalising the protectionists without splitting the Government. Churchill had done the leg work, but the outcome had been by the Prime Minister's design. The triumph belonged to Baldwin.

ENDNOTES

1 In his memoirs [II: 346], Amery erroneously claims that the Marketing Fund solution had been his idea, a fact gainsaid by his own diary in which he wrote that he 'was anything but happy' with the plan [*Amery Diaries*, 8 December 1924: 394].

CHAPTER 5

CITIZENS AND STATESMEN IN CHURCHILL'S *THOUGHTS AND ADVENTURES*[I]

JAMES W. MULLER
University of Alaska, Anchorage

> ...Churchill devoted much of the 1930s to literary endeavours. [...] In the intervals between writing history and making it, he poured out a stream of articles for the press...
>
> Paul Addison, *Churchill: The Unexpected Hero*

More than half a century after his death, as personal memories of Winston Churchill's statesmanship grow rarer and dimmer, the books he wrote afford a window into his soul, allowing us to recover his understanding of the world he experienced. Successive decades of his life, as he recognised, ushered in enormous and momentous changes, both in politics and in science and technology. As a scion of one of Britain's most prominent aristocratic families, Churchill lived to see the disappearance of aristocratic privilege and the transformation of Britain's government into a democracy. Born into the Victorian world before the invention of the internal combustion engine, he also lived to see the beginning of the atomic age and the diplomacy of mutual assured destruction.

The First World War was in many ways the turning point of these changes. In his autobiography, *My Early Life: A Roving Commission* (*MEL*), Churchill tells us that in 1920, he invited Paul Cambon, before he retired after twenty years as French ambassador to the Court of St. James's, to luncheon at his house. They talked about "the giant events through which we had passed and the distance the world had travelled since the beginning of the century" [*MEL*: 104–105]. The ambassador told him that over the past two decades he had 'witnessed an English Revolution more profound and searching than the French Revolution itself. The governing class have been almost entirely deprived of their property and estates; and this has been accomplished almost imperceptibly and without the loss of a single life' [105]. Recalling this observation in *My Early Life* a decade later, Churchill found that in writing an account of his youth and early manhood, with a focus on the years in his early twenties between 1895 and 1900 which he called 'the staple of this story' [74], he had indeed 'drawn a picture of a vanished age', looking back on changes he 'should not have believed possible in so short a space without any violent domestic revolution' [9].

These two revolutions, in science and in politics, were the focus of the books he wrote in his middle period as an author, in the years between the two world wars. In the preface to a book of his essays published in 1932, *Thoughts and Adventures*,[2] Churchill remarks on 'the extreme diversity of event and atmosphere through which a man of my generation, now in its twelfth lustre, has passed and is passing' [*T&A*: 1]. He warns of 'two alternative Infernos'—'two nightmares'—that may come upon us, 'if Civilisation cannot take itself in hand and turn its back on those Cities of Destruction and Enslavement to which Science holds the keys'. Churchill tells us he has 'tried to adumbrate' these Infernos in two essays toward the end of the book, 'Shall We All Commit Suicide?' and 'Fifty Years Hence' [2].

In 'Shall We All Commit Suicide?' Churchill apprehends the coming of a City of Destruction, a term that he borrows from the Old Testament prophet Isaiah, who foresees such a city in Egypt [*Isaiah*

19:18], or from the seventeenth-century author John Bunyan, whose protagonist Christian begins his journey in *Pilgrim's Progress* there. In both of these cities, citizens' faithlessness to God causes their destruction. Churchill's City of Destruction is distinctly modern. As our author explains it, 'the story of the human race is War'. Yet up till now, human beings have been spared the ability to destroy their own species, not for want of ferocity but because 'the means of destruction at the disposal of man have not kept pace with his ferocity'. His needs 'to live and hunt and sleep' fortunately distracted him from the 'murderous strife' that 'was universal and unending' in prehistoric times, preventing anything like 'reciprocal extermination'. The human race stayed alive, gradually developing 'tribes, villages, and governments' [*T&A*: 259]. With their aid, roads were built and considerable armies assembled, who attacked their enemies with deadlier weapons. But governments remained insecure, armies were riven by violent struggles, and it was difficult to feed so many men concentrated in one place—all of which hampered men's efforts to destroy each other.

Therefore, Churchill argues, 'it was not until the dawn of the twentieth century of the Christian era that War really began to enter into its kingdom as the potential destroyer of the human race'. He gives eight reasons for this change: (1) Great states, empires, and nations could wage bigger and longer wars. (2) Individuals' 'noblest virtues' were combined in 'the destructive capacity of the mass'. (3) Finance, credit, trade, and capital reserves allowed men to concentrate on devastation. (4) Democratic institutions reflected the will of millions. (5) Education explained war to everyone and helped everyone wage it. (6) The press unified and encouraged the people. (7) Religion provided encouragement and consolation. Finally, (8) 'Science unfolded her treasures and her secrets to the desperate demands of men, and placed in their hands agencies and apparatus almost decisive in their character' [260].

These changes came together in the great climacteric we know as the First World War. Europe, much of Asia, and then North America as well were wrenched into a new kind of struggle in which not just professional armies but whole peoples were subjected to all the rigours of war. Churchill points out that technological innovations would have made the unfought 1919 campaign even more destructive than those of preceding years [260–262]. Nor were the grievances that provoked war put to rest by peace settlements afterwards: he refers to 'fires of hatred burning deep in the hearts of some of the greatest peoples in the world, fanned by continual provocation and unceasing fear, and fed by the deepest sense of national wrong or national danger!' [265]. Russia chafed under the loss of 'her Baltic Provinces'—Estonia, Latvia, and Lithuania—under the 1918 Treaty of Brest-Litovsk, and 'intense hatred of France' was even more potent in Germany [263]. Hence Churchill calls what we know as the interwar years a 'period of Exhaustion' rather than one of 'Peace'. But he tells readers they have at least at present 'an opportunity to consider the general situation':

> Certain sombre facts emerge solid, inexorable, like the shapes of mountains from drifting mist. It is established that henceforward whole populations will take part in war, all doing their utmost, all subjected to the fury of the enemy. It is established that nations who believe their life is at stake will not be restrained from using any means to secure their existence. It is probable—nay, certain—that among the means which will next time be at their disposal will be agencies and processes of destruction wholesale, unlimited, and perhaps, once launched, uncontrollable.

In the first of the two 'nightmares' that Churchill mentions in his preface—as this essay's startling title 'Shall We All Commit Suicide?' makes clear—mankind, having 'got into its hands for the first time the tools by which it can unfailingly accomplish its own extermination', actually does use them to destroy the human race [262].

Churchill indicates that this nightmare is still a few steps away from being real. Although he acknowledges that human 'virtue' or 'wiser guidance' might help prevent human beings from destroying themselves and claims that is now among 'their new responsibilities', he cannot realistically expect nations to shrink from any extreme if they 'believe their life is at stake' [262]. How acute that danger is may be judged from two observations he makes.

First, he foresees new, more powerful weapons of all kinds—metallic [steel or aluminum], electrical, explosive, poison, chemical, and biological. He brushes aside the forlorn hope of developing some universal remote-controlled detonating ray to set off dangerous explosives in the hands of aggressors before they could use them against others [265]. Instead, he imagines 'methods of using explosive energy incomparably more intense than anything heretofore discovered. Might not a bomb no bigger than an orange be found', he asks, 'to possess a secret power to destroy a whole block of buildings—nay, to concentrate the force of a thousand tons of cordite and blast a township at a stroke?' If we are not quite there yet, he observes that 'military science is remorselessly advancing' [264], its march 'unfolding ever more appalling possibilities' [265]. The weapons of the future 'will be incomparably more formidable and fatal' than those which laid so much of the world in waste after the Great War [262].

Second, he observes that, unlike the 'superior martial virtues—physical strength, courage, skill, discipline'—that allowed 'the best and fittest' to prevail 'in barbarous times', the scientific knowledge required to gain 'supremacy' over one's enemies may belong to 'a base, degenerate, immoral race' [264]. Thus even 'the liberties of men are no longer to be guarded by their natural qualities, but by their dodges', through some scientific artifice that is no respecter of morality or justice [265]. Whereas classical magnanimity, self-respect, or Christian mercy might cause men possessing these traditional virtues to forbear from iniquity, modern science in the hands of base men might allow them to prevail over 'an enemy far above them in quality' [264]: Churchill warns that 'superior virtue and valour may fall an easy prey to the latest diabolical trick' that has no relation 'to any form of human merit' [265]. Therefore the science and technology of warfare, especially new developments that might upset the balance of power among nations, must be carefully studied by decent statesmen as well as arrant aggressors—as he did throughout his career. Otherwise 'possession by one side of some overwhelming scientific advantage would lead to the complete enslavement of the unwary party', since those who got the jump on the others could reduce 'their opponents to absolute helplessness' [264].

To be sure, Churchill concedes that 'the blessed respite of Exhaustion' after the Great War [265]—which might produce no more than 'a sullen passivity' arising from 'the horror of war' and subjecting the human soul to 'stupor' and 'collapse' [262]—offers 'the nations a final chance to control their destinies and avert what may well be a general doom' [265]. Yet the inexorable grinding mechanisms of mobilising and deploying huge armies that went into motion after the assassination of the Archduke Ferdinand in Sarajevo, which Churchill describes in the final volume of his memoirs of the First World War, *The World Crisis: The Eastern Front*, tracing the outbreak of the unknown war on the eastern front, prevented statesmen from stopping that war. Indeed, the sudden subjection of decent, well-meaning men to imperious necessities, so that the war escaped from human ability to guide and control it, is a central theme of Churchill's memoirs, *The World Crisis, 1911–1914*.

It is not given to human beings to have certain knowledge of the future. Readers seeking respite from the apocalyptic tone of this essay's title may protest that, despite their firm intentions, future combatants in a scientific war may fail to exterminate the entire human race. If a diabolical opponent secures an iniquitous advantage over a more decent nation, Churchill writes, the loser faces 'complete enslavement' as the ignoble alternative to personal suicide—an enslavement tantamount to the suicide of the nation. To exchange liberty for a life not worth living is a hard and poor bargain. On the other hand, the hopeful reader may reply that asymmetric warfare or the unpredictable chances of war might produce a lesser punishment for one side or both—at least an incomplete extermination of the human race. Churchill admits this possibility, which anticipates only 'the ruin of the world' and 'an immeasurable diminution of the human race' [*T&A*: 264]. This lesser disaster would 'shear away the peoples *en masse*', if not *tout entiers*, and would 'pulverise, without hope of repair, what is left of civilisation' [262].

What Churchill means by civilisation is mankind's success in forsaking the violence and insecurity of primitive barbarism by founding cities and eventually nations that allow people to live in liberty and safety. While civilisation does not guarantee that justice will be achieved, it is the indispensable condition for pursuing that human aspiration. The preservation of some men on one side or the other, or even both sides, after an apocalyptic future war, leading lives not worth living in a ruined world with no civilisation left, so far from affording solid consolation, is a very bleak alternative to complete extermination.

Readers who are hopeful, rather than simply exhausted, may persist in believing the world has left these dangers behind by the armistice and the peace settlements ending the war to end all wars and by founding the League of Nations to preserve the peace. 'Surely', Churchill agrees, 'if a sense of self-preservation still exists among men, if the will to live resides not merely in individuals or nations but in humanity as a whole, the prevention of the supreme catastrophe ought to be the paramount object of all endeavour' [265]. He does not turn up his nose at the League: on the last page of the essay he calls it the only 'path to safety and salvation', so that 'to sustain and aid the League of Nations is the duty of all' [266].

Yet Churchill combines this exhortation on behalf of the lone choiceworthy alternative to the two Cities of Destruction or Enslavement with a douche in ice-cold water for anyone who trusts in the League to achieve it:

> Against the gathering but still distant tempest the League of Nations, deserted by the United States, scorned by Soviet Russia, flouted by Italy, distrusted equally by France and Germany, raises feebly but faithfully its standards of sanity and hope. Its structure, airy and unsubstantial, framed of shining but too often visionary idealism, is in its present form incapable of guarding the world from its dangers and of protecting mankind from itself. [265–266]

The League, which can boast neither the armed force of the powerful nations that might break the peace nor the long-sustained allegiance of the citizens of those nations, is too weak a reed to uphold mankind's hopes for maintaining liberty, civilisation, and peace. Churchill argued that only support of the League's aims by the prudent efforts of the strongest nations in the world, including application of their armed forces against potential aggressors, could preserve civilisation and enable the League's aims to be achieved.

After the next war and its defeat of inhuman tyrannies with the eventual explosion of the atomic bomb, in his last prime ministry he had to come to grips with the invention of the far more powerful hydrogen bomb that brought the world still closer to the destruction he had foreseen in this essay and its possession by hard, brutal men who held captive the people of Russia and the eastern half of Europe. Lest his nightmare come true, Churchill sought to open a dialogue with the Soviet rulers, arguing that the communists' denial of liberty was unnatural and that Russians would eventually turn their back on communism if the peace could be preserved, but that the world could not afford a nuclear war that threatened, if not to destroy the human race, at least to kill hundreds of millions and to destroy civilisation.

The danger comes from the increase of human power without a corresponding increase in human virtue or wisdom: moral and political progress has not kept pace with scientific progress in the power of human beings to destroy or enslave their fellows. Human beings have always been subject to death and capable of killing each other before death would catch up to them after the span of years allowed by nature. The power to master nature, even if it has not enabled human beings to overcome death, has enabled them to inflict death on whole cities and peoples: 'mankind has never been in this position before', but 'that is the point in human destinies to which all the glories and toils of men have at last led them'. Churchill observes this awful power in the hands of 'a frail, bewildered being' [262], whom he endeavors to guide to prudent preservation of the civilisation mankind has achieved up till now.

In the second of the two essays exploring the nightmares of Churchill's preface to *Thoughts and Adventures*, 'Fifty Years Hence', we learn more about the possibility that we might find ourselves in a City of Enslavement, which he briefly mentions in 'Shall We All Commit Suicide?' Churchill began thinking about this essay with the aid of a memorandum written by his scientific adviser, Professor Frederick Lindemann of Oxford University (afterwards Lord Cherwell), whom he had asked to speculate on advancements in science and technology to be expected in the next half-century.[3] Noticing that the twentieth century 'has witnessed an enormous revolution in material things, in scientific appliances, in political institutions, in manner and customs', Churchill argues that 'the greatest change of all' is 'the far greater numbers which in every civilised country participate in the fuller life of man'. The world of aristocracy, in which 'England was for the few and for the very few' [*T&A*: 283] in words he quotes from Disraeli,[4] has been replaced by a new world of democracy, in which life in Britain 'has become larger, safer, more varied, more full of hope and choice' for 'many millions'. This democracy is even more advanced across the ocean in the United States, where 'scores of millions have lifted themselves above primary necessities and comforts, and aspire to culture—at least for their children'. Across the Channel, Europe has experienced 'a similar if less general advance', although a continent 'stunned and lacerated by Armageddon' [*T&A*: 283].

Churchill explains that in modern times 'we assume that progress will be constant'. If it were to stop now or be reversed, we could not maintain the comforts or even the existence of everyone who depends on it. Science, with 'a vast organised united class-conscious army' which cares nothing for our laws, customs, beliefs, or instincts, has caused our pace of life to increase. When it comes to making prophecies about the future, Churchill denies that the historians' method of likening our situation to a similar period in the past is of any avail [288], since the changes during the last century 'have been so sudden and so gigantic that no period in history' is comparable [286]. Only through the scientists' method of 'observing all that Science has achieved in modern times, and the knowledge and power now in her possession', can we foresee inventions and discoveries that may be coming next. Churchill wonders 'what reactions these discoveries and their applications will produce upon the habits, the outlook and the spirit of men' [288].

He expects science to advance even more quickly, increasing man's power over nature and allowing 'schemes of cosmic magnitude', so that 'geography and climate would obey our orders' [289]. He predicts we will have 'materials thirty times stronger than the best steel', new forms of transportation and communication by land, water, and air, and wireless telephones and television. Claiming that 'civilised races' have learned to get all the food they need [290], he imagines new kinds of synthetic food and underground farms where food can be grown without sunlight [291].

Just over the horizon he espies 'startling developments' in breeding human beings and in shaping human nature [291]. After seeing the Czech playwright Karel Čapek's play *Rossum's Universal Robots* in London, which pioneered the idea of robots, Churchill thought they might be among us within fifty years. More than eighty-five years later, we hear plenty of breathless talk about the internet of things—computerised speakers, refrigerators, automobiles, and whatnot, sometimes with minds of their own, or with native mechanical cussedness not so different from our own—but Churchill's prophecy is more ominous. He imagines the production of 'beings specialised to thought or toil'—creatures of 'admirable physical development', but 'with their mental endowment stunted in particular directions'. Such a creature might be willing to spend its life taking care of a machine, without having any other ambition. While Churchill is confident that 'the laws of a Christian civilisation' will prevent 'such fearful eventualities' among us, he is not so sure about other regimes:

> [M]ight not lop-sided creatures of this type fit in well with the Communist doctrines of Russia? Might not the Union of Soviet

> Republics armed with all the power of science find it in harmony with all their aims to produce a race adapted to mechanical tasks and with no other ideas but to obey the Communist State? The present nature of man is tough and resilient. It casts up its sparks of genius in the darkest and most unexpected places. But Robots could be made to fit the grisly theories of Communism. There is nothing in the philosophy of Communists to prevent their creation.

He fears that 'despotisms and tyrannies will be able to prescribe the lives and even the wishes of their subjects in a manner never known since time began'—in short, that science will show iniquitous rulers how to usher not only defeated enemies but even their own citizens into modern Cities of Enslavement. Observing that 'one of the most powerful reigning governments' has leaders with 'pitiless sub-human wickedness' [292], he asks, 'who shall say that the world itself will not be wrecked, or indeed that it ought not to be wrecked?' [292–293]. A tough and resilient man might prefer death to slavery: 'There are nightmares of the future', Churchill writes, 'from which a fortunate collision with some wandering star, reducing the earth to incandescent gas, might be a merciful deliverance' [293].

Thence he comes back down to Britain to consider the effect of these impending discoveries 'upon the structure of Parliamentary institutions', admitting that it is 'a descent almost to the ridiculous'. In a blunt, uncompromising critique, Churchill states that 'democracy as a guide or motive to progress has long been known to be incompetent'. He finds it simply unimaginable that 'the whole mass of the people' could decide by their votes in an election 'the right course to adopt amid these cataclysmic changes'. Britain as he wrote was in the depths of the Great Depression, which by 1931 had crossed the ocean from America and was causing a worldwide economic decline. Churchill tells us that 'Parliaments of every country' have been at a loss to find their way out of this crisis [293]. Among earlier essays in *Thoughts and Adventures* is 'Parliamentary Government and the Economic Problem', which he had delivered as the Romanes Lecture at Oxford in 1930, arguing that people wanted 'more prosperity', yet 'neither the electors nor their representatives' knew how to achieve it [254]. He recommends establishment of 'an Economic sub-Parliament' of experts to advise the parliamentarians [255].

In the face of still greater challenges from 'the tremendous and terrifying discoveries which are approaching', Churchill dismisses as inadequate 'the claptrap of the hustings and the stunts of the newspapers'. Nor does he think any of the 'legislative assemblies of the great modern states' possess, in the new era of universal suffrage, 'even a fraction of the strength or wisdom of the community'. In an argument reminiscent of Alexis de Tocqueville's assessment of popular government in *Democracy in America*, he rues the fact that

> Great nations are no longer led by their ablest men, or by those who know most about their immediate affairs, or even by those who have a coherent doctrine. Democratic governments drift along the line of least resistance, taking short views, paying their way with sops and doles and smoothing their path with pleasant-sounding platitudes. Never was there less continuity or design in their affairs, and yet towards them are coming swiftly changes which will revolutionise for good or ill not only the whole economic structure of the world but the social habits and moral outlook of every family. Only the Communists have a plan and a gospel. It is a plan fatal to personal freedom and a gospel founded upon Hate. [293]

In this argument we discern the human attributes that Churchill considers qualifications to rule: ability, expertise in a nation's immediate affairs, and possession of a coherent doctrine. The attributes are in descending order. A ruler with knowledge limited to immediate affairs will be incapable of handling wider questions, and a coherent doctrine all by itself may take a nation the wrong way in immediate affairs or in larger challenges. The line of least resistance, short-sightedness, sops, doles, and plausible platitudes characterise rule by those with none of these attributes, resulting in a lack of continuity or design. Having to face swift, revolutionary change makes such absent-minded rule all the more dangerous. Democratic governments are at a loss not only in coping with this change, but also in competition with communists, who have at least a coherent doctrine. The trouble is that their plan and gospel makes life not worth living.

An able ruler might be able to lead fellow parliamentarians toward better comprehension of the nation's good. An able man who was not a ruler might be less able to do so. That may be why Churchill, taking his bearings from the effect of the approaching changes caused by science on the habits and outlook of every family, turns in the rest of 'Fifty Years Hence' to 'the moral philosophy and spiritual conceptions of men and nations', since he might have the opportunity to influence his countrymen's thinking. Here he argues that the modern increase in scientific knowledge and power has not improved men's virtues and wisdom:

> The brain of a modern man does not differ in essentials from that of the human beings who fought and loved here millions of years ago. The nature of man has remained hitherto practically unchanged. Under sufficient stress,—starvation, terror, warlike passion, or even cold intellectual frenzy, the modern man we know so well will do the most terrible deeds, and his modern woman will back him up.

Churchill observes that man's weapons and powers have outstripped his intelligence and his intelligence has outstripped his nobility, so that, in the words of Thomas Babington Macaulay, we have civilisation's strength without its mercy. Hence it is crucial for our moral philosophy and spiritual conceptions to hold their own against all these scientific changes, lest we be enslaved 'by our own apparatus and the forces which it directs'. The danger is that, 'without an equal growth of Mercy, Pity, Peace and Love, Science herself may destroy all that makes human life majestic and tolerable'. Churchill emphasises the importance of expressing 'the inherent virtue of human beings' strongly and confidently in our daily lives, disdaining 'earthly power and achievement' and hoping for immortality for the sake of our safety [294–295].

It turns out, he concludes, that 'material progress, in itself so splendid, does not meet any of the real needs of the human race'. Churchill suggests why by appealing to a science fiction book he had read 'the other day' [295] about the 'far future' of the human race.[5] The book told the story of mankind 'from the birth of the solar system to its extinction', tracing human history through 'fifteen or sixteen races of men' over 'tens of millions of years'. Eventually they learned to master nature:

> A state was created whose citizens lived as long as they chose, enjoyed pleasures and sympathies incomparably wider than our own, navigated the inter-planetary spaces, could recall the panorama of the past and foresee the future. But what was the good of all that to them? What did they know more than we know about the answers to the simple questions which man has asked since the earliest dawn of reason—'Why are we here? What is the purpose of life? Whither are we going?' No material progress, even though it takes shapes we cannot now conceive, or however it may expand the faculties of man, can bring comfort to his soul. It is this fact, more wonderful than any that Science can reveal, which gives the best hope that all will be well.

While modern science concentrates on ministering to the material needs of our bodies, Churchill reminds us that our 'tough and resilient' human nature has made us beings who have souls. Whatever changes may come about in the future to our material surroundings or even to our bodies, the human nature that gives us souls is enduring. Our souls have needs of their own; and Churchill foresees that, despite the material powers that science may eventually vouchsafe to our descendants, 'their hearts will ache, their lives will be barren, if they have not a vision above material things'. Long ago Moses offered the Israelites a choice between life and death, between blessing and cursing. Churchill tells us that mankind is facing that choice again, and 'never was the answer that will be given harder to foretell' [295].

Our author recognises in the preface to *Thoughts and Adventures* that he has tucked his 'two nightmares', the two essays we have considered here, into a book full of papers many of which 'touch on the lighter side of grave affairs'. Yet he writes that he 'should be sorry if on this account' anyone took them 'merely as the amusing speculations of a dilettante Cassandra', imagining that his prophecies about the two 'alternative Infernos' of destruction and enslavement might not find readers who were willing to consider them seriously. Churchill assures us that he means them 'in deadly earnest as a warning of what may easily come to pass' [2]. The lapse of nine decades since he wrote them has made them not a whit less timely. May this essay help them find new readers.

ENDNOTES

1 An earlier version of this essay was presented to the International Churchill Society's related group panel 'Winston Churchill on Democracy and Its Discontents' at the annual meeting of the American Political Science Association in Boston, August 31, 2018.

2 Winston S. CHURCHILL, *Thoughts and Adventures* (London: Thornton Butterworth Limited, 1932). The current edition cited here is Winston S. Churchill, *Thoughts and Adventures: Churchill Reflects on Spies, Cartoons, Flying and the Future*, ed. James W. MULLER (Wilmington, DE: ISI Books, 2009), hereafter referred to as *T&A*. In fact, although Churchill approved of the book's preface, it was written not by him but by his former secretary Edward Marsh, since Churchill was recuperating from illness [*T&A:* 339].

3 For a description of this memorandum, see *T&A*: 360.

4 Churchill gives no source for the quotation, and I have never been able to trace its origin.

5 He does not name the book, but it was Olaf Stapledon, *Last and First Men: A Story of the Near and Far Future* (London: Methuen & Co. Ltd., 1930).

CHAPTER 6

THE PEOPLE'S CONVENTION, 1940–1941: A SOVIET STALKING HORSE?

RICHARD OVERY
University of Exeter

On 12 January 1941, at the Royal Hotel in central London, the self-styled 'People's Convention' assembled to launch a wartime political movement to demand a British government that genuinely reflected the needs of the people, and could broker a people's peace. The popular response to the Convention was muted and within a year the organisers suspended its activity. Historians have given the movement scant regard.

Andrew Thorpe in his study of wartime political parties gives the Convention no more than a passing mention as part of the perceived though limited threat of Communist activism in 1940–41 [THORPE, *Parties at War:* 129, 201]. Sonya Rose in her study of Britain's 'people's war' gives it no mention at all [ROSE, 2003]; Paul Addison's *Road to 1945* is equally silent about a movement whose temporary publicity in 1940–41 makes wartime consensus at best a relative reality. Dan Todman in his panoramic history of Britain [TODMAN: 611–612] and Geoffrey Field in his study of Britain's wartime working class give a brief and not wholly accurate account of a movement they see as entirely communist-inspired

[FIELD: 90–91, 314–316]. It is necessary to go back to Angus Calder's 1969 classic *The People's War* to find at least an account of the Convention conference itself, though Calder viewed the initiative in largely negative terms. At the time, and since, the People's Convention movement has been regarded as a thinly-veiled Communist front set up to compensate for the unpopularity of the Communist Party of Great Britain in the shadow of the German-Soviet Pact of August 1939 and the Soviet war on Finland [THORPE, *The British Commmunist Party and Moscow*: 264]. A week after the meeting in London, the Communist mouthpiece, *The Daily Worker*, a consistent supporter of the People's Convention, was closed down on the orders of the Home Secretary. The People's Convention was defined by the Ministry of Home Security as 'subversive' [TNA, HO 199/478].

There is little doubt that British Communists and their sympathisers contributed to the establishment of the People's Convention, though not only Communists; nor can it be argued that the movement in the end had anything but a marginal impact on British politics in the first two years of war. It is nevertheless of more than historical curiosity to understand how a vocal anti-government movement could function in wartime at a time when Britain faced the deepest crisis of the war, and be tolerated by authorities keen to minimise any evidence that the home front was not solidly united behind the war effort. It is the purpose of this article to argue that the movement must be understood as something more than a short-term Communist political gambit. The People's Convention movement says something about the complex and contested nature of British public engagement with the war effort and about public imagination of a postwar world which was not exclusively Communist. Like the Bombing Restriction Committee, which emerged a few months after the founding of the People's Convention in order to campaign head-on against the strategy of bombing German cities by night, the movement challenged the mood of wartime consensus and demonstrated the possibility of multiple, and sometimes discordant discourses in shaping public perception of the war and its leaders [OVERY, 'Constructing Space for Dissent in War'].

To understand the origins and evolution of the People's Convention, it must be set in the broader historical context of the late 1930s and the onset of war. The notion of a 'People's Government' or popular front was hardly new in 1941. The hostility to waging an imperialist, bosses' war, was also a product of left-wing and pacifist anti-militarism from at least the mid-1930s, if not earlier. The practical concern that not enough was being done to provide the working class with adequate air-raid shelter, which was the most immediately relevant plank in the movement's platform, had been a bone of contention before the war as left-wing scientists, architects and local officials tried to persuade the government unsuccessfully of the need for 'deep shelters'. Political sympathy for the Soviet Union and its people, which was point five of the movement's programme, ran as a thick thread through the 1930s and continued into wartime, despite the German-Soviet Pact and the Soviet invasion of Finland in November 1939, which the mainstream labour movement in Britain strongly condemned. Finally, the movement's decision to identify with the anti-colonial lobby and freedom for India, linked it to a decade or more of British protest against the abuses of Empire. The 500 sponsors who signed in support of the meeting in January 1941 included some well-known names identified with pre-war movements, protests or petitions—the scientists J.H.B. Haldane and Hyman Levy, the clerics Hewlett Johnson (the Red Dean), Mervyn Stockwood, and Stanley Evans, the actors Michael Redgrave and Beatrix Lehmann—but chiefly a large number of trade union officials and organisers who saw the Convention in terms of the longer struggle to protect working-class interests after the inter-war depression.[1] Seen from the perspective of continutities with the 1930s, the People's Convention appears at once less anomalous, building on initiatives and mobilising sentiments that are historically recognisable from the pre-war years.

This article seeks to explore the context more fully in order to give the movement greater historical depth, but it is first necessary to outline its immediate origins and brief history. The People's Convention left little archival footprint, which may well explain the lack of historical interest in its brief flourishing. It is necessary to rely on the Convention's own publications, broadsheets, conference programmes and propaganda as the movement's principal archive. Mass Observation provides a full account of the initial People's Convention congress in London, and subsequent comment, while the survey of the movement's 'subversive' status provides some additional material in The National Archives from the Ministry of Home Security and the Ministry of Information. There are brief references in the Pritt papers in the London School of Economics, and in the Communist Party of Great Britain collection in the People's History Museum in Manchester. The broader context in which the movement can be placed is more easily accessed through private papers, organisational records and the publicity generated by a variety of movements and lobby groups from the 1930s and on into the war, while contemporary publications on issues from air-raid shelters to popular fronts supply much of the evidence of continuity.

The People's Convention emerged from initiatives taken in June 1940, after the disaster in France, by left-wing circles highly critical of the way the war had been handled by a predominantly Conservative National Government. The Hammersmith branch of the Labour Party and the Hammersmith Trades Council set up informal discussions to establish a provisional committee to mobilise the discontent, encouraged by the Labour MP for Hammersmith, Denis Pritt, who had been expelled from the Party earlier in the year for his support of the Soviet war against Finland. At a meeting in Holborn Hall, Kingsway on 7 July 1940, attended by a range of Labour Party, Trade Union and Communist Party members, a 'People's Vigilance Committee' was established consisting of Pritt, Harry Adams, the London organiser of the Amalgamated Union of Building Trade Workers, W. 'Dick' Squance, former secretary of ASLEF, and Labour councillor J.E. Skilbeck, London organiser of the

Woodworkers' Union [Branson: 290–291; Pritt: I, 247–249]. The latter three were still Labour Party members, but were immediately expelled, like Pritt, from the Party. The Hammersmith Labour Party and Trades Council were also disaffiliated and then reorganised, along with a number of other Labour Party branches who supported People's Vigilance; by February 1941 33 members had been expelled by Labour's executive and 55 by local Labour Party branches [Thorpe, *Parties at War*: 129, 201]. The initiative was supported by Rajani Palme Dutt, appointed in October 1939 as effective general secretary of the Communist Party of Great Britain following the reignation of Harry Pollitt, who found it hard to embrace the party line from Moscow after the Pact. Dutt used the *Labour Monthly*, which he edited, to advertise the new committee and to encourage the development of local Vigilance Committees to raise the profile of the new movement [Callaghan: 193–194; Stammers: 103]. The movement was helped by the sudden expansion of readership for the *Labour Monthly*, whose sales leapt from 7,500 in August 1939 to more than 20,000 by December 1940. *Labour Monthly* discussion groups also rapidly expanded countrywide across 1940–41, from only a handful in early 1940, to 83 a year later, and over 200 by June 1941 [*Labour Monthly* 23/1 (January 1941): 2]. The Communist *Daily Worker* added to support for the movement. In June 1940 the composition of the editorial board was made public for the first time. The chairman was the Marxist scientist J.B.S. Haldane (he joined the Communist Party only in 1942), who became a key member of the future Convention for his promotion of effective bomb-proof shelters in working-class districts [Branson: 291–292].

The National People's Vigilance Committee initially drew up five principal demands at the initial congress: to get rid of the 'men of Munich' still in the government; to develop friendship with the Soviet Union; to reestablish democratic rights; to defend living standards and end alleged profiteering; and finally to form a new 'people's government' to provide the conditions for establishing a 'people's peace'. The central ambition of the new movement was to organise a People's Convention which would publicly rally all the forces opposed to the current government around the slogans adopted in July 1940. A national organisation was set up based in High Holborn, London and the communist Ben Bradley appointed as national organiser of what was now called the People's Convention. While local vigilance committees were established principally across the major industrial regions and the London area, the national organisation drew up a manifesto in September 1940 for the forthcoming People's Convention congress in which the original five demands were replaced by six 'points'. The demand to get rid of the 'men of Munich' was dropped, the call for a people's government and a people's peace was separated into two points, and adequate air raid precautions and post-raid welfare added as a distinct demand, consistent with the growth of popular protest over poorly constructed and insanitary shelters with the onset of the Blitz [TNA, INF 1/319; GALLACHER, 'A Letter to all Trade Unionists', 1 November 1941: 4]. Some sense of how widely the new movement was to be publicised comes from the decision to print 250,000 copies of the manifesto leaflet. National Committee Members undertook to speak to local vigilance groups or informal meetings of shop stewards and union members, who formed the bulk of support [PRITT: 248–252].

The venue for the congress was the Free Trade Hall in Manchester, but it was damaged in the German air raids in December 1940, and a new venue had to be found at short notice. With only a week to go, the Royal Hotel in central London, only a short distance from the People's Vigilance headquarters, agreed to house the meeting in its main hall. So large was the number of delegates that the nearby Holborn Halls, both large and small, had to absorb the overflow and the main speakers went during the day from one venue to another to repeat their speeches [*The People Speak:* 3–5]. The Convention meeting on 12 January was the high point of the entire history of the movement. Against expectations that bombing, transport difficulties and cost would inhibit attendance, 2,234 delegates were present from all over the country. London was heavily overrepresented with 1,099 delegates, but 387 made the journey from northern England, and 117 from Scotland, even four from North Wales

[*The People Speak* (appendix 'Delegates Present'): 59]. Among those invited to attend was Indira Nehru, daughter of the Indian Congress leader, Jawaharlal Nehru, serving four years in prison under the British raj. Paul Robeson, the singer and campaigner for American civil rights sent a message of goodwill; so too did Mao Zedong from his embattled enclave in north-west China, hoping, perhaps rather optimistically, 'for a strengthening of international militant solidarity between the British and Chinese peoples'. Three of the National Committee, Denis Pritt, Harry Adams and Dick Squance, gave the main speeches. Krishna Menon, the future Indian defence minister, spoke about empire independence and was warmly applauded. Harold Moody, the black doctor who led the London-based League of Coloured Peoples, spoke about racism, which his son, who had recently joined the Royal Air Force, experienced at first hand [BOURNE: 23–26].

Among those attending the meeting was a Mass Observation reporter, working now ostensibly for the Ministry of Information's Home Intelligence department, who listened closely to the delegates in the lobbies and auditorium. The report concluded that men outnumbered women by three-to-one; that most delegates were between 25 and 35, with very few over 50; and that the delegates were overwhelmingly from the skilled working class, with a leavening of unskilled workers, but very few visibly 'middle class' [MO 54/3: 1]. Talk in the meeting and in the lobbies focused on peace, although the Convention was not intended to be pacifist. The reporter thought the meeting displayed a 'general feeling of ideological and spiritual starvation and bewilderment', reflecting a desire to address major issues rather than focus on material problems such as shelters, food, and labour conditions, which the Convention speakers addressed in detail. The atmosphere was hopeful and enthusiastic, but the widely discussed question 'what is the Convention going to lead to?' suggested that the Convention was a starting point with no clear direction [MO 54/3: 2–3].

The main practical issue was to appoint a national committee. The executive consisted of Harry Adams as chair, the former naval officer Edgar Young, a prominent anti-war campaigner in the 1930s, as vice-chair, Dick Squance as secretary and Denis Pritt as treasurer, all four recently expelled from the Labour Party; the full national committee had 26 members, drawn chiefly from among trade union delegates (including the communist Arthur Horner, president of the South Wales Miners' Federation) but also including public figures who supported the campaign, among them Haldane, the Dean of Canterbury, and Krishna Menon representing the India League [*Forward to a People's Government*: 3]. The committee then presented to the Convention each aspect of the Convention programme, but two additional points were added, both more radical in content than the original six. Point (4) of the programme now read 'Emergency powers to take over the banks, land, transport, armaments and other large industries…', echoing demands already evident in the 1930s for a more state-run economy. Point (5) called for independence for India, self-determination for the colonies, and an end to the 'enforced partition of Ireland' [*The People Speak:* 20]. Both of these additions represented very large issues over the future of the British economy and the Empire, but there is little to indicate why they were added at this juncture, although Ben Bradley, the Convention national organiser, also drafted the Communist Party study syllabus on 'The Colonies and the Future' endorsing self-determination [Bradley, *The Colonies and the Future*], while the inclusion of Menon on the National Committee demonstrated that the People's Convention was now intended to apply to the wider Empire. The issue of a united Ireland, however, remained dormant in the year of publications that followed.

The question of where the Convention was going to lead was indeed an apt one. The organisers saw the meeting itself as 'something momentous in the history of our country', but the direct consequences scarcely matched the rhetoric [*The People Speak:* 3]. Local Convention meetings continued, but the emphasis of the national committee was to identify with current protests, publishing special newssheets and pamphlets on food, the role of women in wartime and the campaign for better shelter accommodation, rather than mobilise protest more fully for a people's government and a people's peace. The London People's Convention met again at the Royal Hotel on 16 March, but the national committee recalled an emergency session of the Convention only once more after January, on 5 July 1941, in response to the German invasion of the Soviet Union [*Labour Monthly*, 23/3 (March 1941); PRITT: 272]. The venue was the Stoll Picture House in Kingsway, again only a few hundred yards from the movement's headquarters, and once again around 2,500 delegates attended, this time, noted a second Mass Observation reporter, more middle-class in composition, and largely men and women under 30 years of age. The reason for the meeting was to rally Anglo-Soviet co-operation now that the Soviet Union could once again return to fighting fascism, and, according to the report, 'enthusiasm was immense' [MO File 775: 10]. A manifesto calling for a 'Second Front' was issued a month later in an edition of 200,000, and a second manifesto in October called for supreme efforts by Britain's working class to help produce goods for the Soviet Union, and 'offensive action' to ease the pressure on the Red Army [*Manifesto*, October 1941: 1–2; PRITT: 274–275]. A decision to recall a national congress was, however, set aside and by January 1942 the National Committee reached the decision that the organisation should be suspended indefinitely. By this date the organisation could count only 1,650 active supporters countrywide [Edgar Young papers]. The resolution of the committee, adopted on 3 January 1942 acknowledged that with government support for the Soviet war effort, the main aim of the People's Convention had been met—which was scarcely the case—and supporters were now free to work hard for joint victory as part of the national effort [People's History Museum, CP/ORG/MISC/1/5]. The Convention began with a bang and ended with a whimper.

There is no very precise way of measuring how much support the People's Convention enjoyed during its brief year of activity, or identifying the political allegiance of the delegates that assembled in January and July. The organisers conducted their own statistical survey based on forms that each delegate had to fill in. The results are set out in Table I. The organisers then worked out how many members each delegate or group of delegates 'represented', to arrive at a remarkably precise overall figure of 1,284,413, of which 1,004,953 came from trade union organisations of a variety of kinds. The total of workers included 471 delegates elected directly by the workforce (presumably most of them shop stewards), representing 400,000 workers, and 31 delegates representing 270,000 mineworkers [*The People Speak:* 58–59, 'Delegates Present'].

Table I Delegate Composition at the People's Convention, 12 January 1941

Delegates	Elected from	Representing
471	239 factories and jobs	400,000
87	138 engineering and metal trade unions	67,680
31	26 miners' trade unions	270,000
94	65 building workers' organisations	27,900
153	86 transport ((road and rail unions)	45,450
22	11 unions from the furnishing trade	12,800
95	47 clerical, distributive and administrative unions	52,800
26	20 general workers' unions	4,500
55	55 electrical workers' unions	6,500
75	29 trade union organisations (tailoring, printing, firemen)	24,650
27	20 Trades Councils	92,673
99	89 co-operative organisations	50,000
254	199 political organisations	38,500
17	12 groups of professional workers	460
24	12 colonial organisations	10,000
164	91 youth organisations	20,000
261	131 People's Vigilance Committees	n/a
77	50 tenants' associations and shelter committees	118,000
23	14 housewives' committees	1,500
113	75 cultural, educational and discussion groups	11,000
66	30 miscellaneous organisations	30,000

The degree of representation was certainly exaggerated, since delegates were elected from local, often informal, committees made up of the most politically active workers and outnumbering, as one Home Intelligence report unkindly put it, 'the more moderate and more apathetic majorities' [TNA, INF 1/292]. The number represented by the local People's Vigilance Committees could not be calculated by the organisers, but it was observed that the South Wales Vigilance Conference claimed to represent 220,000 people [*The People Speak:* 59].

The issue that worried the government was the extent to which the organisation and its supporters were communist, though historians of the movement have had fewer doubts. Weekly intelligence reports for the Ministry of Home Security included the People's Convention first under 'Extremist activities', then under 'Communist activity'. According to one weekly report in December 1940, it was only the communists who promoted the Convention, though the 'vagueness of its aims gains the support of left-wing psychopaths' [TNA, INF 1/292]. The official view was adamantly hostile to a movement regarded as a Soviet stalking horse, and there were calls for the suppression, even internment of those involved. On the day the Convention met, 12 January 1941, Churchill wrote to Herbert Morrison, the Labour minister responsible for home security, asking why communists could not be sent to camps: 'I do not see why if Mosley is confined, subversives and Communists like D.N. Pritt [...] should not equally be confined. The Law and regulations ought to be enforced against those who hamper our war effort, whether from the extreme Right or the extreme Left' [*The Churchill Documents* 16: 72]. The attitude of the Labour Party was almost as extreme. Members were told in October 1940 that no association with the Convention movement would be tolerated, and witch-hunts to root out communist 'entryism' continued well into 1941. The Labour journal *Tribune*, assuming a communist conspiracy behind the Convention, dubbed it to be 'mischevious, phoney, dishonest, a fraud, a swindle, snare and delusion from start to finish' [CALLAGHAN: 194]. The National Council of Labour distributed to Labour Party and trade union branches a leaflet on 'The

Truth about the People's Convention' which claimed that the movement had been founded by prominent communist leaders who had duped what was called 'an Innocents' Club' of fellow travellers to support their strategy of 'revolutionary defeatism'—the term associated with radical left-wing resistance to war in 1914 [*The People's Convention Reply to the National Council of Labour*: 1]. Clement Attlee, the Labour Party leader, went even further in a speech in the South Wales town of Tonypandy on 13 February when he accused the 'Communist Party' Convention of assisting Hitler in dividing the nation: 'When Hitler starts to destroy a country from within he buys some traitors, but always manages to find a number of gratuitous asses who become his unconscious tools... All these people are useful to Hitler' [PRITT: 264]. Attlee went on to report that news of the Convention had been published in the German press and broadcast on German radio, an accusation that Denis Pritt, who took up the challenge, was able to demonstrate from a statement by the Ministry of Information, was untrue, but Attlee refused publicly to recant. Pritt insisted, with some justice, that the Convention leaders were all committed anti-fascists [*Another Lie Nailed:* 7–10].

The extent to which the government and Labour Party identified the People's Convention with communism was evident in Morrison's treatment of the *Daily Worker*, which was suppressed together with the Communist *The Week*, nine days after the congress in London under Defence Regulation 2D. The issue was raised at cabinet the day following the Convention assembly, and it is difficult not to see the connection between the two. Morrison hesitated to impose the ban which he had first suggested in December, though he regarded the paper as the mouthpiece of communist circles who sought to frustrate and confuse the war effort by advocating a negotiated peace and a people's government: '"Through chaos to triumph"', he wrote in a memorandum for cabinet, 'might well be the slogan of British Communism as of German Nazism' [CAB 66/14: 4]. He worried that current public concern with government intervention might provoke a backlash because of the tension between attacking 'subversion' and the accusation that the government used totalitarian methods, but cabinet backed his decision [Donoughue & Jones: 298–299; Stammers: 107]. On the same day as the cabinet approved the ban, the *Daily Worker* ran a full double-page spread on the Convention as a historic moment in British politics [*Daily Worker* (13 January 1941): 1, 4–5, 8]. A week later, on 21 January, the day that the police were ordered to occupy the paper's premises and confiscate the printing equipment, the paper led with a major headline 'Workers mobilise against government threats' thanks to the support of the People's Convention [*Daily Worker* (21 January 1941): 1]. More worrying for the government was the suggestion that soldiers too were now being induced to participate. Military policemen were posted to prevent soldiers attending a speech by the Communist MP, William Gallacher, a member of the People's Convention National Committee, while two unnamed soldiers present on the podium at the Convention earlier in January won enthusiastic applause. The Convention itself had to be approached more circumspectly, but Morrison's ministry was assured in January by Home Intelligence, based on local police reports following the Convention meeting, of 'the ineffectiveness of Communist activities' [INF 1/292 (15 January 1941)]. There was also the example of wartime France, where communisim had been banned and communists interned in primitive and insanitary camps. That this repression had damaged the French war effort was assumed in British government circles, and made Morrison reluctant to go further than a press ban. He was, however, directed by the cabinet to ban further publications and propaganda deemed to be subversive, but the many People's Convention pamphlets and newssheets were left in the end unmolested.

The limits of restriction were illustrated a few weeks later, when apparently at official suggestion, the BBC decided in March 1941 to ban a number of musicians and actors from BBC programmes because they were supporters of the People's Convention. These included the composer Alan Bush, and the actors Michael Redgrave (a Convention sponsor) and Beatrix Lehmann (a member of the National Committee). It was a small issue, but it immediately attracted public attention after the protests against the ban on the *Daily Worker*. When the news of the BBC decision was published in the press on 4 March, there was an immediate reaction from other well-known broadcasters. The composer Ralph Vaughan Williams withdrew a commissioned choral work, returning the fee and a torn-up contract; the novelist E.M. Forster threatened to withdraw from work for the BBC, and the writer Rosamund Lehmann cancelled a broadcast. Letters of protest arrived from, among others, the actor Leslie Howard, the author J.B. Priestley and the cartoonist David Low. The *News Chronicle* deplored 'this arbitrary, illogical and and illiberal censorship' in a country committed to freedom', but other papers pilloried the Convention as a defeatist organisation, seeking a peace with Hitler [BRANSON: 327; STAMMERS: 155; *People's Convention Special* (March 1941): 1–2]. Michael Redgrave wrote to the National Committee on 6 March dismayed by the accusation of defeatism and received a reply from Harry Adams allowing him to make clear publicly that the Convention was not 'a stop-the-war' movement. 'It is not a movement for a deal with Hitler, or for "peace at any price"', Adams continued, 'All the supporters of the People's Convention are irreconcilably opposed to Fascism or to any victory of Fascism' [Letter reproduced in *People's Convention Special*: 4–5]. The issue led to an intervention by 40 MPs who tabled a Commons motion against political discrimination in a state corporation. By the time Churchill answered the motion on 20 March, the BBC had already agreed to reverse the threatened ban. Churchill made it clear that the government would not 'accord the special facilities of the microphone to persons whose words and actions are calculated to hamper the nation in its struggle for life', but he considered the effort of linking political opinion to musical or dramatic performances 'not apparent or worth establishing' [*Hansard* (20 March 1941)]. The Convention organisers made the most of the opportunity presented by the BBC, but the government step-down reflected a growing popular concern about the challenge to civil liberties exposed in the first months of 1941.

The government obsession with alleged communist conspiracies to subvert the war effort has masked the broader, though brief, appeal that the People's Convention enjoyed among working-class circles and left-wing professionals. All four Convention executive committee members had been Labour Party members until their expulsion. Edgar Young, the vice-chairman, was an anti-war activist, who had helped to run the International Peace Campaign between its foundation in Brussels in 1936 and the decision, which Young opposed, to abandon the campaign in early 1941 [Edgar Young papers, DYO 10/45 (6 February 1941)]. How many of the shop stewards and union organisers who elected delegates to the Convention were Communists is unknown and unknowable, but the scale of support and the wide variety of organisations represented make it evident that they represented a broader section of progressive working-class opinion than the estimated 15,000 current members of the Communist Party [THORPE, 'The Membership': 781]. The publications of the Convention were produced in large numbers intended for a wide audience: 631,930 copies of pamphlets and 1,336,000 leaflets and manifestoes [PHM, CP/ORG/MISC/1/5 (circular letter, 12 January 1941): 1]. Scepticism about the number of 1.2 million represented at the Convention in January 1941 should not overturn the reality that substantial numbers of electors at factory and trade union level identified with the call for a change of government and the protection of working-class interests. The Mass Observation reporter at the Convention was impressed by the absence of what the report called 'the old gang' of the left and the predominance of the skilled working-class. Even *Tribune*, so hostile to the malign intent of the Communist Party, thought the Convention full of 'honest-to-God workers', whose social and political grievances reflected 'the authentic voice of large and growing bodies of opinion'. The *Daily Mirror* also saw support for the Convention in terms of working-class disillusionment with Labour participation in the Churchill coalition: 'They expected Labour ministers in the government to be their champions. They are disappointed in them...So the people feel themselves leaderless' [CALLAGHAN: 194; BRANSON: 310].

It is perhaps easy to overlook the extent to which the Labour Party Bournemouth conference in early May 1940, when the Executive decided to join a Churchill government, acted rather like the British equivalent of the German-Soviet Pact. Overnight the Labour Party, strongly critical of the Chamberlain National Government, hostile to the remaining 'men of Munich', and with a long-standing distrust of the fiercely anti-socialist Churchill, became part of the government side-by-side with former political enemies. Disillusionment on the left of the Party, already evident in the late 1930s, was understandable and it was from this constituency that the early moves to creation of the Vigilance Committee were directed. Convention publicity on its origins claimed that 'it developed out of the Labour Party', a claim that was economical with the truth, but not wrong. Workers who now had to adjust to labour conscription under the trade union leader Ernest Bevin and accept the restrictions imposed under the Defence Regulations faced a war effort that appeared loaded against working-class interests. Despite the Trade Union Congress agreement with the government to avoid strike action, there were 940 stoppages in Britain in 1940, prompting the trade union leader Ernest Bevin, Minister of Labour in the new wartime coalition, to introduce Order 1305 on 19 July 1940, removing the right to strike. There was also the issue of war aims. There was widespread concern, made evident in Home Intelligence reports, over the failure of the government to make clear what its aims were during the war and for the postwar world. The People's Convention, according to Harry Pollitt, appealed to a wide spectrum of those 'who realise the significance of the Government's refusal to state concretely what it is fighting for'. The failure appeared to justify left-wing criticism that the war really was about protecting empire rather than fighting fascism and building a better world. In January 1941, the day before the ban on the *Daily Worker*, the War Cabinet debated the issue of war aims which Churchill's government had refused to articulate. Although there was recognition that the absence of any statement left public opinion dissatisfied, generalities were deemed to be ineffective, while specific proposals 'would be bound to give rise to difficulties'. In the end the cabinet instructed Churchill to tell Parliament that a statement would be forthcoming but not for the foreseeable future' [CAB 65 (20 January 1941)].

It is also evident that the Convention manifesto was not simply a Communist one, except to the extent that Communists obviously shared concerns common to the left in Britain to safeguard labour interests and living standards, preserve democratic liberties, and promote self-determination for the colonies. The Convention did not pursue the formal Communist line, dictated from Moscow, that the war was a conflict of rival imperialisms which Communists should not support, and indeed the Convention movement seems to have attracted little if any attention from Comintern. The Soviet ambassador in London, Ivan Maisky, gave it no mention in his diary.[2] By contrast with the formal Communist Party line, the Convention leadership wanted fascism defeated, but argued that the present government was not adequate to the task given its political outlook and the string of early defeats, whose significance in shaping popular disillusionment is too easily overlooked. It is also the case that the argument for a 'People's Government' or 'People's Front' representing democratic forces in Britain was not new in 1940. Calls for a popular front or people's front went back to the mid-1930s, and they were clearly not the monopoly of the Communist Party, which followed the Comintern line of collaboration with other progressive political forces in a 'popular front' in order to combat fascism [Horner, *Towards a Popular Front*, 1936].[3] In 1934, centre-left intellectuals tried to rally support for a progressive bloc committed to saving democracy, but the initiative petered out for lack of any political base [Overy, *The Morbid Age:* 299–301]. In late 1936, the Conservative MP, Harold Macmillan, launched together with a number of Labour politicians and intellectuals the idea of a 'People's Front' (the name was deliberately designed to avoid imitating the French 'Popular Front', elected in May 1936) which would unite the centre-left in British politics in defence of democratic and liberal values [Horne, *Macmillan, 1894–1956*: 105; G.D.H. Cole papers, D/5/2/2]. Though this movement was far from being communist, in March 1937 the Labour Party executive began an investigation to see whether those who supported a 'People's Front' should be expelled, to prevent the Communist Party from 'capturing the leadership of the British Labour Movement', an early iteration of the Party's hostile response to the later Convention movement [NEC minutes, 17 and 24 March 1937; Blaazer: 175–176]. The 'People's Front' again fizzled out because of political differences between the groups that supported it. The residual supporters of the idea called a meeting in October 1937 to establish a 'National Progressive Council' but only sixteen people attended [Layton papers, 1937].

A more significant attempt to construct a popular front materialised in spring 1938, only two years before the launch of People's Vigilance. Throughout late 1937 and 1938 there were regular resolutions from Labour Party members and branches calling for a 'United Front' or 'Peace Alliance' despite the Party ban on any involvement in popular or united fronts. In a number of cities, Councils of Action were established to promote a united front between the Labour Party and other left-wing groups [Noel-Baker papers; Labour Party reports, May 1938]. On 14 February a 'Unity Conference' was organised in Battersea Town Hall, chaired by Dutt, and addressed by Harry Adams, later chairman of the Convention [Pritt: 100]. In May 1938, Labour MPs Stafford Cripps, Ellen Wilkinson and Denis Pritt, appealed to the Labour National Executive to create a 'National Unity' movement together with the Communist Party, the Independent Labour Party, and the Co-operative Party to defend democracy and defeat 'capitalist totalitarianism', a language repeated in later Convention publications. The same month the Labour Party published 'Labour and the Popular Front', rejecting a strategy in which communists 'would be capable of stabbing us in the back at any time.' In July the National Executive rejected unequivocally any contact with the unity movement [*Labour and the Popular Front*: 6; Labour Party memorandum, 5 May 1938: 3]. Cripps was the leading spokesman on unity and tried to keep a popular front policy going, without including communists. In January 1939, Cripps issued an appeal to all Labour Party members over the heads of the executive to form a progressive bloc by abandoning narrow party interests. He was expelled from the Party on 25 January 1939, while the Executive issued a statement 'Socialism or

Surrender: Labour Rejects the Popular Front' [NEC Minutes, 13 January 1939; Noel-Baker papers, Labour Party leaflet, No. 85; Layton papers, 27 March 1939; Blaazer: 187–189]. Cripps then launched what he called the 'Petition Campaign' in favour of a popular front in Newcastle in February, and by May there were 450 'Petition Committees' with local support from some Labour branches [Mates, 'The North East…': 276–279, 283–286]. The organising secretary of the petition movement was Edgar Young, future vice-chair of the People's Convention, who was also expelled from the Labour Party in March, two months after Cripps [Edgar Young papers, DYO/2/32]. Support for Cripps from inside and outside the Party showed that a constituency favouring some kind of popular or people's front was already in place before the outbreak of war, with or without communism, and it survived to resurface with the call for popular unity against the National Government expressed in summer 1940. Cripps might well have joined Pritt had he not been sent as ambassador to Moscow in June. In a letter to constituents in September 1939 he wrote that his aim was 'to Maximise the drive to get rid of the present Government…with the ultimate hope of breaking the power of capitalism before the war is ended', a view not out of place in the future Convention. He organised a meeting with Pritt and Hewlett Johnson in early 1940 to discuss creating a real opposition for which he claimed to have drawn up plans, but nothing materialised before he left for Moscow [Gorodetsky, *Cripps*: 2; Pritt, *Autobiography*: 235].

Like the earlier unity appeals, the demand for a 'People's Government' in 1940–41 lacked political realism. Indeed, the Convention can be seen as the end point of a brief six-year period of 'popular frontism', rather than a movement of the future. Although the Convention talked about a government that was more representative of the common people, rather than a ruling class regime, there was little written about how it might be achieved in a parliamentary system with a duly elected House of Commons. Before the Convention met, Pritt wrote a pamphlet on *Forward to a People's Government* to flesh out the movement's principal commitment but it contained no practical strategy for changing the government except to suggest that working-class organisations 'have a magnificent record of solidarity and determination' which would allow them to take 'decisive action' to establish a 'People's Government' [PRITT, *Forward to a People's Government:* 14]. This had revolutionary implications, although the movement in general eschewed any revolutionary language. In February 1941, Harry Pollitt, still out in the cold in the Communist Party, wrote about the People's Government in *Labour Monthly* in terms that were more obviously insurrectionary:

> The demand for a new Government will take an irresistible character, the mass movement demanding and organising to secure a new form of Government—a People's Government—will grow stronger and stronger, and lead to new forms of political crisis, where the masses will find the means of securing this People's Government. [*Labour Monthly* 23/2 (February 1941): 63]

The main Convention publications, however, used the concept of a 'People's Government' as a stick with which to beat the existing regime, with a remarkable absence of any political strategy to achieve it, revolutionary or otherwise.[4]

Much the same could be said of the demand for a 'People's Peace', which was intimately linked to the call for a popular government, and an equally unreal aspiration. The Convention movement was not formally pacifist, nor could it afford to be opposed to the current war, but at the same time the demand for peace reflected a longer anti-war movement in the 1930s, in Britain and elsewhere, in which popular initiative between peoples was expected to overcome the menace of war. The chief spokesman of the Convention on peace was Edgar Young, who had helped to establish the British branch of an international peace organisation, the *Rassemblement universel de la paix*, founded in Brussels at a vast anti-war congress in September 1936. The conclusion of the Congress organisers was that 'humanity, in its immense majority, rejects with horror the idea of a fatal war' [Edgar Young papers, DYO 10/26]. The British branch was known as the International Peace Campaign, and was chaired by the president of the British League of Nations Union, Lord Cecil, and run by the Labour politician, Philip Noel-Baker. The new movement argued for unity among those opposed to war, apparently inspired, to an extent that worried British anti-war campaigners, by the communist desire for popular front initiatives. The left-wing character of the new movement created tensions with the League of Nations Union, to which it was united at Cecil's insistence, while the IPC lacked unity with any of the other pacifist or anti-war organisations [Overy, *Morbid Age*: 257–261]. Edgar Young was among those who thought that war could only be averted and peace saved through collaboration with the Soviet Union, and when that failed and war broke out, Young was one of a minority on the IPC National Committee who condemned the war and wanted to keep alive the idea that the people would act to save peace [Edgar Young papers, DYO 10/39–44]. He was an original sponsor of the People's Vigilance Committee, along with the Rev Stanley Evans, who worked with him on the International Peace Campaign National Committee. He authored the Convention pamphlet on a people's peace in which he elaborated views that stretched back to the early discussion of popular participation to achieve peace expressed by the *Rassemblement*.

The 'People's Peace' was as fanciful an aim as a 'People's Government'. Indeed a peace was only possible, in Young's view, once a people's government was in power. The object was not to seek a peace with Hitler on any account, but to use the people's government to advertise to the enemy peoples the idea that they should throw off their fascist ruling class and embrace a peace without annexations or penalties, in which every people would be free to determine their own future. Young suggested, as the IPC had argued in 1938, that Soviet involvement was essential because here was a people's government able to assist in persuading other peoples that they could take their future into their own hands, even those under German occupation, even in Germany itself, The argument mirrored the situation in the early stages of the First World War, when radical socialists hoped that international socialist solidarity between the working class in every warring state would make it impossible for the war to continue.

In Convention writing, however, there is no historical reflection on the failure of international collaboration in the earlier conflict, or of the stark implausibility of a peace created through the initiative of the common people. As Pritt wrote late in 1940:

> Is it not almost certain that such action on the part of the working people of Britain, and the prospect of such a peace, would at once release all the pent-up hatred for the ruling class of Germany…? Is it not almost certain that the coming to power of a People's Government in Britain would be the signal for decisive action by the French, Austrian, Czech, and other workers to throw off their oppressors? [*Forward to a People's Government*: 12–13]

Deluded as such views now appear, the idea that a peace might be brokered very different from the Versailles Settlement clearly appealed to the cross-section of working-class organisations represented at the Convention, where, according to the Mass Observer, 'Peace and all the accessories of peace definitely formed the main theme both in the meeting and in the lobby conversations' [MO File 54 3/1: 1–2]. A progressive peace settlement was a mainstream concern, not least because there were few clues from the Churchill government about how they viewed the future.

The other area of clear continuity with the 1930s was the decision by the People's Vigilance Committee to include as a manifesto point in September, when urban bombing began, of 'adequate air-raid precautions, deep bomb-proof shelters, rehousing and relief of victims' [*Why Britain Needs a People's Government*: 2]. The issue of effective air-raid precautions became politicised in the last years of preparation for a possible bombing campaign before the outbreak of war. Government policy on the provision of shelters was governed by reluctance to bear the substantial cost of constructing protection for the entire vulnerable population, but also by a belief that bomb-proof shelters would encourage a 'shelter mentality' that would discourage workers from returning to work. Sir Alexander Rouse, chief technical adviser to the Home Office on air-raid precautions claimed in March 1939 that if bomb-proof shelters were provided for the population 'they are going to go underground. They go underground and the war is won—but not by us. We cannot expect, as civilians, to have more protection than our soldiers and sailors' [HALDANE, 'A.R.P. and a People's Government': 23]. The policy was opposed by a diverse group of scientists and architects, including the Marxist geneticist J.B.S. Haldane, whose strident championship of deep 'Haldane' shelters was used to mobilise popular protest against the failure to provide effective security against bombing in predominantly working-class areas [MEISEL, 'Air Raid Shelter Policy': 308–311]. The emigré architect, Berthold Lubetkin, was another champion of deep shelters. His firm, Tecton, designed a comprehensive programme of deep shelters for the London Borough of Finsbury in early 1939, but when the programme was submitted to the Home Office for approval, it was turned down on the grounds, among others, that providing deep shelters would divert national effort from more urgent defence tasks [MEISEL: 311–314]. Both the Communist Party and, significantly, the Labour Party took up the political challenge. In November 1938, the London Labour Party published *London Undefended: A Record of Shameful Government Neglect*, which claimed that government failure to provide effective air-raid protection for the working-class was 'treachery to the nation' [*London Undefended!*: 6]. In late 1938 an A.R.P. Co-ordinating Committee was established under Haldane's chairmanship, including architects, engineers and politicians—among them Herbert Morrisson, the later Minister of Home Security. The committee led the agitation over the following two years for adequate shelter, but was banned in 1940 by the Labour Party Executive as a 'subversive' organisation, with Morrison in the lead against what he now claimed was Communist-inspired agitation [BRANSON: 301–302].

Under these circumstances, Haldane was an obvious recruit for the People's Convention. He was an initial sponsor, and in January 1941 a member of the National Committee, and almost certainly the driving force behind the movement's decision to highlight the shelter crisis. In the late autumn, People's Vigilance began collecting signatures in shelters for a petition to the government but thousands of posters and pamphlets condemning shelter provision were seized by the police [ADDISON & CRANG, *Listening to Britain:* 435]. The ARP Co-ordinating Committee lobbied Morrison to change policy on providing shelter, but the shelter campaign soon developed its own momentum at local level, since the trench shelters and surface brick shelters provided in many working-class districts were quite inadequate protection [Haldane papers, 4/3/2/15]. The government scientist, Solly Zuckerman, later calculated that over 50 per cent of the urban population had no access to a shelter and ran their luck at home [Zuckerman Archive, OEMU/59/13].[5] In London's East End, the principal target in the first months of the Blitz, local councils tried to persuade the government to let them develop deep shelters, but schemes developed by Islington and West Ham were rejected by the Home Office [IDLE, *War over West Ham*: 70–71; TNA, HO 207/644]. On 14 September 1940, the Stepney Communist and future MP, Phil Piratin, led 70 protestors to the Savoy Hotel in London's Strand and occupied the plush shelters deep beneath the building, where they refused police efforts to get them to leave until they were ready [PIRATIN: 73–74].

Whether the People's Convention made a difference to government policy is difficult to judge, and since Morrison for one regarded shelter committees and organised protest as yet another form of communist subversion, the impact of the Convention on this issue may have been negative. In October 1940, he claimed that demands for deep shelters were politically motivated: 'It is sometimes done in a way that means Fifth Column in effect, and I am not sure it is not Fifth Column in intention' [ADAMS citing the *Daily Herald* for 11 October 1940: 14]. But since there were many non-communist voices warning of poor conditions and the danger to home morale, including the prime minister's wife, Clementine Churchill, who toured shelters to see conditions for herself, the People's Convention was not out of step with wider opinion. The claim that working-class districts had been in general poorly supplied with shelter support was vindicated in the high casualties suffered in areas of dense, poorly constructed housing [OVERY, *The Bombing War:* 145–150].

The final strand of continuity between the People's Convention and the movements of the 1930s was the popular attitude to the Soviet Union. Friendship with the Soviet Union was a major plank in the Convention platform, and one that eventually, thanks to Hitler's invasion on 22 June 1941, led to concrete results. It is easy to argue that Communist Party support for the Convention was an expedient way to try to reverse the public hostility to the Soviet Union over the German-Soviet Pact, the invasion of Finland and the occupation of the Baltic States. But this would be to overlook the popular image of the Soviet Union in the 1930s among left-wing and progressive circles that were not Communist, even if they have often been dismissed by the imprecise and pejorative term 'fellow traveller'. This Cold War construct obscures the wide range of avenues of approach to assessment of the Soviet Union in the 1930s. Socialists of all shades were bound to respond to the apparent evidence of social and economic progress under Stalin, and if they often did so uncritically, it was in order to highlight what were deemed to be the defects of free-enterprise capitalism and ruling-class power. When the British Institute of Public Opinion ran a survey in January 1939 on the question 'If you HAD to choose between Fascism and Communism which would you choose?', 63 per cent opted for Communism, though few, if any, would have been Communists ['What Britain Thinks': 19–20]. There was a healthy appetite for information on the Soviet Union and public lectures, art displays, and concerts highlighted Soviet achievements. The Society for Cultural Relations with the U.S.S.R., founded in 1924, counted among its sponsors John Maynard Keynes, Norman Angell, Aldous Huxley, H.G. Wells, Virginia Woolf, Bertrand Russell, and a handful of peers and knights [Gollancz papers, MSS 157/3/RU/14]. In 1935 a Committee for Peace and Friendship with the USSR was established in London under the chairmanship of the Labour peer, the Earl of Listowel, whose prominent, but non-Communist supporters, included Ralph Vaughan Williams, George Bernard Shaw, Vera Brittain, and the economist J.A. Hobson [Gollancz papers, MSS 157/3/RU/9&10]. A stream of equally distinguished visitors went to the Soviet Union during the 1930s, and returned in most, though not all cases, impressed by what they had seen. Best known were Sidney and Beatrice Webb, Fabian Socialists whose book *Soviet Communism: A New Civilisation* sold tens of thousands of copies and received widespread publicity [Overy, *Morbid Age*: 294–295].

By the time the People's Convention had made 'friendship with the Soviet Union' point (6) of the programme, there lay behind a decade or more of enthusiasm in Britain for the Soviet experiment that embraced many beyond the Communist Party. Pritt, Edgar Young and Harry Adams had all visited the Soviet Union in the 1930s and returned impressed by what they saw. The difficulty in 1940 was to overcome public disillusionment and hostility to Stalin's pact with Hitler and territorial expansion in Eastern Europe. Pritt was at the forefront of circles in 1939 and 1940 trying to demonstrate that the Pact was a necessity after the failure of Britain and France to reach a collective agreement, and to support the security needs of the Soviet Union that made necessary the conflict with Finland. The publication of Pritt's Penguin Special, *Must the War Spread?* in January 1940, in which he justifed Soviet action, led to his expulsion from the Labour Party and prompted Allen Lane, the publisher, to cancel Pritt's next book while it was in press shortly before the Convention met in January 1941 [Pritt, *Autobiography*: 258–259]. Pritt and the Convention stayed loyal to the idea that only friendship with the Soviet Union rather than the wide talk of possible war against it, current in the spring of 1940, would make it possible to achieve the 'People's Peace'. Harry Adams found that point (6) always aroused the most enthusiasm in Vigilance and Convention meetings 'among audiences whose political views on many other matters differed very widely' [Adams, *The People's Convention Fights for British-Soviet Unity*: 7]. When Gallup Polls asked a survey audience in March 1940 'Would you like to see our government establish friendly relations with Russia?' there were still 41 per cent in favour of the proposition, the month that Finland was forced to accept an armistice; a further survey in April 1941 had 70 per cent in favour, and only 13 per cent against [Gallup: 16, 44]. Despite persistent press and government hostility to the Soviet Union, a substantial residue of the earlier positive view remained, sustained, among other sources, by the People's Convention.

The German invasion of the Soviet Union transformed British attitudes, both at government and popular level. The Convention was able to make the most of its long support for closer friendship, and began at once to promote the idea that unity in the fight against fascism meant support for the Churchill government, and for maximum war production, in this case a clear identity with the overnight switch in the Communist Party line dictated from Moscow (though it is worth recalling that the 'party line' of the Churchill government switched just as rapidly the day the German-Soviet war broke out). The agreement signed in Moscow on 12 July 1941 by Stafford Cripps and Vyachslav Molotov for mutual assistance and no separate peace prompted one of the last of the Convention's publications, Pritt's *Together against Hitler* in August 1941, which reproduced the National Committee's statement of 26 July summoning the movement's supporters to make the Anglo-Soviet alliance a reality by pressing the government to honour its pledge. Pritt now argued that together with the Soviet Union 'an honest and trustworthy peace', a 'people's peace' in effect, was a possibility at last [Pritt, *Together against Hitler*; Pritt, *Autobiography*: 272]. The Convention began to agitate for offensive action, soon for a Second Front. But the changed circumstances made the movement less necessary and support soon waned. Pritt and other Convention workers threw support behind the movement for British-Soviet Committees to raise money for the Soviet war effort, promote news of the Soviet armed forces, and create a culture of friendly relations. In February 1942, a National Council of British-Soviet Committees was established a month after the Convention suspended activity [*British-Soviet Committees:* 5].

Even at this point, the Labour Party could not abandon its deep dislike and distrust of Communism, although many of the committees were run with local Conservative support and participation, representing in political and social terms a broad if temporary pro-Soviet front. Transport House organised its own 'Aid-to-Russia Fund' and the National Executive announced in July that 'no association with the Communist Party was possible', despite the changed wartime circumstances and the unmistakable evidence that sympathy for the Soviet Union was non-partisan. Labour supporters were sent guidelines directing them not to appear on any platform where there might be communist involvement, but this proved almost impossible to enforce [BRANSON: 13–15]. Ironically when the Labour intellectual Harold Laski, a severe critic of the Convention, proposed in spring 1942 a strategy for unifying the international labour movement, Comintern advised the British Communist Party to refuse 'any obligations towards the Labour Party' [Alexander Dimitrov to Stalin and Molotov, 5 May 1942. DALLIN & FIRSOV: 193–194].

The People's Convention was not, on the evidence presented here, simply a Communist stalking horse as almost all of the literature implies.[62] Its immediate appeal did reflect genuine grievances, and disillusionment with the sudden switch of Labour to support of the despised National Government, while the organisation was run by men only recently expelled as members of the Labour Party. The background of the 1930s, the age of 'causes' that flared up, flourished briefly, and fizzled out, whether peace initiatives, popular fronts or unity movements, provides a sounder historical context for what happened in 1940 and 1941 than the wartime history of British Communism. Apart from the alarm the Convention raised among the Government, not least its Labour members who were much more inclined to suppress non-Labour socialism and engage in heresy hunts in the Party, the Convention was able to organise and distribute literature without the same regular police intervention suffered by known communists, whose houses could be searched without warrant, papers and records seized, employers notified so that the offending worker could be sacked, and placed under threat not to attend any further meetings [BRANSON: 294–297]. Indeed the level of police intervention and surveillance may well have discouraged communists and communist sympathisers from participating too fully in the Convention. Communist

Party membership languished over the whole period of the movement at around 15–20,000. The Convention itself was protected from serious intervention by the failure to secure a real mass base of support and the difficulty of defining it legally as subversive. Government intelligence reports regularly reported how limited radical ('extremist') participation was, and therefore how ineffective, while the head of Home Intelligence, Mary Adams, argued that in her view criticism of the government did not amount to subversion [Hinton: 154]. For all the rhetoric of people's action, a combination of wartime conditions, the crisis caused by the Blitz, fear of official reprisals and concern that the movement might be too clearly communist, almost certainly kept a broader constituency from emerging. Nor was the commitment to People's Government and People's Peace a plausible call to action, any more than they had been in the 1930s. The People's Convention was nevertheless for the eighteen months of its activity from July 1940 to January 1942 a reminder that wartime consensus was both fragile and challengeable, a more democratic reality than the Convention's own fears of growing totalitarianism allowed.

ENDNOTES

1 List of 500 sponsors in *The People's Convention for a People's Government: Free Trade Hall Manchester, January 12 1941*, National Committee, People's Vigilance, November 1940.

2 On the day of the Convention, 12 January, Maisky wrote at length about an incendiary bomb attack on Kensington Gardens but had no comment on current politics. See Gorodetsky, *The Maisky Diaries:* 328–329.

3 On the origins of the 'Popular front' strategy see Myant, '1935: The Turning Point'.

4 For example Adams, *Why Britain Needs a People's Government* (December 1940).

5 His survey of sheltering during the Blitz showed that 51 per cent did not shelter in dedicated shelters, and only eight per cent sheltered in public shelters.

6 [2]'The convention's programme was essentially that of the CPGB': Thorpe, *British Communist Party:* 264.

CHAPTER 7

PER ABCA AD ATTLEE?

THE ORIGINS AND EARLY RECEPTION OF PAUL ADDISON'S *THE ROAD TO 1945*[1]

RICHARD TOYE
University of Exeter

> As for the popular radicalism which gave Labour its majority, it's possible that some historians will argue that strike statistics and Ministry of Information reports reinforce the impression, but I am beginning to wonder whether the 1945 victory, like the referendum on the Common Market, was not another example of the successful management of popular opinion by an elite, albeit in wartime the elite was a left-wing intelligentsia headed by Michael Foot.
>
> Paul Addison, *c.*1976.[2]

INTRODUCTION

The politician and historian Roy Jenkins once suggested that a suitable title for Paul Addison's *The Road to 1945* would have been *Per ABCA ad Attlee*—an adaptation of the RAF motto, *Per Ardua ad Astra*. The formulation was erudite, elegant, and rather unfair. The idea that the Army Bureau of Current Affairs (ABCA) had radicalised servicemen and thus paved the way for Labour's landslide was in Addison's view an exaggeration [Addison, 'Suggested blurb for *The Road to 1945*'].[3] But Jenkins was certainly right that he had sought to account for 'the influences which moved British politics to the left in World War II.'[4] Although many scholars have disputed the conclusions of Addison's book, his first, its seminal status is not in doubt. One of his obituarists, the historian Ian S. Wood, recalled being short of money at the time that it was published. He sold a suit to raise the cash to buy it: 'It was worth every penny and has never been out of print since, setting a new standard for the analysis of the social, cultural and political forces behind Labour's great 1945 election victory' [Obituary of Paul Addison, *The Scotsman*, 12 February 2020].

The book needs to be understood in three historiographical contexts. First, the development of the discipline of contemporary history from the 1940s, in parallel with new social science approaches to politics [Hayton: 290–292]. Second, the growth of interest in social history in the 1960s and 1970s [Harvey, 'History and the social sciences']. Third, contemporaneous with the start of Addison's career, the rise of the study of 'high politics' in a fashion at first glance far removed from the popular or 'low' political concerns of *The Road to 1945*. *The Road* has been described as 'a classic text' [Hickson: 142] and as 'a key point of reference' [Readman: 229] in the field; one could enumerate many more tributes of this type. Reviewing Addison's book *No Turning Back: The Peacetime Revolutions of Post-war Britain* (2010), Rodney Lowe wrote that *The Road* had provided

> the construction of political consensus as both a 'positive and purposeful' structure for historians studying domestic politics during the Second World War and a goad for those 'conviction' politicians who, since its publication in 1975, have condemned such a consensus as the principal cause of Britain's relative decline [Lowe: 502].

Crucial to *The Road*'s long-lasting appeal, then, was the apparent potential it offered to extract lessons from the past to illuminate political problems in the present. As Addison acknowledged in a 1992 interview, 'If you think a good historian is one who is interested in the past for its own sake, I would never have been one, I am always thinking about origins' [Zweiniger Bargiełowska: 190]. It has, of course, been common for historians to approach the issue of 1945 with some degree of political commitment [Burgess: 155–170].

This helps explain why a classic book also stimulated a classic *debate*—not something that all excellent works succeed in doing. Another classic on a similar topic, Angus Calder's *The People's War* (1969), failed to achieve *The Road*'s degree of historiographical purchase, for reasons to which we will return. Equally, Addison's own two books on Churchill, which are authoritative and superbly written, are widely read and cited and yet have not provoked heavyweight counterattacks in the same way that *The Road* did. Addison's claim that the wartime coalition laid the groundwork for a 'post-war consensus' on the Attlee government's terms was at the heart of the controversy. Harriet Jones, co-editor of the 1996 volume *The Myth of Consensus*, recalled:

> As young postgraduates, we spent a lot more time than we ought to have done in the canteen at the PRO derisively unpicking Addison's arguments with the smug cynicism that is the irritating trait of young postgraduates everywhere. [...] Debunking the postwar consensus has led to a tiresome series of heated seminars and conferences over the years, and defenders of the idea often cling to it with an orthodox fundamentalism calling to mind some of the wackier Christian sects I grew up with in the Bible Belt [Jones, 'Speaking Volumes'].

Jones noted that Addison comported himself through these debates with grace; certainly he was not one of the fanatics on his own behalf [*Ibid.*]. In his afterword to the 1994 edition, he acknowledged that some of the criticisms he had received had been well founded, and clarified that the consensus he was talking about was a 'Whitehall consensus' rather than one with a wider embrace.

> But some of my critics are wide of the mark in attributing to me the idea that wartime politics were characterized by consensus alone—a seamless web of public spirit that embraced everyone from [Sir Stafford] Cripps and the Archbishop of Canterbury to Jeeves and Bertie Wooster'. [*The Road to 1945* (1994 Reissue): 280]

The purpose of this article is not to re-adjudicate the debate but rather to cast light on its origins.[5] It is sometimes suggested that *The Road* established a new orthodoxy which then came under attack. 'Addison's interpretation established a dominant new narrative of the period', suggests Daniel Ritschel.

> Yet, no sooner had this narrative established itself, than a new revisionist school emerged in the late 1980s, highly critical of the 'consensus paradigm' and firmly convinced that its supporters had greatly exaggerated both the depth of ideological agreement on reconstruction during the war and the extent of the policy parallels between the Labour and Conservative governments afterward [Ritschel: 176].

Writing in 2009, Paul Readman presented a similar picture, although he was less specific about the time-frame: 'while Addison's views have been influential, the idea of consensus both during and after the war has been subjected to damaging criticism, with many scholars now questioning its purchase, and even suggesting it to be a myth' [Readman: 229].

This is a chronology which makes a good deal of sense if the evidence is confined to books and full-dress articles; contributions from Kevin Jefferys in 1987 ['British Politics and Social Policy during the Second World War'] and Ben Pimlott in 1989 ['Is the "Postwar Consensus" a Myth?'] suggest a turning point at this time. However, examining the original reviews of *The Road* shows that some scholars offered, along with a lot of enthusiastic commendation, important reservations and criticisms which foreshadowed later, lengthier responses. Jones was surely right to suggest that by the early eighties 'consensus had become a central concept in our understanding of post-war Britain', but, as the canteen arguments she described make clear, that did not mean that it had achieved unquestioned acceptance ['Speaking Volumes']. But it would be wrong to dwell only on the scepticism. It is worth paying attention, too, to the praise that Addison received. What did he say that was perceived to be new? Which orthodoxies was he thought to be overturning? And what longstanding suspicions did his impressive research appear to confirm? Above all, what were the frames of reference through which reviewers regarded the book? The most important frame of all, it is worth emphasising, was not always explicitly stated. 'To write of post-war Britain is to enter a long-running debate over the state of the nation which began about 1960 and has continued ever since', Addison wrote in 1991. 'Many conflicting views have been expressed, but strange to say there is one assumption on which almost all participants agree. They all conceive of British history since 1945 as a record of decline' ['The Road to 1989'].'

ORIGINS

Addison was born in Staffordshire in 1943 and was raised by his mother Pauline; he never knew his father, Stanley, who was in the US Army and who returned to America when Paul was an infant. In middle age, Addison identified as 'a secularised Anglican of Lib-Lab outlook' ['Destiny, History and Providence': 236] but as a child, he imbibed the views of his grandfather, 'a strong Tory who detested the Labour government and all its works. Only Mr. Attlee commanded his respect as a decent Englishman who had somehow strayed into the wrong party' [*The Road*: 281]. Addison attended the King Edward VI Grammar School in Lichfield, where he had two inspirational History teachers. One was 'one of nature's Tories', and the other, a former conscientious objector, 'taught us that history was all about the class struggle'. Addison's belief in 'progress' underlay much of his work as an historian, though the rise of 'the permissive society' and then of the new Right left him slightly baffled. He recalled in *No Turning Back* [1–2], 'At some barely conscious level of my imagination the England of which I was a part in the late 1950s is forever the norm, and almost everything that has happened since a puzzling deviation'. When he wrote *The Road* he assumed that 'the brave new world of Attlee, Beveridge and Keynes' was an 'enduring structure', or at the very least was worth preserving 'as a memorial to a more civilized era' [*The Road*: 280]. Addison admired Labour's 1945 leaders as 'moderate social patriots' [276]. This is a label that could well be applied to him too.

Addison graduated with a First from Pembroke College, Oxford, in 1964. He then started as a research student at Nuffield College. He recalled:

> When I began my research, Harold Wilson, who had of course acted as secretary to the Beveridge report, was campaigning for office on a platform which, had I realised it at the time, was a re-run of wartime social reconstruction, demanding efficiency on the one hand and better social services on the other. ['The Politics and Historiography of the Second World War']

While working towards his thesis, Addison helped Randolph Churchill assemble the documentary companion volumes to the official biography of Winston Churchill, alongside Martin Gilbert and Cameron Hazlehurst ['Achievement on a Colossal Scale': 21]. In 1967, well before he completed his D. Phil.—on 'Political Change in Britain, September 1939 to December 1940' (1971)—he secured a lectureship at Edinburgh University, where he remained for the rest of his career [Obituary of Paul Addison, *The Times*, 23 March 2020]. The influence of his supervisor, A.J.P. Taylor, was critical. Addison, who felt 'a bit of a misfit' in Oxford ['Achievement on a Colossal Scale': 21], credited Taylor with keeping him 'emotionally alive' by giving him 'constant encouragement to go on with tasks that seemed to be very very difficult at times' [ZWEINIGER BARGIEŁOWSKA: 188]. Taylor was Director of the Beaverbrook Library, the short-but-brilliant life of which (1967–75) was an important influence on Addison's early historical work.[6] One imagines that his links with Randolph Churchill and Taylor opened a few door; the Nuffield psephologist David Butler lent a hand [David Butler to Quintin Hogg, 28 May 1966]; and Addison was able to secure an impressive roster of interviewees for *The Road.* These included Attlee, Lord Boothby, Lord Reith, and Sir Horace Wilson [*The Road*: 10].

Addison recalled that, when he started researching the politics of World War II, the topic was 'barely distinguishable in many ways from current affairs. [...] Probably in a rather crude way, I wanted to know what the origins of the present were' [ZWEINIGER BARGIEŁOWSKA: 189]. He found a friend and ally in Angus Calder, who was studying for a Ph.D. at Sussex University on the radical wartime party Common Wealth, and also working on the book that would become *The People's War* ['Angus Calder (1942–2008)'].[7] Angus was the son of the radical journalist Ritchie Calder, who had reported vividly on the Blitz, and who became one of Addison's interviewees. Though it is standard to cite *The Road* as the starting point for the consensus debate, *The People's War* used the term six years earlier; indeed it appeared on the book's dustjacket. 'The consensus, while serving in the long run to preserve private capitalism, had shifted the debate on to ground which Labour had made its own', Calder argued [CALDER: 575]. Although Calder's contribution deserves to be better recognised, this is not to say that he should be credited, over Addison, with having coined the concept of 'consensus'. On the one hand, as we will see, the roots of that idea were to be found earlier. On the other hand, the two men had worked so closely together that their 'convergent work' had sometimes amounted 'almost to collaboration' [16].

Although Addison and Calder exchanged ideas freely, their respective works had different emphases. As Addison recalled,

> We both regarded it as axiomatic that the drawing up of post-war plans was an elitist exercise in the creation of 'blueprints from above'. But whereas Dr Calder regarded the consensus as a victory for the forces of privilege and bureaucracy over the 'participatory democracy' of 1940–42, I regarded it as 'positive and

> purposeful': the basis of a more enlightened and humane society. [*The Road*: 288–289]

The basic difference between them was over the question of whether or not it was possible to obtain meaningful social democratic reform within capitalism. Addison's book has been described as the restatement of an 'earlier orthodoxy' of wartime national solidarity that Calder had disrupted [Eley: 816 n.15]. True, Addison regarded the Labour Party as 'speaking for England' in 1945 [*The Road:* 269]. Yet, given that both scholars saw consensus as a form of elite imposition, benign or otherwise, it is clear that Addison was not merely peddling nostalgia. In the later debate, Calder inclined towards Addison's side, as his review of Jefferys' 1991 book shows [*Albion*: 369–370]. Calder also revised his own views, having deduced that many readers of *The People's War* had regarded it as a confirmation of wartime myth rather than as a challenge to it, and having concluded that he himself had accepted aspects of the myth without sufficient questioning [*The Myth of the Blitz*: xiii].

In the Sixties, archive-based research on the politics of World War II was a novelty—in fact, Addison and Calder's respective Ph.D.s were classified not as History but as Social Studies. Addison located (and drew Calder's attention to), the papers of the sociological research organisation Mass Observation (MO). By this time, MO had mutated into a market research body, with offices in London's Cromwell Road. 'In the basement, all higgledy-piggledy under layers of dust, were the archives.' At this time, naturally, the notetaking had to be done by hand ['Angus Calder': 300]. The MO material was only one part of the incredibly rich range of sources upon which Addison drew. He benefitted from the Wilson government's Public Records Act (1967) which meant that official documents were in general to be made available after thirty years instead of fifty. As a bonus, the records for the whole of World War II were released by 1972. The Cabinet Papers were obviously crucial, but so too were the Ministry of Information's Home Intelligence Reports.

In addition to the Public Record Office (now known as the National Archives), Addison exploited holdings elsewhere. These included those of the British Library of Political and Economic Science at the LSE (notably the Hugh Dalton diary) and at Churchill College. He also tracked down a number of collections that were still in private hands. The papers of Churchill himself were not at this stage generally available to researchers, and although Addison was permitted to consult the papers of Neville Chamberlain for background, he was allowed to make use of only one short quotation from them [*The Road*: 329]. Of course the opening later on of further archives, such as those of the Conservative Party, contributed to the revision by others of some of Addison's claims [Jones, 'A Bloodless Counter Revolution': 2]. But his diligent detective work meant that his interpretation of the war drew on thickets of new information—and this in itself made his book a critical point of reference for subsequent historians.

Addison might well have written a very different book; or rather, he might have turned sooner to the second major theme of his career. In 1969, he wrote to Taylor to ask his advice with an issue that was worrying him. The publishers Jonathan Cape had offered him an advance of £10,000 to write 'a one volume and scholarly biography of Churchill to be done by 1975/6'. In 2019 prices this was over £165,000. It was an extraordinary sum to offer to a scholar in his twenties who, as yet, had no publications to his name, but the fact that they published Calder shows their openness to youthful talent. Addison seems to have contemplated either giving up his lectureship or at least taking a lengthy leave of absence, as he noted that Cape 'would keep me while I spent the time writing it'. He wanted to know whether Taylor thought a) that it was a professionally honourable assignment, and b) whether he Addison, was up to the job [11 Jan. 1969, BBL/11].

In reply, Taylor offered sage advice, but did not commit himself as to whether Addison's 'great historical judgement' would equip him to be a satisfactory biographer: 'I know from experience that these gifts are different from those required from a historian'. He also pointed out a practical problem. After Randolph Churchill's death, Martin Gilbert had replaced him as Churchill's official biographer. If Gilbert did not allow

Addison access to the Churchill Papers, he would have to wait until the official Life was finished; or if he did, Addison would in effect have to duplicate all of Gilbert's work [14 Jan. 1969, BBL/11]. Addison judged: 'Martin has the popular market, and more of that kind of thing would be one chimp too may at the tea-party'. When it came to Churchill, what was needed was 'a Schlesinger-style analysis of Churchillian politics' [Addison to Taylor, 20 May 1969, BBL/11]. The reference was to Arthur M. Schlesinger Jr., the Harvard historian who, prior to his service in the Kennedy administration, had published *The Age of Jackson* (1945) and *The Age of Roosevelt* (1957–60). Addison did in fact contract with Cape to write both a one-volume biography of Churchill and—jointly with Owen Dudley Edwards—a work called *The Politics of Winston Churchill*, but neither book was delivered.[8] The comment about Schlesinger gives a clue as to what Addison wanted to achieve with *The Road to 1945*. By this point Addison had a draft of his Ph.D. 'all in rough though typed' but the eventual book would be considerably more ambitious than the thesis [Addison to Taylor, 20 May 1969, BBL/11].

Addison later recalled that '*The Road to 1945* was written during the latter half of the Heath government of 1972–4, and the first year or so of the Labour governments of 1974–9. That problems were mounting was obvious: the "post-war consensus" was under pressure' [*The Road*: 280]. Contemporaneously, he described the book as 'a tough political property which could be very timely from the point of view of current debates' [Addison to Machin, 10 June 1975, JC217]. Unbeknownst to Addison at the time—but highlighted later in *No Turning Back*—a few months before publication of *The Road* Margaret Thatcher's Shadow Cabinet debated the term vigorously [Addison, *No Turning Back*: 276–277]. Ideologically divided, they differed amongst themselves over the nature, extent and desirability of the post-war consensus, but none of them seemed to doubt it existed [Joseph; Hailsham; official minutes]. In fact, uses of the term can be traced back to the 1940s, thus showing that, contrary to what has been argued by some of Addison's critics, the idea of consensus was not a retrospective nostalgic invention. However, such statements need to be read as interventions in political debate and not as incontrovertible proof that consensus actually existed [Toye, 'From "Consensus" to "Common Ground"': *passim*]. For our purposes, the point is that the language of consensus was available to Addison in the primary sources (as it was also to Calder). Although, somewhat surprisingly, he did not quote any examples of historical actors using the term itself, he did note that it had held many different meanings from the time of Disraeli onwards. He also quoted Churchill and Labour's Arthur Greenwood to the effect that the war stimulated cooperation and comradeship between the Coalition's members [*The Road*: 165]. Although Addison did not coin the concept of consensus, he gave it new substance and definition and was responsible for giving it prominence within the academic literature.

But as he freely acknowledged, he was not painting on a blank canvas. Writing (with Harriet Jones) in a book published in 2005, he observed:

> The first drafts of history are seldom the work of historians. The conceptual framework of contemporary British history was initially the work of politicians, media commentators, economists, social scientists and social policy experts. It is to them that we owe such concepts as the 'relative economic decline' of Britain, the 'missed opportunity' of British participation in 'Europe', the 'post-war consensus', 'Thatcherism', 'consumer society', 'globalization', 'racism', 'gender', the 'decline of the welfare state', the 'permissive society', the 'classless society', the 'North-South divide'. The first challenge for anyone seeking to historicize contemporary Britain is therefore to test the validity of these concepts. [Addison & Jones, 'Introduction'. *A Companion to Contemporary Britain*: 2].

Since the early 1950s, as Simon Burgess has shown, political scientists had been debating the degree to which the Labour and Conservative parties had become ideologically closer ['1945 observed': 161–167]. An article in *The Economist*, published in 1954, had created the figure of 'Mr. Butskell' a composite of Conservative Chancellor R.A. Butler and his Labour predecessor Hugh Gaitskell ['Mr Butskell's Dilemma', 13 Feb. 1954]. *The Road* made only two mentions of 'Butskellism' (or 'Butskellites')—one of them, though, in the book's last sentence—but it was a term that would have been familiar to the readers of the day [278].

It was not only social scientists and journalists who influenced Addison. Amongst historians, Arthur Marwick (along with Calder and Taylor) stands out. Seven years Addison's senior, he was the author of several books, including *War and Social Change in the Twentieth Century: A Comparative Study of Britain, France, Germany, Russia and the United States* (1974). Addison cited this work, but perhaps more critical was Marwick's seminal article tracing the growth of 'middle opinion' in the 1930s.[9] In his acknowledgements, Addison thanked Marwick 'for many wise observations which cleared my mind and broadened my understanding'. Both Marwick and Calder read the book's first draft and offered criticisms and suggestions [*The Road*: 10]. But, just as he disagreed with 'Calder's vision of a betrayed people', so too was he a little sceptical of scholars 'like Richard Titmuss and Arthur Marwick, who sympathise with Labour, and argue that wartime government was under pressure from below to change its pre-war ways.' In Addison's view, in fact, there had been 'an intense bureaucratic drive to power' ['Politics and Historiography'].

ADDISON'S MODEL OF POLITICS

Addison, in his 1994 afterword, admitted: It is clear to me in retrospect that I applied to the later stages of the war a model of British politics that I never explained in the text, and probably thought of as quite unproblematical.' Addison's description of this model—which he counter-posed to Margaret Thatcher's model of 'government as an instrument of party, and party as an instrument of ideology'—is worth quoting at length:

> My own model of politics allowed [...] for a large measure of administrative and political autonomy at the top. To simplify, it assumed

> that whichever party was in office, the Whigs were in power. Party conflicts were compromised, and ideology relegated to the margins of government, by countervailing factors which impelled all administrations towards the middle ground. Among these factors were the influence of the civil service, the electoral imperatives of a party system in which the two parties were evenly balanced, the pragmatism of party leaders, and the practical value of maintaining a large measure of continuity between one administration and the next.
>
> This model owed something to Marxist ideas of the nature of the state, something to the political history of Maurice Cowling, and something to the notion of 'the Establishment' [*The Road*: 282–283].

Taylor used the term 'the Establishment' in a 1953 book review; whether or not he actually coined it is unclear, but it was subsequently popularised by the journalist Henry Fairlie [TAYLOR, 'Books in General'; *Oxford Dictionary of National Biography*]. The mention of Cowling is striking. Addison was clearly a little surprised, in the early 1990s, to be asked to contribute to a *Festschrift* for Cowling, whom he had met only once, twenty years earlier: 'If I were to be set down in the middle of Cambridge [...] I would not know the way to Peterhouse' ['Destiny, History and Providence: The Religion of Winston Churchill': 236]. As the book's editor explains, he invited Addison because he wanted to include critics, knowing that Cowling would approve.[10] Yet Addison's comment about his 'model' suggests, he should not be seen simply as a Cowling antagonist. There were also areas of overlap between *The Road* and Cowling's ostensibly very different 'high politics' approach.

A few months before *The Road* came out, Cowling had published *The Impact of Hitler: British Politics and British Policy, 1933–40*. Addison had spent his days in a dusty basement trawling through the forgotten files of Mass Observation, whereas Cowling contended that there were only fifty or sixty people in politics who mattered [*The Impact of Labour, 1920–1924:* 3]. Cowling called into the question whether it had been necessary for the British to fight Hitler; Addison harboured no such heretical doubts. Yet as David M. Craig has argued, Cowling has been misrepresented. He concentrated on elite manoeuvre but did not think that this was the only factor in politics that counted; the fifty or sixty people who mattered did so in terms of *national decisions*, but this did not mean that backbench and public opinion held no significance [CRAIG, '"High Politics" and the "New Political History"', *passim*]. Addison—whose single meeting with Cowling had perhaps made more impression than he realised—was thanked in the acknowledgements to the Hitler book as one of three scholars who 'made helpful remarks or read helpful papers at Mr A.J.P. Taylor's seminar' [*The Impact of Hitler*: x].

Addison and Cowling's books had some specific points of agreement [*The Impact of Hitler*: 387–388]. As Burgess has remarked, both saw the formation of the Coalition as more significant than the 1945 election ['1945 observed': 165]. Robert Blake noted in his review of *The Impact* that

> To Mr. Cowling its creation made a permanent imprint on British history [...] as the medium through which the Labour Party became the dominant intellectual and political force after 1945 (Mr. Cowling evidently regards post-war Conservative governments as little different from Lib-Lab).

Blake's article, it so happened, was headlined 'The road to coalition' [*Times Literary Supplement*, 25 July 1975].

In one of his last pieces of writing Addison described Cowling as 'the cantankerous historian whose reactionary imagination enlivened a trilogy of works on the history of British democracy' [Review of *The End is Nigh*]. Paradoxically, Cowling actually formed a link of sorts to Addison's interest in Marxist ideas. Cowling was well versed in Marx's writings; indeed, he sometimes described himself as a 'Tory Marxist' [WILLIAMSON, 'Maurice Cowling and modern British political history': 113–114]. Both Addison and Cowling, moreover, were archival pioneers, skilled at digging out previously unavailable sources. *The Impact of Hitler* appeared too late to influence *The Road*. Though *The Road* cited none of Cowling's work Addison had by this point likely read *1867: Disraeli, Gladstone and Revolution* (1967) and, even more probably, *The Impact of Labour, 1920–1924* (1971).[11] Addison once told an interviewer that he had been 'at the start a very old-fashioned political historian' [Zweiniger Bargiełowska, 'The road from 1945': 189]. Clearly, by the time of *The Road*, his interests had broadened, but he still had a considerable interest in elite manoeuvre in addition to popular politics. As one reviewer noted, two chapters were devoted 'to explaining the political miscalculations of Chamberlain in the months after September 1939' [MORGAN, 'Westminster at War', 1975]. Another, with Peterhouse connections, thought that the 'outstanding chapter' was that on Stafford Cripps's 'bid to oust Churchill in 1942' [VINCENT, 'Brave New World', 1975]. This all helps explain why Addison—well aware of the then-current wave of appeasement revisionism—received *The Impact of Hitler* quite warmly. Cowling had succeeded in making the Churchill of the 1930s appear 'as one professional politician among many, and not perhaps a very good politician' ['Politics and Historiography']. The book offered 'an exciting and thoroughgoing revision, from a radical conservative viewpoint', although Addison could not of course accept its most controversial judgements. 'Whether or not other historians agree with Cowling's conclusions, they are bound to be influenced by his approach' [Review of Pelling and Cowling in *History* (1977): 537].

In a strongly negative review of a later and more eccentric book, Addison noted of Cowling's previous work:

> Though his views were regarded by most historians as distinctly rum, they were wholly intelligible from a professional point of view as a methodical interpretation of the archives. For this very reason many of Cowling's findings have been tactfully assimilated by historians of quite different political outlook. ['Getting on'. *London Review of Books* (1986)]

This makes it harder to dismiss Addison's comments, in the Cowling *Festschrift*, about 'bracing revisionism' and 'a very much needed scepticism', as merely polite ['Destiny, History and Providence': 236]. We need not argue here about the true extent of Cowling's influence on left-leaning historians more broadly.[12] It is enough to note the areas of convergence between Addison's thinking and his, even though Addison had reached his specific conclusions about Labour in World War II completely independently of Cowling.

Cowling's position was that democratic politics are never quite what they seem. This is because politicians have to 'make decisions in the light of the wishes and ambitions of other politicians', and also justify themselves to a public which might disapprove of their own motivations. This was not corruption, but simply the way that the system had to operate.[13] Addison's 'model' was also based on the idea that politicians' statements of ideological belief masked the real reasons for their actions. He had sympathy for 'the very common human predicament' of those like Attlee who were 'compelled to believe in certain aims' and then 'compelled to behave' as though they did not [*The Road*: 271]. Unlike Cowling, he believed that this dynamic had, during World War II, delivered positive outcomes for society. As we will see, the points of contact between *The Impact* and *The Road* were visible to contemporary reviewers.

THE ROAD TO PUBLICATION

A typescript of the book was complete by the end of 1973. At this stage it was called *The Impact of War: Conservatism and Change in British Politics, 1939–45*. Jonathan Cape, who had had great success with Calder's *People's War*, was a logical choice of publisher; Addison was by this point serving as their modern history adviser. However, the initial report, by an internal reader was unenthusiastic. Its author, identified only by the initials 'A.C.', was probably Anthony Colwell, one of the firm's directors. Had it not been for Addison's advisory role, the reader would have confidently turned the book down after reading a third of the text and skimming the remainder. Even a full and careful reading did not convince. Using rather scathing language, the report postulated that Addison was hostile to ideological interpretations of history. High political manoeuvre was more important to him than ideas—yet the book nonetheless admitted quite often that ideas were significant. The reader felt that there was a lot of waffle about trends of opinion and changes in public mood, and that everything ended up being explained by vague references to immediate conditions. Colwell—if it was indeed he—felt that he had learned a lot of facts about wartime politics but had gained no clarity about what they all signified ['Report by AC', 15 Jan. 1974, JC 217].

In the absence of the original typescript, it is impossible to say whether the above criticisms were at all fair; but they may suggest that Addison was still struggling to reconcile his interest in high politics with his understanding of social change and intellectual currents. He now made revisions. A new report by another reader was written in October 1974. This time the verdict was very positive. Though there were still a few stylistic infelicities to be ironed out, the book was well organised and remarkably readable. By this point, though, the book had a new title: *The Triumph of Mr. Attlee: The Impact of World War II on British Politics, 1939–1945*. The reader found this problematic. According to him or her, Attlee's success was simply the accident that he happened to be leader of the Labour party at the vital moment ['Report by MJP', 4 Oct. 1974, JC 217]. Addison had some difficulty settling on an alternative. 'I played a small part in helping Paul decide the title', recalls John Campbell, a former Addison student. 'It was on a long train journey from Edinburgh to London on which, as I remember it, we had to stand most of the way, when he was agonising about the title. He was afraid *The Road to 1945* sounded like a Bob Hope / Bing Crosby film. I don't know if I helped persuade him to go with it, but it is odd to think that he ever had doubts.'[14]

With the book accepted, Addison worried about the jacket copy. By his own confession, he, like many 'pregnant authors', was 'hyper-maternal', but he was likely right to imagine that the book's reception was likely to be influenced by para-textual material such as the blurb. He was anxious that the publisher's draft actually reinforced various myths that the book was intended to challenge. The first of these was that it was not generally realised until 1945 that radical change had taken place: 'if this were true, half the text would be redundant. I go on at great length about people pushing for change and resenting the changes which took place in wartime'. The second was that war exposed the nation's ills: 'I argue that it did not, and that most wartime reforms had been thought out before the war, although they were encouraged by wartime circumstances.' Third, the book did not claim that the *extent* of left-wing propaganda had been overstated; rather, it suggested that its *influence* had been exaggerated. Fourth, Addison was not claiming that the war had strengthened working-class morale; in fact the book described evidence showing that the working classes were very pessimistic about the future. Fifth, there had not been 'a growing conviction that Britain could be superbly rebuilt, though one or two idealists thought so'. Finally, the book revolved around two themes, 'all-party consensus at the top, and a swing to the left in popular opinion, and the two ought to be distinguished' [Addison to Machin, 30 June 1975, JC217]. Addison's comments were taken on board, although the final jacket copy seemed to emphasise ABCA's role more than he perhaps wished.[15]

THE REVIEWS

The Road was published in September 1975. The ever-modest Addison awaited the reaction anxiously, but, to the publishers' delight, the first run of press notices was extremely positive.[16] It has been possible to locate seventeen reviews, which are listed in Table 1. Several of the surviving authors were contacted; they kindly offered their reflections. Several things stand out. Unsurprisingly for the era, all of the reviewers (with the possible exception of *The Economist*'s anonymous contributor) were men. Almost all of the interest was from within the UK. Addison scored a brief, praising review in the US journal *Foreign Affairs*, but not in the *American Historical Review* or even in *Albion*, then the leading

North American British Studies journal. Lothar Kettenacker, the sole reviewer for a non-English-language journal, was based at the German Historical Institute in London. Lord Boothby was the only reviewer who had been directly involved in the political events that the book described. He thought that Addison had 'got it all right—at last'. But he spent so many words dealing with his own role as a Conservative MP in the machinations of 1940 that he had 'no space to deal adequately with the remainder of this admirable book' [Boothby, 'Politics and War', 1975].

Amongst the rest of the major reviewers, Henry Pelling and John Grigg had served in the war, but others had experienced it only as children or (like Michael Bentley) had been born afterwards. The war years and post-war reconstruction were now moving from current affairs to history and the commentators were changing accordingly. Addison thus avoided the fate of the 1960s essayists ticked off by Attlee for having the cheek to write about his government in spite of being too young to have first-hand knowledge [Attlee, 'When Labour Had the Whip Hand' (1963); Burgess: 160–161]. The reviewers included journalists, political scientists, and historians. Many were academic heavyweights. One of them was Taylor, who, gratifyingly, praised his former pupil's 'wit, scholarship and imagination' but did not offer any striking contribution to the debate. [Taylor, 'Warfare to Welfare' (1975)]. Another was Kenneth O. Morgan, a personal friend of Addison (from Oxford days) [Morgan, *My Histories:* 88]. In other cases the acquaintance was slight or was only established later.[17] At least one of the reviewers never met Addison in spite of working in a closely related field.[18] Morgan notes today the broader context of the book's appearance: 'the industrial struggles of the 1970s though before the "winter of discontent"'.[19]

In terms of political views the reviewers ranged from Morgan, a biographer of Keir Hardie, on the moderate left, to John Vincent, a Nineteenth Century scholar and former Fellow of Peterhouse, on the Conservative right. In terms of specialism the outlier was Kettenacker, an expert on Nazism rather than British politics. Anthony Howard was the editor of *The New Statesman* and had previously written on the Attlee government. Grigg, a successful journalist and biographer of Lloyd George, was a former Conservative candidate of advanced views who was to join the SDP in the 1980s [*Oxford Dictionary of National Biography*]. Robert Skidelsky was known for *Politicians and the Slump* (1967), which was a study of the second Labour government, and for his recent biography of Oswald Mosley. Some considered the latter book too sympathetic to its subject, though the pre-fascist Mosley's enthusiasm for Keynesian style policies is crucial context here. Skidelsky too later joined the SDP, then became a Conservative peer, and now sits on the cross-benches. Michael Ratcliffe was a regular reviewer for *The Times*. E.L. Ellis was based in Aberystwyth and, much later, wrote a biography of the inter-war civil servant Thomas Jones. G.K. Fry had briefly been a civil servant before becoming an academic expert on Whitehall. P.J. Waller was tutor in Modern History at Merton College, Oxford. His first book, a political and social history of Liverpool, would be published in 1981.

David Howell, of the Department of Government at the University of Manchester, was soon to publish his first book, *British Social Democracy: A Study in Development and Decay* (1976). The underrated Pelling, 'probably the least fashionable of Labour historians', was no radical but enjoyed provoking Maurice Cowling at Cambridge seminars [Macintyre, 'Henry Pelling': 190; Reid, 'Class and politics in the work of Henry Pelling', *passim*; *Oxford Dictionary of National Biography*]. Bentley, who was soon to publish *The Liberal Mind, 1914–1929* (1977), had been Cowling's student. Bentley now reflects that he and Addison 'were poles apart on the political history front. But I liked what he did and I think he was the first to give a clear political shape to British experience of the Second World War'.[20]

Overall there was warm recognition of the depth of Addison's research, the aptness of his quotations, and his ability to conjure a telling phrase. He was seen to be ploughing relatively untilled soil. Morgan, one of many who recognised the high quality and scholarly importance of the book, suggested that only Pelling's *Britain and the Second World War* (1970) covered similar ground. (He might also have mentioned Calder)

[Morgan, 'Westminster at War' (1975)]. *The Economist*'s reviewer appreciated that Addison had moved 'beyond conventional history sources into a much wider range of ephemera', thus adding 'colour to the newly published Cabinet memoranda' ['A party transformed' (1975)]. Vincent, to whom the book was only brilliant 'in parts', found it 'mouth-watering in the naughty, Cecil King sense.' (King was a former press supremo who had published revealing diaries.) 'Alec Home wonders whether Winston should be sacked. Harold Macmillan wants a Centre Party under [Herbert] Morrison. Eden doubts whether Churchill could ever be PM' [Vincent, 'Brave New World' (1975)]. The fact that Home, Macmillan and Eden were all still alive made these revelations particularly spicy.

Grigg thought that Addison was 'fair in his judgements and impartially destructive of myth' [Grigg, 'Enter the Butskellites' (1975)]. But which myths were being destroyed? Grigg did not specify, but others were more explicit. Howard quoted from a speech given by the Labour MP John Freeman on 16 August 1945, when Parliament re-opened after the election: 'Today, we go into action. Today may rightly be regarded as "D-Day" in the Battle of the New Britain'. According to Howard, this represented 'the orthodox "Whig" interpretation of Britain's post-war political history'. In this analysis, 1945 not only marked a landmark in terms of the end of the war; it was then too that a 'social revolution' was launched that led to the birth of the welfare state. 'The importance of Dr. Addison's admirably argued first book is that it challenges this orthodoxy head-on and demolishes it' [Howard, 'Before the Flood' (1975)].

As an example of a specific claim that Addison debunked, Ellis highlighted the notion 'that Labour's electoral machine was kept oiled and ready during the war while the Conservative organisation rusted away in patriotic neglect' [Ellis, *Welsh History Review* (1978)]. Ratcliffe did likewise: 'I suppose the truth has always been known but I have never seen it put so clearly as in this book: after the fall of Chamberlain the whole country shifted irreversibly to the Left, and Labour [...] was the best political machine of the day to express that shift on the Statute Book' [Ratcliffe, 'The People's Peace' (1975)]. Morgan agreed, and argued further that Addison had deflated the myth that Churchill's mistakes during the 1945 campaign, such as his notorious *Gestapo* broadcast, had been responsible for his defeat. Morgan also suggested that the social changes wrought by the war had previously been explained via a series of clichés, such as the impact of evacuation and rationing and 'indoctrination by the army's current affairs bureau'. Addison had dispelled such legends [MORGAN, 'Westminster at War' (1975)]. Pelling thought the book showed that

> Labour's victory in the 1945 general election was due to no sudden popular whim, such as might have been occasioned by Churchill's mistakes in the election campaign itself; nor was it the result of 'left-wing propaganda' through such bodies as the Army Bureau of Current Affairs'. [PELLING, *History* (1977): 150]

So (although *The Economist*'s review placed some emphasis on the Bureau's influence) Addison was not generally understood to be peddling a straightforward *Per ABCA ad Attlee* narrative.

Not all reviewers actually used the word 'consensus'. For *The Economist*, the book's 'main thesis' was 'the transformation of Labour in the war years'. Thus, 'by 1945, Labour was well placed to be the natural party of government, ready to build the welfare state on the changes brought about by the war ['A party transformed']. For Kettenacker, the book meant that the victory of the colourless Attlee over the militarily triumphant Churchill was no longer an unsolvable riddle; Germans would no longer have to fall back on the vague explanations of which they were fond, such as the British national character or the political cleverness of the English. According to his summary, 'The close cooperation of both large parties and the elimination of their previous differences for the duration of the war had created a new political consciousness that one could almost call "national-socialist"'.[21]

Other writers engaged directly with Addison's terminology and several of them gave it a broad endorsement. Morgan, for example, agreed that the war's outcome 'was a progressive shift in political and social attitudes, which led to Baldwin's consensus giving way to that of Attlee—and of the Butskellites that came after'. He added, though, that the degree and the radicalism of the transformation wrought by the war remained debateable, and felt that Addison had neglected the position of the Bevanites ['Westminster at War']. (Addison wrote to Morgan that he agreed with the latter criticism.)[22] Vincent noted the importance of the early years of the war to Addison's account: 'By the end of 1942, Attlee's consensus had been created'. Vincent accepted Addison's picture, but accused him of treating the wartime opponents of consensus as Aunt Sallies. 'The responsible politics for which they stood seem to Addison as dead as the dodo. Alas, how right he is, and how wrong to make it his historical mission to celebrate the fact' ['Brave New World'].

Skidelsky, for his part, felt that Addison's 'very fine, elegantly written book' revealed that the author was trapped in a Butskellite perspective. So though the research was cutting-edge, the outlook was dated, and failed to take account of Britain's relative decline:

> He looks back on the war as one might have done in the late 'fifties or early 'sixties when it still looked all eminently worthwhile. Yet this was the immediate prelude to a collapse in Britain's position and morale sufficiently spectacular to compel a reappraisal of the war experience.

Skidelsky did not doubt the existence of Attlee's consensus, but felt that it 'provided no basis for tackling the "British disease"' [Skidelsky, *Spectator* (1975)]. Skidelsky now reflects: 'I was glad I said so many nice things about Paul's book; sorry that my assessment of the result of the war was so negative. I had just finished my biography of Oswald Mosley & I was unduly swayed by his view that the war had been a disaster'.[23]

Howard found only one fault with Addison's 'first-class' volume. Why, given Labour's strength in 1945 (as diagnosed by Addison) was the Attlee government 'able to do so little to change Britain's economic and social contours in the following six years? [...] Alas, Dr. Addison never even bothers with the question' ['Before the Flood']. Others, though, were more challenging of the notion of consensus as an historical reality. Pelling praised Addison's scholarship and commended 'his valuable exposition of the story of domestic political change'. However:

> Dr. Addison rather exaggerates the changes that occurred in popular feeling in 1940–45. It is not true that the Labour Party gained more than 50 per cent of the vote in the 1945 election. Nor was Conservative opposition to the nationalization programme of the Attlee government a 'token' affair: there was a fierce tussle over the railways as well as over iron and steel. [PELLING, *History*: 150].

Waller was significantly more critical. He noted that the book contained 'both new material and refreshing commentary on old' but found its thesis unconvincing as a whole. Waller found that some of the book's language seemed 'stale, redolent of the academic journalist comment of the 1960s. The wallpaper is very Nuffield' [Waller, *English Historical Review* (1977)]. This was an allusion to an ad campaign for Sanderson wallpaper ('very Sanderson') that was designed to appeal to the upwardly mobile. Thus it was a dig at the aspirations and self-satisfaction of Nuffield scholars. 'That every politician must at some point appear at a Nuffield seminar in the 1960s and early 70s and consult the sages was practically mandatory', Waller recalls:

> Understandably, this gave the place a swagger [...] There was no gainsaying it, Nuffield was influential; but too many people fell for the illusion that the only politicians who mattered were all feeding from the same trough. I suspect that's what I was getting at in my review, that a Nuffield groupthink was being projected back in a self-congratulatory way into the 1940s / 1950s, brushing aside real differences.[24]

Waller's critique noted Marwick's 'middle opinion' article had pre-figured the arguments of *The Road*. Marwick had been writing during the 'thirteen years of Tory misrule' that ended in 1964:

> Dr Addison set to work later, when Labour was in office and claiming to be a 'national' party and future 'natural' party of government. Accordingly he moves his sights from the incipient 'agreement' of the 1930s to the formed 'consensus' of the 1940s, which established Labour's first majority government.

Both the Marwick and Addison theses were attractive at the surface level, Waller argued, but there were problems of definition if the term 'consensus' was to be of much use.

> Does it mean a real absence of controversy about fundamental principles of government in the present and foreseeable future; or is it simply a shorthand for an adjustment to majority opinion or inescapable circumstances prevailing at any one time?

This was a question which anticipated the debates of the eighties and nineties. Waller's answer was: 'The "consensus" that Dr Addison seeks to prove requires something more: that the parties not only responded in similar fashion but actually had beliefs and intentions in common'. [Waller, *English Historical Review* (1977)].

Howell was more critical still, doling out only a soupcon of lukewarm praise. He recalls today that although the review was published in 1977 'it was written between the implementation of the Wilson Government's incomes policy in the summer of 1975 and Wilson's resignation the following March'.[25] He also flags up the context of the miners' strikes of 1972 and 1973–4, the Sunningdale agreement that established power-sharing in Northern Ireland and its subsequent collapse, and of course the election of Thatcher as Tory leader in 1975.[26] Howell was influenced by wider historical debates which included Skidelsky's *Politicians and the Slump* and Peter Clarke's *Lancashire and the New Liberalism* (1971). Clarke had challenged the idea that Edwardian Liberalism 'was played out and that only with its displacement by the Labour party would class find its proper expression in politics'[vii]. 'Paul's book belongs in this company as does David Marquand's biography of [Ramsay] MacDonald published just after the review appeared', Howell explains. 'These were and remain powerful challenges to a simplistic Labour historiography. Sometimes I have felt that the challenges involve a limited understanding of the labour movement. Hence the criticisms in the review'.[27]

The review was long; the criticisms searching. The crucial point was this:

> The whole analysis constitutes an attempt to rewrite history around a particular interpretation of the British Left. Addison wishes to emphasise the centrality of moderation and pragmatism, and to deny the other face of Labour in either its ideal or its industrial aspect. While it is true that most of Labour's political leaders have accepted existing political and economic structures and have always shown a strong predisposition to do so, that is no reason for ignoring or devaluing other strands in the Labour tradition.

Howell believed that Addison, on the one hand, had neglected the fact that, both during the war and after, the fundamental economic interests of certain bodies of workers had provoked them into industrial action, in spite of the appeals of Labour leaders. These forces had led miners to strike in 1944 and to the eventual breakdown of the Attlee government's efforts at wage restraint. On the other hand, he had failed to take seriously the radical socialism of the party's rank and file, a face of Labour that was much on display during the 1945 election. Now, when some trades unionists had shown themselves unwilling to bow to 'Mr. Wilson's consensus', loyalists sought to deny the legitimacy of their attitude. 'The persuasiveness of such denials is obviously increased by the rewriting of the party's past history', Howell concluded. 'It is intellectually and practically important therefore, that the "new myths" of revisionist historians should be subject to critical examination' [Howell (1977): 114].

Three of Addison's reviewers identified similarities between *The Road* and *The Impact of Hitler*. Skidelsky wrote:

> He [Addison] agrees with Maurice Cowling that as late as April 1940, Neville Chamberlain was still hoping to avoid fighting the war he had been forced to declare, relying on a stalemate on the western

> front. His strategy in peace and phony war alike was destroyed by the interaction between Hitler's brutal thrusts and a domestic opposition which wanted Chamberlain out for many reasons of which foreign policy was only one, or perhaps even only the instrument.[28]

According to Pelling:

> His [Addison's] thesis, not so very different from, if somewhat more optimistic than, Mr. Cowling's in his *Impact of Hitler*, is that the crisis of 1940 led to a permanent left-wing swing in British politics, replacing the MacDonald-Baldwin consensus with a new social democratic consensus under Attlee later called 'Butskellism'. [PELLING (1977): 150]

Ratcliffe observed that

> 'Consensus' can be a smothering sort of conspiracy and there is a feeling again now in current books as unlike as Maurice Cowling's *Impact of Hitler*, *The Cecil King Diary*, and Terry Arthur's *95 per cent is Crap*, that Westminster and Whitehall are mutually competitive industries which close ranks the minute they are threatened from outside.

(Arthur's book, subtitled, *A Plain Man's Guide to British Politics*, delivered a libertarian, free market case in a humorous way.) Ratcliffe continued: 'the sharpest of several definitions he [Addison] gives the phrase "consensus politics" is the agreement by which the parties agree to cooperate in order to prevent the political initiative passing out of parliamentary hands' ['The People's Peace'].

In 1975 the post-war settlement seemed under threat from the extremes of Left and Right, as the economic and industrial crisis appeared unresponsive to earlier solutions such as those offered by Keynes and Beveridge. As we have seen, various commentators ascribed political motivations to Addison's writings and revealed preferences of their own. Ratcliffe thought that Addison believed that the system which had informed the government of Britain for the quarter-century after 1945 was 'now irretrievably defunct through overstrain and exhaustion' [*Ibid.*] But to what extent did the reviewers themselves detect or anticipate the death of the old order?

As we have seen, Vincent believed and regretted that 'responsible politics' had become extinct—which suggests he thought that the current order had established itself permanently. Skidelsky, by contrast, regarded Butskellism as old hat. Morgan ended his review on a dark note: 'When consideration is given to the results of Attlee's consensus for the condition of England (not to mention Wales and Scotland) in 1975, the politics of thirty years ago resemble less the politics of hope, than of hope deferred, perhaps for ever' ['Westminster at War']. 'Over 30 years after the war the tide has only now started to turn back', wrote Fry. 'We may be on the brink of or actually experiencing another sea change in British politics' [Fry (1977): 123]. One obvious sign of such a change was Thatcher's recent seizure of the leadership of the Conservative Party, but no reviewer referred to her explicitly. Grigg, however, did make mention of the man who acted as her political mentor, albeit in a way that appeared to underrate the challenge posed by the New Right:

> Now that the particular consensus whose origins he [Addison] describes is, in some respects, breaking down, it is salutary to be reminded that another will have to be found if our Parliamentary democracy is to survive. It is, therefore, encouraging that Sir Keith Joseph has repudiated the middle way only to proclaim the virtues of the common ground.[29]

CONCLUSION

Joseph, in the middle of the next decade, developed an enthusiasm for Correlli Barnett's *The Audit of War* (1986), a book which laid much of the blame for poor British industrial performance on the 'New Jerusalemism' of the advocates of the welfare state. [EDGERTON, 'The Prophet Militant and Industrial': 363].[30] Nigel Lawson, when Chancellor of the Exchequer, cited it as an influence too. [HARRIS, 'Enterprise and Welfare States': 177]. Although *The Road* received mention in comment articles in *The Guardian* in 1977 and 1979,[31] it never attracted political attention in the same way. However, the academic debate triggered by Barnett was effectively shut down by devastating critiques from David Edgerton and others.[32] Another important scholarly wrangle of the era, about the role of the so-called 'franchise factor' in the rise of the Labour Party, had begun in the 1970s but was amicably resolved through the discoveries of Duncan Tanner, a Ph.D. student of Peter Clarke, who was one of the protagonists. [CLARKE, 'In Memoriam: Duncan Tanner': 137–140]. Calder's early work, by contrast, never triggered the debate it arguably deserved—though it was an influence on the playwright David Hare and the director Richard Eyre. Addison judged:

> Such is the profusion of detail in *The People's War* that its importance as a work of interpretation is often overlooked. This is partly because Angus himself was never the kind of didactic or polemical historian (compare Arthur Marwick or Correlli Barnett on wartime Britain) to lay a thesis on with a trowel. Although he provided readers with signposts, he believed that his analysis of events was implicit in the way the story was told. This probably flattered his readers and certainly took no account of the need of students and tutors for concise, user-friendly texts with neatly summarized formulae and conclusions. *The People's War* was not only too long, but cast too much as a large-scale narrative, to sit easily with the demands of the essay list and the lecture theatre. It was, nevertheless, a major landmark in the historiography of twentieth-century Britain. ['Angus Calder': 301–302]

That Addison succeeded in sparking argument where Calder failed suggests that he *did* appreciate the needs of his most likely readers. At the same time, one of the reasons that *The Road* triggered controversy—notwithstanding the lengthy hiatus after the original reviews—was because of certain weaknesses in its construction. As Addison acknowledged in his later reflections, the material in Chapter 10 was

> inconsistent with the emphasis placed in the Introduction on the commitment of both sides before the general election to an economic 'middle way'. Critics, therefore have seized on the Introduction and taken me to task for ignoring quite simple points that are in fact made later on. No matter: I did imply in the Introduction, and also perhaps elsewhere in the book, that social and economic policy followed a common timetable of convergence. This was a mistaken emphasis. [*The Road*: 288–289].

But a more fundamental reason was that Addison, whether or not he had provided the right answer, had set a profound question. Clearly, *circa* 1975–1979, a sea-change did occur in British politics.[33] Everyone could agree that the previous settlement had broken down, even if they could not agree that that settlement had amounted to a consensus. The question of the degree to which, during the first three post-war decades, politicians had in fact agreed with each other had to be answered somehow. Addison was therefore bound to remain an essential point of reference. Yet, in another respect, he was even more successful, so much so that his achievement has been taken for granted. In 1975, to assert the primacy of 1940 over 1945 was a novelty (though here Cowling got into print first). After *The Road*, though scholars might doubt the extent of the wartime 'swing to the left', nobody questioned that the roots of Labour's victory were to be found, in some way, in the experience of Coalition.

Morgan's review rightly recognised *The Road* as 'a landmark in the writing of contemporary Britain' ['Westminster at War']. Addison's determined source work is worth remembering, lest we start to take our access to the relevant archives and the advantages of digital technology too much for granted. Equally, Addison gained seminality to no small extent due to his literary talent. The label '*Per ABCA ad Attlee*' reduced a subtle and complex book to caricature. Peter Stansky notes that 'From Calder on, perhaps even before, scholarship on the period can be ironic and interestingly full of contradictions' [STANSKY, review of Sonya O. Rose, *Which People's War?*: 600]. For Addison that irony and those contradictions were linked to his love of country and his mildly bewildered efforts to get to grips with its changes whilst maintaining hope for the future. As he put it in the 1990s, 'it's that mixture in Orwell of radical critique of Britain plus an immense feeling of attachment to Britain that I think was the emotional charge for me to write about Britain in the Second World War' [Zweiniger Bargiełowska, 'The road from 1945': 189]. *The Road to 1945*, then, deserves to be studied as a foundational text for the understanding of British politics, but not only as that. It should also be read as the authentic expression of the puzzled, progressive patriotism of a brilliant and now fading generation.

Table 1. The reviewers of the first edition of *The Road to 1945*.

Date	Reviewer	Publication	Affiliation, if any
16 Oct. 1975	Lord Boothby	*Guardian*	
17 Oct. 1975	Kenneth O. Morgan	*Times Literary Supplement*	The Queen's College, Oxford
19. Oct. 1975	A.J.P. Taylor	*Observer*	Magdalen College, Oxford
25 Oct. 1975	Robert Skidelsky	*Spectator*	Johns Hopkins University
30 Oct. 1975	Michael Ratcliffe	*Times*	
30 Oct. 1975	Michael Bentley	*Listener*	University of Sheffield
30 Oct. 1975	John Vincent	*New Society*	University of Bristol
31 Oct. 1975	Anthony Howard	*New Statesman*	
2 Nov. 1975	John Grigg	*Sunday Telegraph*	
22 Nov. 1975	Anon.	*The Economist*	
1976	Fritz Stern	*Foreign Affairs*	Columbia University
1977	G.K. Fry	*Political Quarterly*	University of Leeds
1977	David Howell	*Government and Opposition*	University of Manchester
1977	Lothar Kettenacker	*Historische Zeitschrift*	German Historical Institute
1977	Henry Pelling	*History*	St. John's College, Cambridge
1977	P.J. Waller	*English Historical Review*	Merton College, Oxford
1978	E.L. Ellis	*Welsh History Review*	University College Wales, Aberystwyth

ENDNOTES

1 I would like to thank Piers Brendon, John Campbell, Antoine Capet, Peter Clarke, Helena Clarkson, David M. Craig, Jeremy Crang, Warren Dockter, Boyd Hilton, and Edward Skidelsky for valuable information, comments and suggestions, and other forms of help. Rosemary Addison kindly shared her memories and looked through her late husband's papers in search of relevant material. Penguin Random House granted access to relevant files in the Jonathan Cape archive. The staff of the Churchill Archives Centre and of Reading University Library provided timely assistance. I would also like to thank Michael Bentley, David Howell, Lord Morgan, Lord Skidelsky, and P.J. Waller. They were amongst the original reviewers of *The Road to 1945* and generously shared their knowledge and offered their reflections on what they had written. Any omissions or errors are of course my own responsibility.

2 Paul Addison, 'The Politics and Historiography of the Second World War', unpublished and undated paper, Paul Addison Papers (courtesy of Rosemary Addison). Internal evidence dates this to soon after the 1976 Labour leadership contest.

3 On the role of ABCA, see S.P. MacKenzie, *Politics and Military Morale: Current Affairs and Citizenship Education in the British Army 1914–1950*, and J.A. Crang, 'Politics on Parade: Army Education and the 1945 General Election'.

4 Jenkins, Roy. 'Under new management', *The Observer*, 29 Sept. 1985 (reviewing Paul Addison, *Now the War Is Over: A Social History of Britain 1945–51*). *Per Ardua ad Astra* means 'Through struggle (or adversity) to the stars'.

5 For a recent contribution which contains a helpful summary of the debate, see Blackburn, 'Reassessing Britain's "Post-war consensus": The politics of reason 1945–1979'.

6 On the library, see Burk, *Troublemaker: The Life and History of A.J.P. Taylor*: 317–320.

7 See also Addison's 2012 *Oxford Dictionary of National Biography* entry on Calder, and Sue Cameron's obituary of him, *Financial Times*, 21/22 June 2008, which includes quotations from Addison.

8 David Machin, Director's Memorandum, 21 Dec. 1973 and Bruce Hunter to Machin, 2 Dec. 1974, Jonathan Cape Papers, JC217. Cape later published Addison's *Churchill on the Home Front, 1900–1955* (1992). In addition to Addison's extensive published writings on Churchill, note also the existence of a

lengthy interview transcript for a 1993 TV documentary, preserved in the Piers Brendon Papers, BREN 1/14, CAC.

9 Marwick, 'Middle Opinion in the Thirties: Planning, Progress and Political "Agreement"' (1964). See also Calder's review of Jefferys, *The Churchill Coalition*.

10 Michael Bentley, email to the author, 4 May 2020.

11 He certainly read both of these books at some stage but it is unclear when. His review of *The Impact of Hitler* suggests a broad familiarity with Cowling's previous work. See Paul Addison's review of Henry Pelling, *Winston Churchill* and Cowling, *The Impact of Hitler*, in *History* (1977). Also his 'Destiny, History and Providence': 236.

12 Williamson casts doubt upon the depth of this influence: 'Maurice Cowling': 115–116.

13 Institute of Historical Research Interview of Maurice Cowling by Michael Bentley, c. 1998, transcript courtesy of David M. Craig.

14 John Campbell, email to the author, 22 August 2020. Addison held Campbell in high esteem. Addison to Machin, 4 Nov. 1972, JC 263.

15 The published blurb stated: 'He [Addison] maintains that the influence of left-wing propaganda, spread through such channels as the press and the Army Bureau of Current Affairs, has been exaggerated. But, together with the egalitarian emphasis of "the people's war", it helps to explain Labour's decisive victory at the polls in 1945'. A variant of the first of these sentences was present in Addison's 'Suggested blurb' [JC217] but the second was not.

16 Lord Morgan, email to the author, 2 May 2020; Machin to Jim Silbermann, 18 Nov. 1975, Jonathan Cape Papers, JC 217.

17 Lord Skidelsky, email to the author, 11 May 2020; David Howell, email to the author, 6 May 2020.

18 P.J. Waller, email to the author, 1 May 2020.

19 Lord Morgan, email to the author, 8 May 2020.

20 Bentley, email to the author, 4 May 2020.

21 'Die enge Zusammenarbeit der beiden großen Parteien und die Eliminierung der bisherigen Gegensätze für die Dauer des Krieges hatten ein neues politisches Bewußtsein geschaffen, das man beinahe "national-sozialistisch" nennen könnte.' Kettenacker, *Historische Zeitschrift* (1977).

22 Morgan, email to the author, 2 May 2020, citing Addison to Morgan, 3 November 1975.

23 Skidelsky, email to the author, 11 May 2020.

24 P.J. Waller, email to the author, 1 May 2020.

25 D. Howell, email to the author, 30 Apr. 2020.

26 D. Howell, email to the author, 6 May 2020.

27 D. Howell, email to the author, 30 Apr. 2020.

28 Skidelsky, 'Wasted opportunities'. For Skidelsky's review of *The Impact of Hitler*, see 'Robert Skidelsky on Hitler and "high politics"', *The Spectator*, 26 July 1975.

29 Grigg, 'Enter the Butskellites'. For the significance of Joseph's remark, see Toye, 'From "Consensus' to 'Common Ground"'.

30 For Addison's critique, see 'The Road from 1945' (1987): 5–27.

31 'The shrouded spirit of '45', *The Guardian*, 14 December 1977; Malcolm Dean, 'Who's afraid of Mrs T?', *The Guardian*, 19 September 1979.

32 In addition to the works by Edgerton and Harris cited above, see Jim Tomlinson, 'Correlli Barnett's History: the Case of Marshall Aid', *Twentieth Century British History* 8 (1997): 222–238.

33 In a deleted sentence from his paper delivered *c.*1976 Addison noted that 'the Centre is weakening in its intellectual appeal, and the Right and the Left have revived'. Addison, 'Politics and Historiography'.

CHAPTER 8

PAUL ADDISON: WAR, PEACE AND SOCIAL CHANGE

JOHN CAMPBELL

I was enormously lucky to have Paul as my tutor in my final undergraduate year at Edinburgh in 1969–70. He subsequently became my guide, mentor and friend for the next fifty years. Not only did he supervise my doctoral thesis—on Lloyd George between the wars—but he secured his own supervisor, A.J.P. Taylor, as my external examiner and then fixed me up with his agent, Bruce Hunter, and his publishers, Jonathan Cape, who accepted my thesis for publication as a book on the basis of the first chapter: not something that would happen today. It is no exaggeration to say that Paul set the direction that I have followed for the rest of my life.

When I say I was lucky I mean exactly that. At the end of my third year I was all set to take as one of my two final honours courses Arthur Marwick's course on war and British society. I'm sure it would have been an excellent course. But Marwick was a very different character from Paul: though a serious scholar, he was also an aggressively hard-drinking, football-playing Scot. It is safe to say that I would not have found a lot in common with him. That summer, however, he was suddenly appointed to be the first professor of history in the fledgling Open University. It was an inspired appointment in which he was a great success. But it left Edinburgh with a gap to fill. The solution was to ask Paul, then a young lecturer of just two years standing, to bring forward at very short notice an alternative honours course to replace Marwick's: it was called something like 'British Government and the Governing Classes Between the Wars'. I don't remember that I had much choice in the matter. But as it turned out Paul's hastily-concocted course suited me down to the ground: it got me interested in the politics and personalities of the 1920s—specifically Lloyd George and F.E. Smith—and launched me, with his guidance and encouragement, on my career as a political biographer. Through all my later books I could always rely on him for stimulating suggestions and wise advice; the last time I saw him, only a few weeks before he died, we had a typically lively discussion about whether Lloyd George should have resigned on the conclusion of victory in 1918. I already miss him hugely.

As a student in Edinburgh in the late 1960s it was easy to believe that this was where the most exciting work on twentieth-century British history was being done. Three young Edinburgh-based writers were setting the pace. In 1965 Arthur Marwick had published *The Deluge: British Society and the First World War,* which examined the domestic experience of 1914–18 as the catalyst of social, political and economic change; and in 1968 he followed this with *Britain in the Century of Total War,* subtitled *War, Peace and Social Change, 1900–1967*, which extended the same idea to the whole century and developed a controversial view of war as a progressive, not just a destructive, force. This came to be known as the 'Marwick thesis'. Then in 1969 Angus Calder published his epic study of the Second World War on the home front, *The People's War,* which set out to dispel a lot of the myths that had already grown up around the Blitz, rationing, the Home Guard and the self-congratulatory celebration of the war as a socially unifying melting pot.

Paul came slightly later. *The Road to 1945* was not published until 1975. But, as he put it in his Preface, he had been 'dabbling in the subject' ever since starting his doctoral research in Oxford in 1964, so he had been very much aware of Marwick's and Calder's work before he was appointed to Edinburgh in 1967, and he thanked both of them for reading his first draft. Likewise Calder in his Foreword to *The People's*

War thanked Paul for 'conversations and assistance over several years of convergent work, amounting at times almost to collaboration' [CALDER: 16]. *The Road to 1945* is clearly influenced by both Calder and Marwick. How could it not be? Between the three of them it can be said they rewrote the social—as opposed to the military—history of the Second World War. But in charting the transformation of the political landscape between 1939 and 1945 Paul steered his own line between Marwick's broadly positive view of the effects of war and Calder's angry socialist revisionism. And in his two later books of social history—*Now the War is Over* (1985) and *No Turning Back* (2010)—I shall seek to show that he subtly revised and refined his position as his views developed, while retaining his distinctively balanced and humane approach.

The Marwick thesis, in a nutshell, asserted that war is the great driver of social change. Citing social theorists from Marx ('The redeeming feature of war is that it puts a nation to the test.... War passes extreme judgement on social systems that have outlived their vitality') [MARWICK (1970): 13]. to Richard Titmuss ('The aims and content of social policy are determined—at least to a substantial extent—by how far the co-operation of the masses is essential to the successful prosecution of the war') [14], he took it for granted that Britain's twentieth-century history was largely 'a history of the rise of the working classes' and attributed this to the effect of 'the two total wars' [16]. To be fair he acknowledged that war was not the only factor, that other societies experienced the same development without the stimulus of war, and that not all the effects of the wars were progressive. But he still gave his name to the idea that war was the principal driver of social progress, concluding somewhat frivolously that 'Wars are like weddings: essentially extravagant and unnecessary, but a great stimulant in a convention-bound society' [17].

Calder by contrast took a strongly socialist line that the so-called 'People's War' was ultimately a confidence trick pulled on the heroic British people whose efforts had made the victory but were then denied the reward they had earned by the upper class which quickly reverted to normal and restored all the privileges and inherited inequality of the pre-war period. The war, he concluded, 'set off a ferment of participatory democracy' but in the end only reinforced what he called, somewhat apocalyptically, 'the forces of tyranny, pressing Britain forwards towards 1984' [CALDER: 21]. In his view the welfare state created after the war mainly benefitted the middle class, while 'the syndrome of low wages, bad housing, poor health and bad schooling would endure' [675].

Paul, writing slightly later than Marwick and Calder, steered a judicious path between the two. *The Road to 1945,* the book that made his reputation, was mainly devoted to explaining the leftward shift of political opinion during the war that resulted in Labour's unexpected victory in 1945. To this extent he was providing corroboration of the Marwick thesis. But he also showed that not as much really changed as was believed at the time (and for some years afterwards). He agreed with Calder that what the Labour government implemented after 1945 was not 'socialism' as the left understood it; but unlike Calder he did not see this as a betrayal. On the contrary he saw it as putting into practice the ideas developed between the wars by the 'progressive centre' whose leading advocates were Keynes and Beveridge—both of course Liberals. The wartime coalition, in this view, 'proved to be the greatest reforming administration since the Liberal government of 1905–14' [*The Road to 1945*: 14]. As a result of six years of conscription, air raids, rationing and an ethos of fair shares for all, 'all three parties went to the polls in 1945 committed to principles of social and economic reconstruction which their leaders had endorsed as members of the Coalition'. 'The political influence of the ration book', Paul suggested in a typically wry phrase, 'seems to me to have been greater than that of all the left-wing propaganda of the war years put together' [18]. As a result 'a massive new middle ground had arisen in politics.... When Labour swept to victory in 1945 the new consensus fell, like a branch of ripe plums, into the lap of Mr Attlee' [14].

Thus what the war brought about was not socialism but a 'patriotic compromise' between left and right which 'virtually satisfied the desire of the Labour party for social amelioration, without'—a nod to Calder—'in any way attacking the roots of exploitation and injustice' [277].

The Road to 1945 ends with the perhaps complacent conclusion that 'We were all—*almost* all—Butskellites then' [278]. This was written in the early 1970s in the age of Wilson and Heath whose governments were still operating within the assumptions of Attlee's 1945 consensus as accepted and continued by the Conservative governments of the 1950s. But it was published in 1975, just as that Butskellite consensus was breaking down and politics was becoming polarised between a new left and a new right. Margaret Thatcher had just become Tory leader following Heath's defeat in the face of the miners' strike; and Bennism was taking hold of the Labour Party, embodying the left's critique that the Wilson Government had (once again) betrayed socialism. Paul's penultimate sentence recognised that a shift was in the air, but I think it is fair to say that—in common with most observers at the time—he failed to foresee the magnitude of the change that was just around the corner.

Ten years later, in 1985, he recognised this revolution in *Now The War Is Over*. This quite short book was published to accompany a BBC TV series on which he had acted as historical adviser. But in his Preface he explicitly called it a 'sequel' to *The Road to 1945*—'an opportunity ... to revise former impressions', acknowledging that 'the past ten years have been a great education for us all' [*Now The War Is Over*: vi]. The Butskellite consensus that had seemed so secure in the early 1970s, he now wrote, had come under attack simultaneously from left and right, both blaming the post-war settlement for Britain's continued economic decline. While the new left continued to blame the betrayal of the promise of socialism, the neo-liberal right blamed the mixed economy / welfare state for undermining free enterprise. 'Both rejected the social democratic legacy inherited by the Conservatives from Labour in 1951' [vi].

Paul rejected both these critiques, while conceding that each contained some truth, 'in spite of the fallacious ideological baggage with which they are mixed up'. For his part he still unrepentantly applauded 'the heroic scale of social reconstruction and economic recovery' achieved by the Attlee Government in immensely difficult economic conditions immediately after the war. But he went on to explain why some of the hopes of the left had been disappointed:

> The Labour ministers of 1945 expected … to preside over a …more earnest Britain of austere public purpose. They created a new and enduring State: what they did not anticipate was a new consumer society, emancipated from deference and old class ties, in which the new State would have to function. [vii]

On the one hand, middle-class resistance to the restrictions of 'socialism'—embodied in organisations like the Housewives' League—led the Labour government itself to relax of most of the controls on production and consumption imposed during the war; at the same time—and this is Paul's main point—the reality of working class aspirations was rapidly diverging from the lofty ideals of citizenship conceived by social reformers.

Written in eight short chapters corresponding to the eight episodes of the TV series, *Now The War Is Over* vividly charts the nation's recovery through demobilisation, rationing, the housing shortage, the foundation of the NHS and the implementation of the 1944 Education Act; but its underlying theme is the public's pent-up rediscovery of leisure expressed in dancing, the cinema, sport, jazz and Butlin's holidays, culminating in the 1951 Festival of Britain which in his final chapter Paul saw as pointing forward to the new consumer society that would emerge in the 1950s.

> A smattering of adult education and elevating purpose was included in the Festival. But in the main it was a visual romp… an exercise in cultural patriotism accompanied by bread and circuses… In some ways it was another paternalistic exercise in educating the masses and elevating their taste—yet this shaded easily into advance propaganda for a colour supplement way of life. [206–209]

The high-minded moralists—Paul cites Orwell, J.B. Priestley and G.D.H. Cole—deplored this public hedonism. ('G.D.H. Cole was a gloomy old soul') [205]. Both Attlee and Nye Bevan, in their different ways, had looked forward to a society culturally and morally uplifted by collectivism. They were unprepared for the discovery that all people wanted to do when rationing was lifted was to enjoy themselves. As early as 1949 Bevan was lamenting pompously that 'Our people have achieved a material prosperity in excess of their moral stature'.[1] In fact the unintended achievement of the welfare state was to enable the long-suffering British people to cash in on the consumer society. *Now The War Is Over* concludes with Harold Macmillan, just six years after the Festival of Britain, boasting that 'most of our people have never had it so good' [210]. The age of austerity had given way to the affluent society.

What Paul was doing in this book was further qualifying the Marwick thesis, arguing that war was not after all the great catalyst of government-directed social change embodied in reforming legislation, but that the millions of small changes wrought by the people themselves in peacetime were actually much more important. 'Then as now, it was a fiction that governments make society. Society makes governments, and unmakes them too' [vii].

That was 1985. It was to be another twenty-five years before Paul returned to social history in what turned out to be his last solo book, *No Turning Back*, published in 2010. In the interval he had been preoccupied with Churchill and military aspects of the war; but he had never stopped brooding on the way society had evolved over his lifetime, and by now his ideas had evolved again. *No Turning Back* is a more substantial scholarly book than *Now The War Is Over*, but also a more personal one. In a movingly candid Introduction he confessed to being psychologically rooted in the 1950s of his youth and disoriented by all the changes that have happened since. 'At some barely conscious level of my imagination, the England of which I was a part in the late 1950s is forever the norm, and almost everything that has happened since a puzzling deviation'. He included among the illustrations his own school photograph from 1957, with his fourteen-year old self in the front row. 'For me the photo is not only a record of my classmates but a snapshot of a conservative world on the brink of many transformations' [*Now The War Is Over*: 1].

The book bears the subtitle *The Peacetime Revolutions of Post-War Britain*, and its argument is a development over a longer timeframe of the idea—contrary to Marwick—that peace is a greater agent of change than war.

> Historians used to argue that Britain was transformed in the first half of the twentieth century by the social upheavals of the two world wars. With the advantage of a longer perspective we can see that the comparative peace and growing prosperity of the second half of the century were more powerful solvents of tradition than the Battle of the Somme or the Blitz. [2]

No Turning Back describes six 'revolutions': the transformation from an economy founded on manufacturing to one based on finance and services; the transformation of a predominantly working-class society into a predominantly middle-class one; the mutation of the social democratic state of the 1950s into a neo-liberal state founded on privatisation and market forces; the undermining of traditional sexual morality by the permissive society; the rise of feminism challenging the traditional division of roles between the sexes; and the transformation of a homogeneous white nation into a multiracial and multicultural Britain. Of course none of these 'revolutions' was complete. There was always a tension between the forces of conservatism and the forces of change, and Paul was careful not to exaggerate or oversimplify. Through all the changes there survived 'a certain continuity of values.... The British remained a comparatively tolerant and orderly people, and Britain one of the best countries in which to live' [3].

But *No Turning Back* too reflects its time. Writing at the very end of the Blair / Brown decade, Paul saw 'New Labour' as standing 'at the confluence of all the main economic, social and political changes that had taken place since the 1960s' [407]. Of his six 'revolutions', however, only one—the transformation of the economy through privatisation and deregulation—was deliberately directed by the Thatcher Government. The others were largely ignored or even resisted by successive governments, but happened anyway. New Labour was more at ease than the Tories with these cultural revolutions, but at the price of accepting the economic revolution. Before he blew his authority by his support for the Iraq war, 'Tony Blair embodied and articulated a post-Thatcherite settlement at home that marginalised opponents on both Left and Right' [408]:

> At the core of this new social and political order lay the acceptance by virtually the entire political class of the rule of global market forces… The doctrines of economic liberalism, so passionately opposed by the Left in the 1970s and 1980s, had become the truisms and clichés of the twenty-first century… Economic liberalism, like social liberalism, had become an almost unexamined faith, accepted as one of the facts of life against which it was pointless to protest. [409–410]

In 1975 *The Road to 1945* concluded with the triumph of Butskellism. Ten years later *When The War Is Over* ended with Macmillan boasting that 'most of our people have never had it so good'. In both cases Paul was looking back to historical moments on the cusp of changes which he did not—could not—fully anticipate. In the final paragraph of *No Turning Back* he raised briefly the possibility that the financial crisis of 2008–9, requiring massive state intervention by governments around the world to save capitalism from collapse, might lead to another sea-change; but he quickly dismissed it. 'On the Left hopes were briefly raised of a revival of social democracy', but this he thought unlikely. 'Private profit and public policy were more closely allied than ever and there was, it seemed, to be no turning back' [410].

He may be right, or in the long run he may be proved wrong. He could not in 2010 have anticipated the divisive impact of Brexit or the economic shock of coronavirus, the ever more urgent climate crisis or the new cold war with China, all of which will shape the next few decades.

But this is not a criticism. It is not the job of historians to foresee the future. As a grateful beneficiary of the 1944 Education Act Paul remained all his life a champion of the Attlee consensus that he first wrote about in 1975. Rejecting both the social theorising of Marwick on the one hand and the ideological commitment of Calder on the other, he held instead to a quietly optimistic view of British society rooted in empathy for the everyday lives of ordinary men and women. What he did in all his books was to reflect with exceptional clarity, perspective and gentle humour the changing assumptions of the times through which we have all lived.

ENDNOTES

1 Nye Bevan at the 1949 Labour party conference, Blackpool, 8 June 1949.

CHAPTER 9

THE ROAD FROM 1945

KENNETH O. MORGAN
University of Oxford

My old friend, Paul Addison was a comrade in more senses than one. We first met in Oxford in the mid-1960s when Paul was a research fellow at Nuffield College. We were reunited in 1970 when Paul was a lecturer at Edinburgh and I was working on my book on Keir Hardie at the National Library of Scotland. Paul was a man of immense charm, thoughtfulness and personal loyalty, quite apart from our sharing the same centre-left political views. I was very fond of him. He was a man of remarkable modesty. I have some letters of his from late 1975 when his great book *The Road to 1945* was on the point of appearing. Astonishingly, he writes to me that 'I have been in real dejection about it, convinced that it is all but a failure'.[1] Two weeks later he has seen two rightly glowing reviews, by A.J.P. Taylor in the *Observer* [19 October 1975], and by me in the *Times Literary Supplement* [17 October 1975], and his morale is fully restored. Of course, from the day of its publication to the present, it has been acknowledged throughout the academic world as one of the outstanding, most important works ever written on twentieth-century British history. He was to write several other fine books later, on the career of Winston Churchill and on British social change after 1945, but *The Road to 1945* is the masterpiece by which his standing as a fine scholar will always be measured. It is appropriate to recall its qualities here, and to reflect on how its central theme, the influence of wartime politics and social ideas in the years 1939–1945, was taken further and given permanent roots in our history in the years of peace that followed.

Paul's brilliant analysis traces with unparalleled clarity and insight the political, social and ideological background to the Labour Party's landslide triumph in July 1945 (the result, delayed by the counting of servicemen and women's votes in distant locations). The entire political culture had been transformed, remarkably enough, from around the time of the fall of Tobruk in 1942. Key episodes showed how political attitudes were in flux—the neo-Keynesian 1941 budget from the unlikely hand of Kingsley Wood, of course the transformative Beveridge Report on social insurance in November 1942, the White Paper on health services in 1943, the Butler Education Act of 1944, and the Government's report on employment policy in 1944. Every one of them showed the passion of the intellectual elite for social reform and reconstruction. They were variously conveyed to a wider audience by the illustrated magazine *Picture Post*'s special issue on post-war planning, by the ABCA classes on current affairs provided for the troops overseas, and, at the start of the war, by the folksy populist tone of J.B. Priestley's 'Postscript' broadcasts on the 'wireless'. Each one of these conveyed language and ideas that reflected the values of the Labour Party, and left the Conservatives intellectually stranded, even radical Tories like Harold Macmillan. Long before the end of the war, Gallup polls were predicting a huge Labour majority when peacetime politics returned, but few paid much heed at that time to these assessments of the public mood. This transformed political context was what Paul's brilliant diagnosis so memorably spelt out. There were of course, many advantages that Labour enjoyed in domestic politics then, to offset the wartime charisma of the giant Churchill. Its constituency apparatus, often based on the trade unions, was in good fettle. Crucially, the leading figures of the Labour Party, Attlee, Bevin, Morrison, Dalton, Greenwood and Cripps were all familiar, respected, trusted figures in the Cabinet, moderate social patriots, and well-known to the wider public for their roles on the home front. When Churchill, in a disastrous election broadcast on 4 June 1945 suggested that these familiar personalities might introduce a form of post-war 'Gestapo' [Toye, *The Roar of the Lion*: 212ff.], it was greeted with widespread incredulity. They were relatively elderly men—no left-wing cult of youth here and no women either—with clear recollection of the disappointment and sense of betrayal that followed the failures of the so-called 'hard-faced men' who dictated post-war policy after 1918. The evidence of the post-war electoral revolution that was coming was there well before the voters cast their ballots. In April 1945, in a by-election in Colchester in Essex, a town with deep-rooted Conservative traditions, Ernest Millington, an unknown RAF officer, a wartime pilot running for the tiny left-wing Common Wealth Party, overturned a 16,000 majority and triumphed by 6,433.[2] Two months later the deluge descended.

Churchill's wartime coalition resigned on 22 May when the Labour ministers, headed by Attlee, rebuffed the Prime Minister's entreaties, and left the Government. Labour and the unions were well-prepared for electoral battles to come. In effect they gave voice to many of the wartime calls for social and economic reconstruction, although Labour also added important thrusts from its own policies of the thirties. Churchill bleakly headed a 'caretaker' Conservative ministry for two months. Herbert Morrison latterly orchestrated the Labour campaign, starting with the election manifesto. It was unique in Labour's history for its clarity and its self-confidence. Ideas on indicative 'planning' were taken over from the extensive war programmes of individual departments, several of them headed by prominent Labour ministers including Herbert Morrison, the mediator and, to some extent, theorist behind the manifesto's policies. This document, brilliantly entitled *Let us Face the Future*, was compiled by a clutch of research groups. The actual writing up of it was undertaken—an inspired choice—by a young social theorist of broad progressive views, Michael Young, director of the progressive think-tank Political and Economic Planning. The tone of the manifesto owed much to his outlook, especially its commitment to general progressive values such as personal freedom and civil liberties, to which radicals of all kinds from the Liberals to the Communists could be expected to subscribe. But the language of the manifesto was robust. Early on, it proclaimed that 'the Labour Party is a Socialist Party and proud of it'. Its purpose was to create 'a socialist Commonwealth'. The tone was uncompromising and a bold challenge to pre-war social and economic shibboleths. The outcome was a tsunami of anti-Conservative political reaction, with Labour, which had never before won an electoral majority, winning 394 seats to the Conservatives' 210. Labour's leaders, who had generally expected that the war hero Churchill was certain to win by a comfortable margin, were astounded. Some middle-class ministers were full of aggressive self-confidence. Some working-class members of the new government were not so sure. The Welsh miner, Jim Griffiths, who captured Llanelly by over 30,000 votes, asked in amazed tones, 'After all this—*what*'? [Griffiths, *Pages from Memory*: 77]. The answer to this provides the essential thrust of this chapter, what Ken Loach was later to call, in a famous film, 'the Legend of '45'.

◆◇◆

The first major topic of the manifesto was 'Jobs for All', a challenge to the tragic pre-war experience in industrial, working-class communities, the world of Wigan Pier, the Jarrow Hunger Marches, the Welsh and Durham mining valleys, crushed by 'the dole' and the means test. It had spawned a vivid literature of social protest, in which the names of Orwell,, Walter Greenwood, A.J. Cronin, and Gwyn Thomas stood out… The 1945 manifesto gave general suggestions along the lines of centralised economic planning, but the main answer provided was the nationalisation of major industries, services and the Bank of England (though not the joint-stock private banking institutions). This had been a slow and confused process. Although the 1918 party constitution famously spelt out the social objective of public ownership of the means of production, distribution and control ('control', *i.e.* of the joint-stock banks, was later dropped), it was not until after the financial crisis of 1931 that it became dominant amongst Labour's objectives, in the writings of young economists like Jay, Gaitskell and Durbin, blending democratic socialism with Keynesian expansionist finance [E. Durbin, *New Jerusalems*]. Herbert Morrison's London Passenger Transport Board provided a municipal model in the form of the autonomous public board. These proposals appeared in full in *Labour's Immediate Programme* of 1937 and were broadly echoed in the manifesto of 1945. It was a hugely ambitious project, with varied answers as to what the purpose of nationalisation really was, whether improved labour relations and social justice considerations, or superior industrial efficiency and technical modernisation. Labour remained ambiguous on this crucial point. The 1945 party manifesto itemised fuel and power (notably the coal mines), inland transport (road and rail), and iron and steel. There would also be the public supervision of monopolies and controls. But nevertheless it cannot be seriously disputed that in the five years down to the General Election of February 1950 Labour pledges were met and its proposed reforms were indeed carried out. In the four and a half years of the Attlee Government, twenty per cent of the British economy, run since the dawn of the industrial era on the basis of private enterprise, free trade and the free movement of private capital, was taken into public ownership. Seven central industries and the Bank of England became the domain of the State.

Backed by a huge Commons majority, the Attlee Government embarked briskly on its policies for public ownership. In 1945–1946, there came the nationalisation of the Bank of England, civil aviation, cable and wireless and, most momentously, the coal industry. Long-distance road transport, the railways, and electricity followed in 1947, and gas in 1948, with finally iron and steel in 1949. To these should be added the Cotton (Centralised Buying Act) of 1947 and national development measures like the 1948 Town and Country Planning Act.

It was a highly radical programme, but it should be noted that there was a high degree of consensus over many of these measures and relatively little challenge from the Conservatives; after all, industries such as coal and steel, for instance, were under a high degree of public control during the war. The Bank of England's nationalisation was essentially technlcal and showed little difference from its previous functions; there was scant power awarded over the clearing banks, capital movements or national investment.

Hugh Dalton, Labour's Chancellor, introduced the Cable and Wireless measure with the words 'The Socialist advance continues' [HC Deb 21 May 1946, vol 423 c201], but neither it nor Civil Aviation caused much controversy. Coal nationalisation, accompanied as it happened by bitterly cold wintry weather which led to severe shortage of supplies, was more robustly Labour in its form. From Durham to South Wales, on Vesting Day, 1 January 1947, banners flew at pitheads, bearing the slogan, 'Today the mines belong to the people'. The National Coal Board inspired little affection thereafter, but very little was heard from mining areas of carrying out schemes of workers' control or quasi-syndicalism voiced in the Welsh valleys before 1919. Public ownership again went through swiftly, apart from some grumbling at the generous rates of compensation paid to private share owners. Electricity and Gas were carried through fairly swiftly and so, with more argument, was Road Haulage, where the position of the 'C Licence' small operators aroused much sympathy. But the passage of nationalisation went through without much argument in the three years. As in France, Austria and other European countries, the post-war period saw a large expansion of State enterprise and ownership.

It was from 1949 that the road from 1945 become more rocky. This arose in the highly controversial case of iron and steel. This was less consensual than coal nationalisation. The steel industry had apparently performed well under the pressure of wartime, and the Churchill government had sponsored such powerful new ventures as the Steel Company of Wales with a tinplate strip mill, at Port Talbot in South Wales. As for the workforce, the steel workers were far less enthusiastic for State control than were the coal miners. Indeed Lincoln Evans, general secretary of the steelworkers' trade union actually opposed public ownership. Furthermore, iron and steel appeared to deviate from the original nationalisation idea focussing on services and extractive industry, and veered, alarmingly to some, into manufacturing industry, car and aircraft manufacture, and civil engineering. The Conservatives felt emboldened in attacking it. The Cabinet was seriously divided on the question, Dalton, Cripps and Bevan being in a minority who favoured nationalisation, Morrison, Addison and Jowitt in a larger group who favoured a compromise; Bevin sat on the fence, with Attlee himself anxious to defer a decision until after the general election [MORGAN, *Labour in Power 1945–1951*: 212–213]. In the end, the Government concluded that 'steel is power' and thus went ahead with an Iron and Steel Bill, which was rejected by the Lords and finally made it through Parliament and on to the statute book in 1951, by which time, the Government's landslide majority of 1945 had disappeared. It weakened the Government fundamentally at a period of economic weakness after the devaluation of the pound and the controversial onset of the Korean War.

The problems surrounding iron and steel showed that the momentum was being lost in the drive for nationalisation, and more generally it had left the Government as a whole, many of them elderly men weary of the pressure of government for almost ten continuous years in war and peace. Cripps and Bevin left office through ill-health, and shortly afterwards Michael Young, the author of *Let us Face the Future*, broke with the Attlee government in 1950, claiming it had run out of ideas. Public ownership had been supplanted by centralised economic planning. No model other than the Morrisonian public board was followed: the Co-operative Society for one protested at the failure to follow its own mutualist method. However, the legacy of nationalisation continued, and the great bulk of it was retained during the thirteen years of Conservative rule that followed the Attlee government. In 1960 Gaitskell's demand that Clause Four, the commitment to nationalisation, be abandoned was heavily defeated, and it remained as a symbolic statement of intent until Tony Blair had it jettisoned in 1994. Clearly the Government had carried out its mandate, even though the legislative outcome became less popular. The fact that many of the measures had been carried out in relatively ancient industries with ageing stock and infrastructure did not give State ownership wide support, while the central board model of management made the new public industries seem remote and undemocratic. They reflected Douglas Jay's somewhat bleak phrase, 'the gentleman from Whitehall knows best' [*The Socialist Case*: 258]. On the other hand, many of the publicly-owned utilities coped well with post-war economic pressures—gas, electricity, cable and wireless and civil aviation were notable successes. Labour programmes and manifestos placed a diminishing emphasis on the issue thereafter. In the 1950 General Election, the party proposed a small 'shopping list' of lesser nationalisation measures—cement, wholesale meat, water supply and, mysteriously, sugar refining. The sugar monopolists Tate and Lyle countered the last with the widely advertised cartoon figure, 'Mr Cube', which meant that a prominent advertisement for private enterprise appeared on every family's breakfast table. It was echoed by a Tory women's pressure group, the Housewives' League. As a result, Labour's majority of over 150 plunged to only six. Not until 1983 and then 2019 did nationalisation again play a part in Labour's election programmes, and both elections were heavily lost by huge majorities. Nationalisation was no longer a vote-winner.

On the other hand, 'jobs for all', which nationalisation was proposed to create, was a clear, even triumphant, success. After the desperate economic ordeal of the pre-war years, the road from 1945 saw **full employment** return with a vengeance. Labour had highlighted this priority in its 1945 campaign, a symbol of social justice and also a gendered commitment to masculinity. 'No more dole queues, in order to let the Czars of Big Business remain kings in their own castles'. Stripped of the emotional rhetoric, Labour carried out its promises. There was a slump in employment after the fuel shortage in the severe winter of early 1947, but this passed away. The mass unemployment of the inter-war years never returned. Despite all the difficulties of trade, the balance of payments and the dollar shortage, the level of employment rose steadily with joblessness a mere 1.5 per cent of the insured labour force when the Attlee government resigned after narrow electoral defeat in October 1951. Of the 'depressed areas' of high unemployment in the thirties, north-east England, with 38 per cent unemployment in 1938, now showed only 3 per cent out of work, with Scotland at 4 ½ per cent and South Wales at 5 ½ per cent. Partly this was a happy consequence of peace returning. Exports boomed after the war, especially when Cripps was Chancellor in 1947–1950, especially in the United States where manufactured products like the Land Rover flourished, while potential rivals like Germany and Japan were still recovering from military defeat or occupation. But the Government deserved much of the credit too, with the Board of Trade using the Coalition Government's 1945 Distribution of Industry Act to introduce new modernised industry to the old 'depressed areas'. Much use was made of Industrial Development Certificates and financial incentives through Development Agencies and local trading estates, following on from policies promoted during the wartime years. In late years, Labour's proudest boast was that it was the party of full employment which had exorcised for ever the ghosts of Jarrow, Wigan and Merthyr Tydfil. Until the 1980s, when unemployment began to be replaced by inflation and the money supply as the major source of working class anxiety, this gave Labour much of the intellectual, if not the political, ascendancy. In time, social observers began paying more serious attention to women's employment as well, a cause which received limited attention in the post-war years.

Next to industrial growth, Labour had featured the planned development of **agriculture** in its 1945 manifesto. This was another success, with much cross-party backing. Although Labour was not powerful in most rural areas such as East Anglia, its policies gave post-war farmers something of a golden age. It was, of course, particularly valuable in dealing with post-war food shortages and difficulties with imports from dollar areas. In part it was following the marketing board policies of pre-war, pioneered by Dr. Christopher Addison in the second Labour government of Ramsay MacDonald in 1930–1931—in fact Addison was now in government again as leader of the Lords under his old comrade, Attlee.[3] 'Chris' and 'Clem' were a strong partnership. The manifesto also cited the successful food production strategies of the war years. But Labour's Agriculture Act of 1947, put through by the ex-miner, Tom Williams, added much impetus of its own with guaranteed prices and an annual price review. But what Labour did not attempt to pursue to do was another item in its manifesto—'Labour believes in Land nationalising and will work towards it'. In fact, as Lloyd George found in promoting his land taxes before 1914, this proved very complicated, especially the valuation of land, and was also perhaps an obstacle to a housing programme. Instead Labour followed the wartime Uthwatt report in championing as policy of town and country planning (including several new towns) and this proved to be a far more effective alternative. Down to the present day, land nationalisation has not found many takers amongst the British Left. It was too hard to handle.

Another, immensely important area where Labour carried out much of its policy promises was that of **social policy**, in particular health, housing, education and social insurance. **Health** policy featured the most iconic achievement of the Government's entire programme, Aneurin Bevan's National Health Service. Curiously enough, the idea had only a brief and perfunctory mention in the 1945 manifesto, just three sentences headed 'Health of the Nation and its Children'. The only specific commitment was to multi-task health centres, which in fact, never came about. Labour's ideas had, however, developed in the thirties. The excitement kindled by the Beveridge report in 1942 gave it hugely more prominence. It listed a free universal health care system as 'Assumption B' amongst its preconditions ('Assumption A' was Children's Allowances and 'Assumption C' full employment) [*Social Insurance and Allied Services*: 158–163]. Henceforth Labour in effect took over the message of Beveridge and made it its own. The idea of a universal national health service was pressed with especial determination by the Socialist Medical

Association, a rare left-wing pressure-group within the medical professional, chaired by Dr. Somerville Hastings MP, which included such influential doctors as Christopher (now Lord) Addison. The wartime coalition Government also provided a lead with the 1944 *Health* White Paper, and both Ernest Brown and Henry Willink tried their hands at Health Service Bills, which however made no headway largely because of the self-centred resistance of the medical profession. Labour therefore took over health policy in July 1945 with a largely clean slate.

The eventual triumph of a National Health Service owed almost everything to the dynamism of Aneurin Bevan, the ex-miner and voice of the socialist left, in his first ministerial appointment, whose blend of dynamism and charm forced the bill through. As is well known the next two years and more were occupied by a long conflict between Bevan and the British Medical Association, who resisted key aspects of the government's proposals such as the ending of private medicine, the redistribution of general practitioners to 'under-doctored areas', the sale and purchase of practices by doctors, and their being made a salaried profession in the service of the State. It was noticeable that the most bitter resistance to the bill came from the BMA executive, who tended to represent wealthier suburban doctors. Bevan, however, backed by a highly supportive civil servant, Arthur Rucker, stuck to his guns and won a considerable victory in the Cabinet by pushing through the nationalisation of hospitals, defeating Morrison, former leader of the London County Council, who preferred a system of local control of municipal and voluntary hospitals. Bevan gained the important backing of the elderly Addison, and, crucially, of Attlee himself [*Cabinet Conclusions*, 1945]. The Conservatives, contrary to their later claims, strongly resisted the health service proposals and backed the doctors in their intransigence, Churchill weighing in with bitter personal onslaughts on the Welshman Bevan, 'this Tito from Tonypandy', and 172 Tory MPs voted against the second reading. Eventually in May 1948 Bevan and the BMA reached an agreement, much helped by conciliatory medical leaders like Lord Moran. It did not meet with the approval of many on the left. Bevan had to make large concessions to the medical profession, allowing for private practice and private 'pay beds' in hospitals to continue, and assuring them that they would never be turned into a salaried profession of civil servants. To the great disappointment of the Socialist Medical Association, expensive health centres were not developed, partly on the grounds that they would take away too much from building resources required for housing. Bevan, of all people, was attacked for lack of socialist zeal and ignoring the 1945 manifesto. Even so it was a huge achievement, creating a nationally-financed universal system, free at the point of need. Its official historian, Charles Webster, calls it 'the most ambitious publicly-provided health service to be established by a major western democracy' [*The Health Services since the War* I: 397]. It was also a progressive, redistributive system which reduced inequality. Nye Bevan's work stood the test of time and, even in the economic difficulties of the early twenty-first century, it survived to become everyman's idea of the Welfare State, and what it meant to be British. In that respect it had overtaken the monarchy itself. In the harsh spring of 2020, with the nation stricken by Covid-19 virus, the leaders of the Conservative Party, with unconscious irony, queued up to pay tribute to the NHS as a unique national treasure. Boris Johnson, emerging from intensive care in hospital, declared that it had saved his life.

Housing, another of Bevan's responsibilities at the Ministry of Health, was less contentious, though a mighty problem confronted the minister after the ravages of the wartime blitz. *Let us Face the Future* declared that 'housing will be one of the greatest and one of the earliest tests of a Government's determination to put the nation first'. It pledged that the Government would strive to give every family decent accommodation along with building schools, hospitals and factories, and attractive town planning. In fact, the programme got off to a slow start: Bevan himself unwisely claimed he spent a mere five minutes a week on housing policy. The main emphasis was placed on houses built by local authorities rather than for private purchase, effectively by the middle class, and local councils varied a good deal in their efficiency as Addison had found at the Ministry of Health in 1919–1920. There were shortages of building materials and of skilled labour in the post-war years and not until 1948 was there clear progress, with 230,000 dwellings completed that year, while in many areas housing targets were scaled down from the original 200,000 completions a year. Bevan was accused of being 'too doctrinal' over private housing, and laying too much emphasis on the quality and comfort of council housing. Even so, the housing programme did show results in the end: a total of 194,000 new houses were completed in England and Wales by October 1951 with further temporary homes such as the famous 'pre-fabs' and repair of war destructions amounting to a further half a million damaged properties. It was not the strongest part of the government's achievements, but in view of the immensity of the legacy of wartime bombing and frequent balance of payments and currency crises, it was a respectable record, if no more.

Education was an area where Labour's priorities followed the wartime Coalition's policies, in this case the 1944 Butler Education Act. This created a bold new structure of State education. Secondary establishments were divided into the famous tripartite system of grammar, technical and modern schools. In time this scheme was to be bitterly condemned, as by Anthony Crosland in *The Future of Soclalism*, a famous work in the mid-1950s, as creating rooted social inequality with the notorious 'eleven plus' examinations dividing schoolchildren into the sheep (largely working-class) going to the less prestigious modern schools and the mainly middle-class goats heading to the grammar schools. Labour's instincts in government were notably less radical than in the high noon of 1945. The Minister for Education, the sole woman in the Cabinet, the left-wing La Pasionaria, Ellen Wilkinson, was strongly wedded to the grammar schools of which she was herself a product. She had won a scholarship to Ardwick Higher Elementary Grade School in Manchester, and eventually gained a good history honours degree at Manchester University, and saw grammar schools as the route for bright working-class children which might challenge the 'public' (*i.e.* private) schools in academic effectiveness. She denied that the Butler Act led to a divisive system and moved towards a far more centrist viewpoint, encouraged by Cripps of Winchester and Dalton of Eton in Cabinet—and perhaps by her private lover, Herbert Morrison. There were protests by Labour MPs who had been school teachers, and by an important pressure-group, The National Association of Labour Teachers, headed by W.G. Cove, a former teacher from South Wales. There was only limited enthusiasm and pressure in the Labour Movement for comprehensive schools at this time, although the first such school was created in Anglesey in North Wales in 1951. This relative conservatism in the State system of secondary schooling was matched by a total failure to reform the 'public schools' in any way. Labour repeated the shibboleth of the Fleming report of 1944 for transferring pupils from State-funded elementary schools to the 'public schools' (which never took place). Symbolic of the government's approach was Attlee's own devotion to Haileybury boarding school—he would draw up in No. 10 a list comparing the number of Old Etonians with Old Haileyburians in his government. Equally Oxford and Cambridge, with their largely public-school undergraduates, did not suffer any disturbance. Nor did Wilkinson's successor at Education, Tomlinson, a working-class trade unionist, show any more reformist zeal. He was so impressed by a visit to Eton that he declared that had he gone there (instead of to Rishton Wesleyan school which he left at the age of twelve) he could have won the battle of Waterloo by himself [Blackburn, *George Tomlinson*: 6]. Labour achieved much in education in other ways, in school building, in teachers' pay (though no equal pay for women) and higher budgets which helped to make the education boom of the 1950s possible. But it was not in general an area where the socialist vision of 1945 shone brightly.

The supreme area where Labour's approach was governed by wartime debates was in implementing the Beveridge report on **Social Insurance**. This task fell to another Welsh miner, James Griffiths. His main objective was to implement Beveridge, and this he did in his 1946 National Insurance Act which laid down new scales of health and unemployment benefits, maternity and widows' benefits and retirement benefits, on higher levels than those recommended in Beveridge. It went through with little difficulty. Two other important measures in 1948, the Industrial Injuries Act and the National Assistance Act (introduced by Bevan) added to a complete remapping of social provision. The universalism of the National Insurance Act created the basis of the Welfare State, even if the growth of private insurance schemes was attacked by the left and proposed for nationalisation in the 1950 general election 'shopping list'. It transformed the lives of working-class citizens, the world of 'less eligibility' and the old Poor Law. Unlike Lloyd George's Tory-led coalition in 1918–1922, the legacy of Attlee's Labour government was indeed, in great measure, a land fit for heroes—and heroines too.

A striking difference between Labour's manifesto and all previous programmes the party put forward was in **international affairs**. This time Labour offered a programme for a party intending to govern. The party was more precise in its world role than ever before, anxious to show that the semi-pacifist posture of the party in the appeasement years, during the time of George Lansbury especially, would no longer apply. There were bold statements about Labour's approach to defence and world leadership and in international collaboration. The whole sense was that Labour Britain was a great power. It had, after all, won the war. Winston Churchill had been the most iconic wartime leader. It was one of the big three at Yalta and Potsdam, and one of four occupying powers in Germany, with Britain in charge of the vital industrial region of North-Rhine Westphalia. In addition, it was leader of the Commonwealth, head of the sterling area negotiated at Bretton Woods in 1944, a close ally of the United States (which should never again be allowed to slide into damaging isolationism), an ally of France, China and other victors of the war, committed to the independence of India and the economic development of colonies in Africa, Asia and the Caribbean, a force for peace and a guarantor of global stability. It was British arms which received the surrender of the Germans on Lüneburg Heath, the Italians in Ethiopia in 1941 and the Japanese in French Indo-China and the Dutch East Indies in 1945. These bold objectives were the dominant priorities of the new Foreign Secretary, a massive trade union leader and social patriot supreme, Ernest Bevin. His outlook was shown by his view in 1946 that Britain should pursue a nuclear weapons programme—if there was an atomic bomb, 'it should have the bloody Union Jack upon it' [Peter Hennessy, *The Times*, 29 September 1982; Cabinet Committee on Atomic Energy, 25 October 1946].

This is not the place to spell out the intricate course of international relations in the post-war years of so-called Cold War from the end of the Second World War to the outbreak of the Korean War in 1950. Britain played a central role in all the international conflicts and crises of these years. The Government in general showed a united front at this period. Even a socialist like Aneurin Bevan soon realised that left-wing dreams of 'left speaking to left' after the war were a total illusion. When the Russians blockaded Berlin in 1948–1949, Bevan led the cry for relieving columns of Western allied tanks to be sent through the Soviet zone of Eastern Germany to provide food and other aid for Berlin's citizens. There was, however, serious dissent from the left in the Commons and the Labour movement, feeling that Cold War confrontation was far from the spirit of 1945, there were many calls for 'a socialist foreign policy'. In general, the Attlee Government's foreign policy generated far more dispute than its domestic programme. Some of the critics were far-left neo-Communist Marxists, Platts-Mills, Solley, Hutchinson and Zilliacus, all four of whom were expelled from the Labour Party in 1948–1949. More effective were the 'Keep Left' MPs headed by Richard Crossman, Michael Foot, Tom Driberg and Ian Mikardo, who gave Bevin much trouble in the Commons, calling for a more independent foreign policy, freer from American pressure. They exerted perhaps their maximum strength in May 1947 in their pamphlet *Keep Left* which Bevin angrily referred to as 'a stab in the back'. Their views were reinforced by what was perceived to be Bevin's anti-Israel approach in handling the unending dilemma of disentangling the British mandated territory of Palestine. Anti-semitism was anathema to Labour at that time. But these were minority voices. Bevin stood up to Soviet demands with broad support from his party, at a time when the United States showed signs of reverting to their pre-war isolationism in Europe. A socialist foreign policy with someone as intransigent and aggressive as Stalin made the prospect of a democratic Labour administration forming any kind of common front with him quite unthinkable.

There were several decisive stages in Britain's Cold War stance. One was British involvement in the civil war in Greece and its decision to withdraw its forces in the face of internal financial difficulties; after difficult negotiations, British forces and other aid to Greece were replaced by those from the United States. In 1948 there was acute crisis over Germany with much Soviet pressure and eventually a blockade of West Berlin: the deadlock was made worse by the perceived nationalism of the German Social Democrats' leader, Kurt Schumacher, which Labour felt might rekindle echoes if Nazism. In 1949 the Anglo-American alliance grew all the stronger with the foundation of the North Atlantic Treaty Organisation (NATO), under which Britain committed itself to taking a major role in European defence and the US committed itself indefinitely to defending the frontiers and social fabric of Western Europe, thereby breaking with over a hundred years of American foreign policy, since the days of the Monroe Doctrine in the 1820s. Another phase of acute crisis came in the Far East in June 1950 when North Korea, with Communist Chinese backing, attacked South Korea without warning. At a time of difficult financial issues, Britain rapidly lined up with the US in sending troops to South Korea in the name of the United Nations to confirm its role as 'first in the queue' in Washington.[4]

This, however, ended the harmony of the Attlee Government over international policy. There was furious controversy in the Cabinet between Aneurin Bevan and Hugh Gaitskell, Cripps' strongly pro-American successor as Chancellor. Gaitskell's 1951 budget involved a large new defence programme of £4,700m, and, crucially new charges for teeth and spectacles in the previously free National Health Service. Aneurin Bevan angrily resigned following this attack on 'his' health service, and Harold Wilson, President of the Board of Trade and a centrist figure, joined him. Bevan's followers, the so-called 'Bevanities' pursued a furious campaign against Gaitskell, along with Attlee and Morrison thereafter (Bevin had now resigned and then died). Civil war broke out in the Labour Party for the next five years or so. Not surprisingly, Attlee's government was defeated in the October 1951 General Election, and fell from power. Labour's momentous period in power was over.

The course of Labour's foreign policy after 1945 clearly did not arouse either the unanimity or the enthusiasm shown in domestic matters. The crisis which led to Bevan's resignation in April 1951, at the height of the Korean War, could have been avoided (the gap between the rival groups was not large and Attlee's illness made him much less effective in keeping Bevan in line) [MORGAN, *Labour in Power 1945–1951*: 441ff.] But at least it can be said the 1945 promises of Britain taking a major role in world affairs was amply kept. Despite constant financial pressures, and the aftermath of six years of total war, for two years battling alone against the fascist powers, Britain maintained a leading role in confronting Stalin, in keeping land forces across the world from Belize to Hong Kong, and embarking, in strict secrecy, on its own nuclear weapons programme. Only later, from the fifties onwards, did it become clear that the burden, in financial and human terms was impossible and the stance of world leadership, in the face of superpowers like the US and the Soviet Union, an illusion.

There was one huge gap in British policy—the failure to take any leading role in western Europe. There were defence pacts with Western powers, but any effort to lead Europe in political and economic terms was limited. In May 1950, the French Prime Minister, Robert Schuman, along with Jean Monnet, tried to get Britain to agree to joint collaboration in a coal, iron and steel community with the French and the Germans, which was rejected on grounds of sovereignty and insularity much as occurred in the Brexit controversy in 2016–2019. Attlee, Bevin,

Cripps and Dalton were all hostile, while Morrison cited the opposition of the Durham miners to the idea. It was the American alliance, the alleged 'special relationship' that was Labour's overseas priority, buttressed by the Commonwealth. In Europe it would proceed expensively and alone, with little sympathy for any kind of political union with its neighbours.

Looked at generally, the most striking feature of Labour's programme as it was unveiled in 1945 was that it was carried through. Michael Young's manifesto in 1945 had aimed at appealing to progressives and liberals everywhere. In general it succeeded in doing so, even if it offered no great gestures on civil liberties. It did, however, reflect a close symbiosis with the trade unions. The Labour alliance created by Keir Hardie and others after 1900 was never closer. Almost the first measure introduced by the government was the repeal of the hated Trades Disputes Act passed by Baldwin's Conservative Government in 1927 to curb the unions' political levy. This repeal measure was introduced by none other than the Foreign Secretary, Ernest Bevin, the most powerful trade union leader alive.[5] In return, despite a rash of unofficial strikes in 1949–1950, the union membership responded with solidarity and loyalty to their class. It should be noted that in the post-1945 period around three quarters of the population regarded themselves as working class. Even at the height of austerity and food rationing, policies like 'fair shares' and food subsidies in the Cripps period at the Treasury in 1947–1950 kept the workers in line. It helped that the main trade union leadership in these years was right-of-centre and loyalist, men like Will Lawther of the Miners and Arthur Deakin of the Transport Workers. Labour lost no by-elections in Labour-held seats between 1945 and 1951 and individual party membership went up steadily to the mid-1950s. Even in the 1951 election, which it lost, Labour polled more votes than the Conservatives (14m.

votes) and many observers felt that they would soon return to power, certainly not remain out of office for the next thirteen years.

At the same time, several of Labour's pledges were not carried out and there were many gaps in the record. As has been observed, nothing was done on 'public schools', the Universities or the private joint-stock banks. The health centres promised in 1945 never materialised. The whole area of constitutional reform was in general ignored. Herbert Morrison, who had the admittedly difficult task of keeping a large flock of new MPs disciplined and in line, was conservative on the constitution, House of Lords and all. The relationship between Cabinet and Parliament or parliamentary procedure remained essentially unchanged, as did the rule of law, despite the extreme social and judicial conservatism of high court judges like Lord Goddard, a strong supporter among other things of capital and corporal punishment. Throughout, the government's strategic approach remained in its programme—the nationalised industries, the National Health Service, economic planning—strongly centralised. Whitehall prevailed at most levels of government. There was no hint of devolution and appeals on this from the Welshman James Griffiths within the government were unsuccessful [Griffiths, 'A Note on the Electricity Bill', 1946]. There was virtually no recognition of Scottish or Welsh nationality—not surprisingly, since the national parties in those two nations were feeble after the unifying effects of the world war. There was little attempt either to reform the sectarian problems of Northern Ireland, although the Free State to the south achieved Republican status in 1948. In social policy, it is remarkable that a government returned with a strong women's vote did little for sexual equality while equal pay was not attempted—much as the Beveridge report had assumed. Labour's priorities were founded on a man's world, the union, the pub and the football terraces, and it showed. Not until the 1970s did feminism make significant inroads.

There were important gaps, therefore. Yet it is remarkable that almost all the important elements of *Let us Face the Future* were put into practice in these six years. Nationalisation of twenty per cent of the economy, a Welfare State, full employment, regional development meant that the bleak world of the Poor Law, the 'dole' and the means test passed away unlamented. Despite the external weakness of the post-war economy, a bold policy of reform went through—certainly, much assisted by the massive assistance received from the United States under the Marshall Aid programme. In addition, there were huge transformations carried out in external policy with the formation of OEEC and NATO, and in the Commonwealth with the transfer of power in India, Burma and Ceylon, and major development programmes in east and west Africa and the Caribbean. Britain did not experience the traumas of decolonisation that France was to undergo in Algeria and Indo-China, and Portugal to experience almost everywhere. Only in Palestine was there long-lasting failure, whose consequences are still alarmingly evident in our world today. But here it is only fair to mention that responsibility for this lies predominantly with a much earlier British government, that of Lloyd George in 1917 where rival ambiguous pledges given to Jews and Arabs alike in the Balfour Declaration left a totally insoluble legacy. A hundred years of bloodshed resulted.

Further, if there were gaps in Labour's manifesto in 1951, its central achievement survived and created a new social fabric in Britain. The successor Conservative governments in office for the next thirteen years retained most of Labour's inheritance. Much of the nationalised industry (road haulage and iron and steel excepted), the Welfare State and Keynesian policies to promote full employment continued until the Thatcher counter-revolution of the 1980s. A moderate centrist policy of 'Butskellism' prevailed. 'One-nation Conservatives' of the type of Butler, Eden, Macmillan and Heath were all anxious to respond to changing popular demands for social justice, Iain Macleod was notably protective of the NHS, while even the aged Churchill was anxious to bow out with a more benevolent public image than those left by memories of Tonypandy and the General Strike. This was at a time when Labour seemed to have run out of ideas after completing its mission of 1945. The socialist advance seemed to have reached a dead end. As Disraeli said satirically of Gladstone in 1874, they were 'exhausted volcanoes'. Not until the Thatcher era was a neo-liberal response with a radically different perspective dominant which condemned the 'dependency culture' of the Welfare State and State planning as dangers to public morale. And one of Mrs. Thatcher's more memorable observations was 'the national Health Service is safe with us'. What Paul Addison defined as 'Attlee's consensus' [*The Road to 1945:* 270–278] had almost become a new orthodoxy or article of faith. And if the NHS was ever unsafe, there was always stout defiance by its most stalwart of defenders, the British Medical Association.

In the 2019 General Election many believed that a new version of the Attlee government's programme was being put forward. Labour's campaign and manifesto, under the leadership of Jeremy Corbyn, a man almost old enough to remember the Attlee years personally, offered new radical, ambitious programmes of radical reform. There would be a return to nationalisation headed by the railways, there would be higher rates of tax for a wide-ranging, ambitious social programme, and more radical proposals such as the abolition of the 'public schools' and university tuition fees, a chicken in every pot, not to mention free broadband in every computer. But it failed to enthuse the electors and Labour ended up with only 203 seats, the worst result for the party since the war, with the Conservatives winning an 80-seat majority. It came on the back of heavy losses in local government and European elections, the decline of social democratic parties in every country in Continental Europe save for Spain, and of course the defeat of European sympathisers in the Brexit referendum in 2016, when many leading figures in the the party showed themselvess no more zealous for the European union than their predecessors had been in considering the Schuman Plan in 1950. Labour's leadership in 2019 in any case had nothing like the authority or prestige enjoyed by Attlee ('Citizen Clem'), Morrison, Bevin, Cripps or Bevan. Corbyn himself, an elderly fellow-traveller with dated sympathies for Russia and South American dictatorships, inspired little trust. Unlike Attlee, or even Bevan, he did not sound like any kind of patriot. His international views reflected anti-American and anti-Israeli prejudices. Nor did the programme win much support. A huge programme, poorly costed, did not win great endorsement, while nationalisation lacked the appeal it had once had in a nation rebuilding from the rubble after the war. If the programme had moved on, so had the electorate. Psephologists showed that Labour's core vote no longer was based on the mass working class, much of which had broken up after decades of industrial decline, especially in areas of heavy industry. The miners of Durham or South Wales no longer ran up celebratory flags to herald the triumph of socialism because there weren't any miners left. Labour's strength now lay, bizarrely, in the A, B and C1 social groups, largely middle-class professionals in the cities and London, more educated, more ethnically mixed, and also younger, no longer looking to ancestral memories of the depression years [Talk to the Labour peers by Peter Kellner, February 2020]. A more hopeful portent was the growing support amongst women: in the leadership contest in early 2020, five of the six candidates were women. Ethnic minorities were also more prominent and vocal.

But it no longer appeared likely that a programme couched in class-war rhetoric opened up the road to electoral victory. Another important factor was that the voters, especially in Scotland, had for many years rebelled against centralised rule based on Westminster. They felt excluded. Scotland, the homeland of Keir Hardie, Ramsay MacDonald and the 'Red Clydesiders', an impregnable bastion of Labour's traditional 'red wall' was no longer Labour territory. Its world view was dictated by considerations of nationhood, not of class. Labour required a new understanding of its electorate and their felt needs, and leaders freed from antique doctrines of a distant era. But that did not mean that a left-wing programme would no longer find support. After all, Bevan and the National Health Service ideal had retained their magic, decades after the event. Attlee himself was regarded as a man of the left. The party needed to find a new message of hope, a humanised capitalism but fired by the old passion for social justice, and a credible economic message not buried in technocratic managerialism or disinterred Marxism. Labour's approach towards business and technical modernisation should be more intelligently defined, not drowned in ancient clichés. The urgency and immensity of the task was sharply revealed in the electoral results of 2019. The message provided was stark. Labour and the left required a total revitalisation in their purposes and their ideas to face the future with confidence, as it had once done in the era of the uncharismatic but utterly trustworthy 'Citizen Clem' [Bew, 2012]. Otherwise it would be left with no future at all. Perhaps the election of a new centrist leader, Keir Starmer, in April 2020, along with the social solidarity created by the battle against the scourge of the coronavirus, offered new hope that it might do so, three quarters of a century on from the 'Legend of '45'.

ENDNOTES

1 Paul Addison to the author, 29 September, 3 November 1975.

2 He joined Labour after the election. Millington's obituary, *The Guardian*, 14 May 2009.

3 For Christopher Addison, see K. and J. Morgan, *Portrait of a Progressive.*

4 Sir Oliver Franks to Attlee, 15 July 1950 (NA, PREM 8/1405, Pt. I). Franks was the Ambassador to Washington, 1948–1952.

5 See 'The Bristol Giant', my review of Adonis' *Labour's Churchill*, 2020 in *Finest Hour—The Journal of Winston Churchill and his Times* 188 (Second Quarter 2020): 33.https://winstonchurchill.org/publications/churchill-bulletin/bulletin-146-aug-2020/the-bristol-giant/

CHAPTER 10

PAUL ADDISON: PUBLICATIONS 1971–2020

ANTOINE CAPET

1. THESIS

'Political Change in Britain, September 1939 to December 1940'. D. Phil. Thesis. Nuffield College, Oxford, 1971. Supervisor: A.J.P. Taylor. 547 leaves.

2. BOOKS AS SOLE AUTHOR

The Road to 1945: British Politics and the Second World War. London: Jonathan Cape, 1975 (Reissue with new postface: Pimlico Paperbacks, 1994).

Now the War is over: A Social History of Britain, 1945–51. London: Cape, 1985 (Pimlico edition with a new introduction. London: Pimlico, 1995).

Churchill on the Home Front. London: Jonathan Cape, 1992 (*Churchill on the Home Front, 1900–1955.* With a new Preface by the Author. London: Pimlico, 1993. Faber & Faber, 2013).

Churchill: The unexpected Hero. Oxford: University Press, 2005.

Winston Churchill. Very Interesting People Series, vol. 16. Oxford: University Press, 2007 [From his 60,000-word entry in the *New Oxford Dictionary of National Biography*, 2004].

No Turning Back: The Peacetime Revolutions of Post-war Britain. Oxford: University Press, 2010.

The Connell Guide to Winston Churchill. Connell Guides History Series. London: Connell Guides, 2016 ['All you need to know in one concise volume'].

3. BOOKS EDITED AND CO-EDITED

Addison, Paul & Calder, Angus [Editors]. Foreword by Len Deighton. *Time to Kill: The Soldier's Experience of War in the West, 1939–1945.* London: Pimlico, 1996.

Addison, Paul & Crang, Jeremy A. [Editors]. *The Burning Blue: A new History of the Battle of Britain.* London: Pimlico, 2000.

Addison, Paul & Jones, Harriet [Editors]. *A Companion to Contemporary Britain, 1939–2000.* Blackwell Companions to British History. Oxford: Blackwell Publishers, 2005 (Contribution: 'The impact of the Second World War': 3–22).

Addison, Paul & Crang, Jeremy A. [Editors]. *Firestorm: The Bombing of Dresden 1945.* London: Pimlico, 2006.

Addison, Paul & Crang, Jeremy A. [Editors]. *Listening to Britain: Home Intelligence Reports on Britain's Finest Hour, May-September 1940.* London: The Bodley Head, 2010.

Addison, Paul & Crang, Jeremy A. [Editors]. *The Spirit of the Blitz: Home Intelligence and British Morale, September 1940-June 1941.* Oxford: University Press, 2020.

4. ARTICLES AND CHAPTERS ON WINSTON CHURCHILL

'Winston Churchill'. *In* Mackintosh, John [Editor]. *British Prime Ministers in the Twentieth Century. (2) Churchill to Callaghan.* London: Weidenfeld & Nicolson, 1978: 1–36.

'Makers of the twentieth century: Winston Churchill'. *History Today* 30/8 (August 1980): 7–13.

'The political beliefs of Winston Churchill'. *Transactions of the Royal Historical Society* 5th Series 30 (1980): 23–47.

'Winston Churchill and the working class, 1900–1914'. *In* Winter, J.M. [Editor]. *The Working Class in Modern British History: Essays in Honour of Henry Pelling.* Cambridge: University Press, 1983: 43–64.

'Churchill in British Politics, 1940–1955'. *In* Bean, J.M.W. [Editor]. *The Political Culture of Modern Britain: Studies in Memory of Stephen Koss.* London: Hamish Hamilton, 1987: 243–261.

'Churchill and social reform'. *In* Blake, Robert & Louis, William Roger [Editors]. *Churchill: A Major New Assessment of his Life in Peace and War.* Oxford: University Press, 1993: 57–78.

'Destiny, history and providence: The religion of Winston Churchill'. *In* Bentley, Michael [Editor]. *Public and private Doctrine: Essays in British History presented to Maurice Cowling.* Cambridge: University Press, 1993: 236–250.

'Winston Churchill and social reform'. *Modern History Review* 6–3 (1995): 10–12.

'Churchill and the Price of Victory: 1939–1945'. *In* Tiratsoo, Nick [Editor]. *From Blitz to Blair: A New History of Britain since 1939.* London: Weidenfeld & Nicolson, 1997: 53–76.

'The search for peace in Ireland'. *In* Muller, James W. [Editor]. *Churchill as Peacemaker*. Cambridge: University Press, 1997.

'Winston Churchill's concept of the English-speaking peoples'. *In* Pok, Attila [Editor]. *The Fabric of modern Europe: Studies in social and diplomatic History*. Nottingham: University Press, 1999: 103–117.

'The three careers of Winston Churchill'. Churchill in the twenty-first Century: A Conference held at the Institute of Historical Research, University of London, 11–13 January 2001'. *Transactions of the Royal Historical Society* 6th Series 11 (2001): 183–200. (Reprinted as 'Churchill's three careers' in Cannadine, David & Quinault, Roland [Editors]. *Winston Churchill in the Twenty-First Century*. Cambridge: University Press, 2004: 9–26).

'My favourite Churchill books'. *Finest Hour—Journal of the Churchill Center and Societies* 128 (Autumn 2005): 40–41 [Reprinted from *The Guardian*, 13 April 2005].

'Churchill and the sterilisation issue'. *Finest Hour: Journal of the Churchill Center and Societies* 131 (2006): 22–23.

'Churchill as a Liberal'. *Revue française de civilisation britannique* 16–2 (2011): 111–122.

'Churchill and women'. *In* Toye, Richard [Editor]. *Winston Churchill: Politics, Strategy and Statecraft*. London: Bloomsbury, 2017: 93–104.

5. BBC WEB PAGE ON CHURCHILL

'Why Churchill Lost in 1945'. Last updated 2011–02-17. https://www.bbc.co.uk/history/worldwars/wwtwo/election_01.shtml

6. ARTICLES AND CHAPTERS ON OTHER THEMES AND PEOPLE

'Lloyd George and compromise peace in the Second World War'. *In* Taylor, A.J.P. [Editor]. *Lloyd George: Twelve Essays.* London: Hamish Hamilton, 1971: 361–384.

'By-elections of the Second World War'. *In* Chris Cook & John Ramsden [Editors]. *By-elections in British Politics.* London: Macmillan, 1973: 165–190.

'Die Zweite Weltkrieg und die politische Enwticklung Englands, 1939–1945'. *In* Hauser, Oswald [Editor]. *Weltpolitik II, 1939–1945.* Göttingen: Musterschmidt, 1975: 178–196.

'Patriotism under pressure: Lord Rothermere and British Foreign Policy'. *In* Peele, Gillian & Cook, Chris [Editors]. *The Politics of Reappraisal, 1918–1939.* London: Macmillan, 1975: 189–208.

'Journey to the Centre: Churchill and Labour in Coalition, 1940–45'. *In* Sked, A. & Cook, C. [Editors]. *Crisis and Controversy: Essays in Honour of A.J.P. Taylor.* London: Macmillan, 1976: 165–193.

'Labour and politics in the People's War'. *Bulletin for the Study of Labour History* 34 (1977): 8–14.

'Britain and the politics of social patriotism'. *In* Aster, Sidney [Editor]. *The Second World War as a National Experience.* Ottawa Conference, 14–19 November 1979. Toronto: Canadian Committee for the History of the Second World War, 1981: 38–49.

'The Road from 1945'. *In* Peter Hennessy & Anthony Seldon [Editors]. *Ruling Performance: British Governments from Attlee to Thatcher.* Oxford: Basil Blackwell, 1987: 5–27 (Extracts in *Contemporary Record* 1/2 (1987): 11–18 [theme issue, 'Britain's postwar industrial decline']).

'Oxford and the Second World War'. *In* Harrison, Brian [Editor]. *The History of the University of Oxford.* Volume 8: *The Twentieth Century.* Oxford: University Press, 1994: 167–188.

'"On to the New Jerusalem: Could post-war Britain be made a land fit for heroes?": Paul Addison looks at politics and social policy'. *The Guardian*, 20 May 1994.

British Historians and the Debate over the 'post-war Consensus'. British Studies Distinguished Lectures, N°31. Austin (Texas): Harry Ransom Humanities Research Center, University of Texas at Austin, 1996 (Pamphlet. Reprinted *in* Louis, William Roger [Editor]. *More Adventures with Britannia: Personalities, Politics and Culture in Britain.* London: I.B. Tauris, 1998: 255–264).

'The British Conservative Party from Churchill to Heath: Doctrine or men? *Contemporary European History* 8–2 (1999): 289–298.

Addison, Paul & Crang, Jeremy A. 'A battle of many Nations'. *In* Addison, Paul & Crang, Jeremy A. [Editors]. *The Burning Blue: A new History of the Battle of Britain.* London: Pimlico, 2000: 243–266.

'National identity and the Battle of Britain'. *In* Korte, Barbara & Schneider, Ralf [Editors]. *War and the Cultural Construction of Identities in Britain.* Internationale Forschungen zur allgemeinen und vergleichenden Literaturwissenschaft, Band 59. Amsterdam: Rodopi, 2002: 225–240.

'The impact of the Second World War'. *In* Addison, Paul & Jones, Harriet [Editors]. *A Companion to contemporary Britain, 1939–2000.* Blackwell Companions to British History. Oxford: Blackwell, 2005: 3–22.

'Retrospect'. *In* Addison, Paul & Crang, Jeremy A. [Editors]. *Firestorm: The Bombing of Dresden 1945.* London: Pimlico, 2006: 209–219.

'Clement Attlee, 1945–1951'. *In* Bogdanor, Vernon [Editor]. *From New Jerusalem to New Labour: British Prime Ministers from Attlee to Blair.* Basingstoke: Palgrave Macmillan, 2010: 9–22.

'A Conspicuous Failure: Lord Randolph Churchill'. *Finest Hour—The Journal of Winston Churchill and his Times* 176 (Spring 2017): 14–17. Free online access 2020: https://winstonchurchill.org/publications/finest-hour/finest-hour-176/conspicuous-failure-lord-randolph-churchill/

'How Churchill's Mind worked'. *In* Louis, William Roger [Editor]. *Serendipitous Adventures with Britannia: Personalities, Politics and Culture in Britain.* London: I.B. Tauris, 2019: 17–27. Free online access 2020: https://www.openhistorysociety.org/members-articles/how-churchills-mind-worked-by-paul-addison/#_edn15

7. OXFORD DICTIONARY OF NATIONAL BIOGRAPHY

'Churchill, Sir Winston Leonard Spencer (1874–1965)'. *Oxford Dictionary of National Biography.* Oxford: University Press, 2004 (c. 60,000 words).

Sir Winston Leonard Spencer Churchill (1874–1965): doi:10.1093/ref:odnb/32413 Online access 2004, restricted to subscribers: http://www.oxforddnb.com/view/article/32413

'Home front, 1939–1945'. *Oxford Dictionary of National Biography.* Oxford: University Press, 2004. Free online access 2006: https://doi.org/10.1093/ref:odnb/92741

'The Few (act. 1940)'. *Oxford Dictionary of National Biography.* Oxford: University Press, 2006. Free online access 2006: https://doi.org/10.1093/ref:odnb/93788

'Calder, Angus Lindsay Ritchie (1942–2008), historian and literary critic'. *Oxford Dictionary of National Biography*. Oxford: University Press, 2013. Online access 2012, restricted to subscribers: https://doi.org/10.1093/ref:odnb/99794

8. EDITED MICROFILMS

Addison, Paul [Editor]. *The British People and World War 2: Home Intelligence Reports on Opinion and Morale, 1940–1944*. Reel 1: *Inf.1 264, 18 May 1940–23 Oct 1940*. Reel 2: *Inf.1 292, 30 Sept 1940–23 June 1942*. Reel 3: *Inf.1 292, 23 June 1942–24 Aug 1943*. Reel 4: *Inf.1 292, 24 Aug 1943–27 Dec 1944*. 4 microfilms. Hassocks: Harvester Press, 1979 [From Ministry of Information records INF 1/292: *Home Intelligence Weekly Reports, 1940–1944*].

9. FILMS

The Spanish Civil War. Written, researched and narrated by Paul Addison and Owen Dudley Edwards. Edited and directed by Tony Aldgate. British Universities Historical Studies in Film, N°3. University of Leeds, 1972. 2 film reels, b&w, 16mm.

10. AUDIOTAPE

1945: The New Elite. Arts: A Fourth Level Course. Great Britain, 1750–1950: Sources and Historiography. Milton Keynes: Open University, 1973.

11. TRANSLATION

German Foreign and Defence Policy after Unification. By Lothar Gutjahr. Translation by Lothar Gutjahr and Paul Addison. The New Germany Series. London: Pinter, 1994.

12. OBITUARIES

'Wizard of Ox: Paul Addison pays tribute to A.J.P. Taylor'. *London Review of Books* (8 November 1990): 3–5.

'Angus Calder (1942–2008)'. *History Workshop Journal* 70 (2010): 299–304.

'Achievement on a Colossal Scale' [Sir Martin Gilbert]. *Finest Hour—The Journal of Winston Churchill and his Times* 165 (Autumn 2014): 21. https://winstonchurchill.org/uncategorised/achievement-on-a-colossal-scale/

13. INTERVIEW

Zweiniger-Bargielowska, Ina. 'The road from 1945: An Interview with Paul Addison'. *Contemporary Record* 6–1 (Summer 1992): 186–193 [The genesis of historical studies on the Second World War].

14. BOOK REVIEWS

American Historical Review

The American Historical Review 104/5 (December 1999): 1758 1759.

Crowson N.J. *Facing Fascism: The Conservative Party and the European Dictators, 1935–1940.* Routledge Studies in Modern European History. Routledge, 1997. Accessible to subscribers on the American Historical Association site: https://doi.org/10.1086/ahr/104.5.1758

English Historical Review (EHR)

EHR 89/351 (April 1974): 469–470:

Marder, Arthur J. *Winston is Back: Churchill at the Admiralty, 1939–1940.* Supplement, N°5, *The English Historical Review.* Longman, 1972.

EHR 98/387 (April 1983): 463:

Honigsbaum, Frank. *The Division in British Medicine: A History of the Separation of General Practice from Hospital Care, 1911–1968.* Kogan Page, 1979.

EHR 99/392 (July 1984): 671:

Ball, Alan R. *British Political Parties: The Emergence of a Modern Party System.* Macmillan, 1981.

EHR 100/394 (January 1985): 214:

Burk, Kathleen [Editor]. *War and the State: The Transformation of British Government, 1914–1919.* Allen & Unwin, 1982.

EHR 101/400 (July 1986): 748–749:

Anderson, Gerald D. *Fascists, Communists, and the National Government: Civil Liberties in Great Britain, 1931–1937.* University of Missouri Press, 1983.

EHR 102/404 (July 1987): 755–756:

Beloff, Max. *Wars and Welfare: Britain 1914–1945.* Edward Arnold, 1984.

EHR 104/410 (January 1989) :162–163:

Middlemas, Keith. *Power, Competition and the State.* Vol. 1, *Britain in Search of Balance, 1940–61.* Macmillan, 1986.

EHR 105/417 (October 1990): 1089:

Pressnell, L.S. *External Economic Policy since the War.* Volume 1, *The Post-War Financial Settlement.* H.M.S.O., 1987.

EHR 108/426 (January 1993): 268–269:

Post-war Britain, 1945–64: Themes And Perspectives: 1st Summer School: Papers. Edited by Anthony Gorst, Lewis Johnman and W. Scott Lucas. Pinter in association with Institute of Contemporary British History, 1989.

EHR 108/427 (April 1993): 423–425:

Middlemas, Keith. *Power, Competition and the State*. Vol. II, *Threats to the Postwar Settlement: Britain, 1961–74*. Vol. III, *The End of the Postwar Era: Britain since 1974*. Macmillan, 1990.

EHR 111/441 (April 1996): 542–544:

Brivati, Brian & Jones, Harriet [Editors]. *What Difference Did The War Make ?* Leicester University Press, 1993.

EHR 116/467 (June 2001): 764–765:

Muller, James W. *Churchill's 'Iron Curtain' Speech Fifty Years Later*. University of Missouri Press, 1999.

EHR 119/484 (November 2004): 1365–1368:

Rose, Sonya O. *Which People's War? National Identity and Citizenship in Wartime Britain, 1939–1945*. Oxford University Press, 2003.

Mackay, Robert. *Half the Battle: Civilian Morale in Britain during the Second World War*. Manchester University Press, 2002.

History

History 62/206 (1977): 536–538.

Pelling, Henry. *Winston Churchill.*

Cowling, Maurice. *The Impact of Hitler: British Politics and British Policy, 1933–1940.*

The New Statesman

NB: Paul was a regular contributor to the *New Statesman* (*NS*) from 1976 to 1979. All his reviews are accessible to subscribers on the *New Statesman* site:

NS (April 30, 1976)—'The Nine-Day Wonder':

Skelley, Jeffrey [Editor]. *The General Strike, 1926*. Lawrence & Wishart, 1976.

NS (May 21, 1976)—'Sitting Bull':

Young, Kenneth. *Stanley Baldwin*. Weidenfeld & Nicolson, 1976.

NS (June 18, 1976)—'Rose Watered':

Rhodes James, Robert. *Victor Cazalet.* Hamish Hamilton, 1976

NS (November 26, 1976)—'Carry on Winnie':

Colville, John. *Footprints in Time.* Collins, 1976.

NS (June 3, 1977)—'Big Fish':

Lash, Joseph P. *Roosevelt and Churchill, 1939–1941*. A. Deutsch, 1977

NS (July 1, 1977)—'The Burden of Proof':

Irving, David. *Hitler's War.* Hodder & Stoughton, 1977

NS (July 15, 1977)—'Pax':

Cross, John Arthur. *Sir Samuel Hoare: A Political Biography.* London: Jonathan Cape, 1977.

NS (August 12, 1977)—'Hate Couture':

Becker, Jillian. *Hitler's Children.* Michael Joseph, 1977.

NS (September 2, 1977)—'Rowse's Law':

Barclay, Glen St. John. *Their Finest Hour.* Weidenfeld & Nicolson, 1977.

NS (March 24, 1978)—'East is East':

Thorne, Christopher. *Allies of a Kind.* Hamish Hamilton, 1978

NS (June 16, 1978)—'Brick in Hand':

Sellwood, Arthur. *Police Strike—1919.* W.H. Allen, 1978.

NS (July 28, 1978)—'Fawlty Powers':

Harvey, John [Editor]. *The War Diaries of Oliver Harvey, 1941–1945.* Collins, 1978.

NS (October 27, 1978)—'Max, Cicero, Josefine':

Kahn, David. *Hitler's Spies.* Macmillan, 1978

NS (December 1, 1978)—'The Goat-Footed Bard':

Grigg, John. *Lloyd George: The People's Champion, 1902–1911.* Eyre Methuen, 1978.

NS (April 27, 1979)—'Smiling Through':

McLaine, Ian. *Ministry of Morale.* Allen & Unwin, 1979.

London Review of Books

NB: The *Review* was founded in 1979, and Paul was among its earliest contributors. All his reviews are accessible to subscribers on the *London Review of Books (LRB)* site: https://www.lrb.co.uk/contributors/paul-addison

LRB 1/4 (6 December 1979)—'Middle Way':

Morgan, Kenneth O. *Consensus and Disunity: The Lloyd George Coalition Government, 1918–1922.* Oxford: Clarendon Press, 1979.

LRB 2/14 (17 July 1980)—'For Church and State':

Wormell, Deborah. *Sir John Seeley and the Uses of History*. Cambridge University Press, 1980.

LRB 2/16 (21 August 1980)—'Prince Arthur':

Egremont, Max, *Balfour*. Collins, 1980.

LRB 2/22 (20 November 1980)—'Mount Amery':

The Leo Amery Diaries. Edited by John Barnes & David Nicholson. Foreword by Julian Amery. Hutchinson, 1980.

LRB 3/12 (2 July 1981)—'Jingo Joe':

Jay, Richard. *Joseph Chamberlain: A Political Study*. Oxford: Clarendon Press, 1981.

LRB 3/22 (3 December 1981)—'Lord Randolph's Coming-Out':

Foster, R.F. *Lord Randolph Churchill: A Political Life*. Oxford: Clarendon Press, 1981.

LRB 4/8 (6 May 1982)—'Early Hillhead Man':

Gilbert, Martin. *Churchill's Political Philosophy*. Oxford University Press, 1981.

Gilbert, Martin. *Winston Churchill: The Wilderness Years*. Macmillan, 1981.

Kersaudy, François. *Churchill and de Gaulle*. Collins, 1981.

Young, Kenneth [Editor]. *The Diaries of Sir Robert Bruce Lockhart*. Macmillan, 1981.

Seldon, Anthony. *Churchill's Indian Summer*. Hodder & Stoughton, 1981.

LRB 5/13 (21 July 1983)—'Buggering on':

Winston S. Churchill. Volume IV: *Companion.* Part 3: *Documents: The Coming of War, 1936–1939.* Edited by Martin Gilbert. Heinemann, 1982.

Gilbert, Martin. *Finest Hour: Winston S. Churchill, 1939–1941.* Heinemann, 1983.

Morgan, Ted. *Churchill: 1874–1915.* Jonathan Cape, 1983.

Manchester, William. *The Last Lion: Winston Spencer Churchill: Visions of Glory, 1874–1932.* Michael Joseph, 1983.

LRB 6/6 (5 April 1984)—'When Neil Kinnock was in his pram':

Morgan, Kenneth O. *Labour in Power, 1945–1951.* Oxford University Press, 1984

LRB 7/1 (24 January 1985)—'Naked except for a bath towel':

Kimball, Warren F. [Editor]. *Churchill and Roosevelt: The Complete Correspondence.* Princeton University Press, 1984.

LRB 7/19 (7 November 1985)—'Churchill by moonlight':

Colville, John. *The Fringes of Power: Downing Street Diaries, 1939–1955.* Hodder & Stoughton, 1985.

LRB 8/1 (23 January 1986)—'Permissiveness'.

Whitehead, Phillip. *The Writing on the Wall: Britain in the Seventies.* Michael Joseph, 1985.

LRB 8/7 (17 April 1986)—'Darling Clem':

Burridge, Trevor. *Clement Attlee: A Political Biography.* Jonathan Cape, 1985.

Pimlott, Ben [Editor]. *The Second World War Diary of Hugh Dalton, 1940–1945.* Jonathan Cape, 1986

Michael Foot. *Loyalists and Loners.* Collins, 1986.

LRB 8/13 (24 July 1986)—'Warfare and Welfare':

Barnett, Correlli. *The Audit of War: The Illusion and Reality of Britain as a Great Nation*. Macmillan, 1986.

Winter, J.M. *The Great War and the British People*. Macmillan, 1986.

LRB 8/17 (9 October 1986)—'Getting on':

Wright, Patrick. *On Living in an Old Country*. Verso, 1985.

Cowling, Maurice. *Religion and Public Doctrine in Modern England*. Volume II: *Assaults*. Cambridge University Press, 1985.

LRB 9/9 (7 May 1987)—'Churchill has nothing to hide':

Gilbert, Martin. *Road to Victory: Winston S. Churchill, 1941–1945*. Heinemann, 1986.

LRB 10/13 (7 July 1988)—'Peacemonger':

Gilbert, Martin. *Never Despair: Winston S. Churchill, 1945–1965*. Heinemann, 1988.

LRB 12/12 (28 June 1990)—'Garbo & Co':

Ponting, Clive. *1940: Myth and Reality*. Hamish Hamilton, 1990.

Hinsley, Francis Harry & Simkins, C.A.G. *British Intelligence in the Second World War*. Vol. IV: *Security and Counter-Intelligence*. HMSO, 1990.

Villa, Brian Loring. *Unauthorized Action: Mountbatten and the Dieppe Raid*. Oxford University Press, 1990.

LRB 13/4 (21 February 1991)—'The Road to 1989':

Morgan, Kenneth O. *The People's Peace: British History, 1945–1990*. Oxford University Press, 1990.

LRB 13/14 (25 July 1991)—'Dismantling the class war':

The Cambridge Social History of Britain, 1750–1950. Vol. I: *Regions and Communities.* Edited by F.M.L. Thompson. Cambridge University Press, 1990.

The Cambridge Social History of Britain 1750–1950. Vol. II: *People and their Environment.* Edited by F.M.L. Thompson. Cambridge University Press, 1990.

Williamson, Bill. *The Temper of the Times: British Society since World War II.* Basil Blackwell, 1990.

LRB 14/21 (5 November 1992)—'War within wars':

Freedman, Lawrence, Hayes, Paul & O'Neill, Robert [Editors]. *War, Strategy and International Politics: Essays in Honour of Sir Michael Howard.* Oxford University Press, 1992.

LRB 15/1 (7 January 1993)—'How Left was he?':

Skidelsky, Robert. *John Maynard Keynes: The Economist as Saviour, 1920–1937.* Macmillan, 1992.

Moggridge, D.E. *Maynard Keynes: An Economist's Biography.* Routledge, 1992.

LRB 17/9 (11 May 1995)—'Sixtysomethings':

Whiteley, Paul; Seyd, Patrick & Richardson, Jeremy. *True Blues: The Politics of Conservative Party Membership.* Oxford University Press, 1994

Pimlott, Ben. *Frustrate Their Knavish Tricks: Writings on Biography, History and Politics.* HarperCollins, 1994.

Literary Review

NB: Paul was a regular contributor to the *Literary Review (LR)* from 2006 to 2017. All his reviews are accessible to subscribers on the

Literary Review site: https://literaryreview.co.uk/contributors/paul-addison

LR 337 (October 2006)—'Anything But Dull':

Hennessy, Peter. *Having It So Good: Britain in the Fifties*. Allen Lane / The Penguin Press, 2006.

LR 347 (August 2007)—'A Nation of Shoppers':

Marr, Andrew. *A History of Modern Britain*. Macmillan, 2007.

LR 352 (March 2008)—'Are We Declining?':

Garnett, Mark. *From Anger to Apathy: The British Experience since 1975*. Jonathan Cape, 2007.

LR 359 (October 2008)—'Gabbo & Bovril':

Rankin, Nicholas. *Churchill's Wizards: The British Genius for Deception, 1914–1945*. Faber & Faber, 2008.

LR 364 (April 2009)—'No Turning Back':

Vinen, Richard. *Thatcher's Britain: The Politics and Social Upheaval of the Thatcher Era*. Simon & Schuster, 2009.

LR 366 (June 2009)—'Events, Dear Boy, Events':

Williams, Charles. *Harold Macmillan*. Weidenfeld & Nicolson, 2009.

LR 372 (December 2009)—'Authoritarian, Illiberal, Puritanical':

Kynaston, David. *Family Britain, 1951–1957*. Bloomsbury, 2009.

LR 380 (September 2010)—'After Eden':

Thorpe, D.R. *Supermac: The Life of Harold Macmillan*. Chatto & Windus, 2010.

LR 400 (July 2012)—'Prime Scribbler':

Clarke, Peter. *Mr Churchill's Profession: Statesman, Orator, Writer.* Bloomsbury, 2012.

LR 409 (May 2013)—'People Watching':

Hinton, James. *The Mass Observers: A History,* 1937–1949. Oxford University Press, 2013.

LR 410 (June 2013)—'Messy Old Life':

Kynaston, David. *Modernity Britain: Opening the Box,* 1957–59. Bloomsbury, 2013.

LR 414 (October 2013)—'Speaking for England':

Toye, Richard. *The Roar of the Lion: The Untold Story of Churchill's World War II Speeches.* Oxford University Press, 2013.

James, Lawrence. *Churchill and Empire.* Weidenfeld & Nicolson, 2013.

LR 416 (December 2013)—'Don't Mention the Tube Alloys':

Farmelo, Graham. *Churchill's Bomb: A Hidden History of Science, War and Politics.* Faber & Faber, 2013.

LR 430 (April 2015)—'Partisans in Whitehall':

Schneer, Jonathan. *Ministers at War: Winston Churchill and his War Cabinet.* Oneworld, 2015.

LR 448 (November 2016)—'Governing in Prose':

Bew, John. *Citizen Clem: A Biography of Attlee.* Riverrun, 2016.

LR 455 (July 2017)—'Picking up the Pieces'

Lowe, Keith. *The Fear and Freedom: How the Second World War changed us.* Viking, 2017.

Times Literary Supplement

TLS (2 December 1977)—'For the general good'

Harris, Jose. *William Beveridge*. Oxford: Clarendon Press, 1977.

TLS (1 December 1978)—'Men beware women'

Harrison, Brian. *Separate Spheres: The Opposition to Women's Suffrage in Britain*. London: Croom Helm, 1978.

TLS (23 November 1979)—'When Lab was Lib'

Clarke, Peter. *Liberals and Social Democrats*. Cambridge: University Press, 1978.

TLS (2 May 1980)—'Parties and pressure groups'

Middlemas, Keith. *Politics in Industrial Society: The Experience of the British System since 1911*. London: André Deutsch, 1979.

TLS (11 September 1981)—'The burden of decline'

Carlton, David. *Anthony Eden*. London: Allen Lane, 1981.

TLS (31 August 1984)—'Attlee's new order'

Pelling, Henry. *The Labour Governments, 1945–51*. London: Macmillan, 1984.

TLS (14 March 1986)—'Seeking popular consent'

Abrams, Mark; Gerard, David & Timms, Noel [Editors]. *Values and Social Change in Britain*. London: Macmillan, 1985.

Brenton, Maria & Jones, Catherine [Editors]. *The Year Book of Social Policy in Britain 1984–5*. London: Routledge & Kegan Paul, 1985.

TLS (5 August 1988)—'Claiming a tradition'

Warner, Gerald. *The Scottish Tory Party: A History*. London: Weidenfeld & Nicolson, 1988.

TLS (2 November 1990)—'Free-wheeling idealists'

Annan, Lord. *Our Age: Portrait of a Generation*. London: Weidenfeld & Nicolson, 1990.

TLS (10 September 1999)—'Rivals at war'

Stewart, Graham. *Burying Caesar: Churchill, Chamberlain and the Battle for the Tory Party*. London: Weidenfeld & Nicolson, 1999.

TLS (14 October 2005)—'Oswald's folk'

Pugh, Martin. *Hurrah for the Blackshirts! Fascists and Fascism in Britain between the Wars*. London: Jonathan Cape, 2005.

TLS (24 November 2006)—'The Bummel, the bad and the bombers'

Ramsden, John. *Don't Mention the War: The British and Germans since 1890*. London: Little, Brown, 2006.

TLS (10 August 2007)—'Home front heroes'

Magee, Bryan. *Growing up in a War*. London: Pimlico, 2007.

Wheal, Donald James. *White City*. London: Century, 2007.

TLS (6 May 2011)—'Unmentionable'

Jalland, Pat. *Death in War and Peace: A History of Loss and Grief in England, 1914–1970*. Oxford: University Press, 2012.

TLS (8 June 2012)—'Big-tent Battle '

North, Richard. *The Many Not The Few: The Stolen History of the Battle of Britain*. London: Continuum, 2012.

TLS (8 May 2013)—'You Rang m'lord?':

Lethbridge, Lucy. *Servants: A Downstairs View of Twentieth-Century Britain*. Bloomsbury, 2013.

TLS (16 & 23 August 2013)—'High roads'

Mills James H. *Cannabis Nation: Control and Consumption in Britain, 1928–2008*. Oxford: University Press, 2013.

Hitchens, Peter. *The War we never fought: The British Establishment's Surrender to Drugs*. London: Bloomsbury, 2012.

TLS (19 September 2014)—'Spent'

Todd, Selina. *The People: The Rise and Fall of the Working Class, 1910–2010*. London: John Murray, 2014.

TLS (24 October 2014)—'From we to me'

Marquand, David. *Mammon's Kingdom: An Essay on Britain, now*. London: Allen Lane, 2014.

TLS (17 July 2015)—'Top down'

Skidelsky, Robert. *Britain since 1900: A Success Story?* London: Vintage Books, 2014.

TLS (19 & 26 August 2016)—'All-out war: Panoramic view of Britain from 1937 to 1941'

Todman, Daniel. *Britain's War: Into Battle, 1937–1941*. London: Allen Lane, 2016.

History Today

HT 30/7 (July 1980)

Grigg, John. *1943: The Victory that never was*. Eyre Methuen, 1980.

HT 30/8 (August 1980)

Harman, Nicholas. *Dunkirk: The Necessary Myth*. Hodder & Stoughton, 1980.

HT 31/9 (September 1981)

Cowling, Maurice. *Religion and Public Doctrine in Modern England*, Volume 1. Cambridge University Press, 1980.

HT 52/7 (July 2002)

Hennessy, Peter. *The Secret State: Whitehall and the Cold War*. Allen Lane, 2002.

Cradock, Percy. *Know Your Enemy: How the Joint Intelligence Committee saw the World*. John Murray, 2002.

HT 60/6 (June 2010)

Toye, Richard. *Churchill's Empire: The World that made him and the World he made*. Macmillan, 2010.

HT 64/5 (May 2014)

Biffen, John. *Semi-detached*. Biteback Publishing, 2013.

HT 66/8 (August 2016)

Hermiston, Roger. *All behind you, Winston: Churchill's Great Coalition, 1940–45*. Aurum Press, 2016.

HT 67/11 (November 2017)

Bell, Christopher M. *Churchill and the Dardanelles*. Oxford University Press, 2017.

***The Observer* (2 January 1983)—'The collectivist scramble'**

Beer, Samuel H. *Britain against Itself: The Political Contradictions of Collectivism*. Faber, 1982.

Finest Hour—The Journal of Winston Churchill and his Times

FH 172 (Spring 2016)

Arthur, Max. *Churchill, The Life: An Authorised Pictorial Biography.* London: Cassell Illustrated, 2015. Free online access 2020: https://winstonchurchill.org/publications/finest-hour/finest-hour-172/churchill-biography/

Hillsdale College—The Churchill Project

Crowcroft, Robert. *The End is Nigh: British Politics, Power and the Road to the Second World War.* Oxford: University Press, 2019: https://winstonchurchill.hillsdale.edu/crowcroft-end-nigh-addison/

Cercles

Reynolds, David. *In Command of History: Churchill Fighting and Writing the Second World War.* London: Allen Lane, 2004: http://www.cercles.com/review/r24/reynolds.htm

Campion, Garry. *The Good Fight: Battle of Britain Propaganda and the Few*. London: Palgrave Macmillan, 2010: http://www.cercles.com/review/r47/Campion.html

Capet, Antoine. *Churchill: Le Dictionnaire*. Paris: Perrin, 2018: http://www.cercles.com/review/r83/Capet.html

SELECTED BOOK REVIEWS BY PAUL ADDISON

REVIEW I

IN COMMAND OF HISTORY: CHURCHILL FIGHTING AND WRITING THE SECOND WORLD WAR

by

DAVID REYNOLDS

London: Allen Lane, 2004
£30.00, xxvi-646 pages, ISBN 0-713-99819-9

At the end of the Second World War Churchill was hailed as the saviour of his country and more widely as the saviour of freedom and democracy. He basked in the applause, but long and painful experience of the vicissitudes of politics had taught him that memories were short and reputation a highly perishable commodity. The lesson was reinforced by his defeat in the general election of July 1945, but as his wife predicted, it turned out to be a blessing in disguise. Opposition set him free to fight a battle that would ensure his place in history for decades to come: the battle of the war memoirs. He embarked on a six-volume history of the Second World War to which he brought all the energy and vision, and the aggressive political skills, of his war leadership. It was a literary campaign which ended with a decisive victory for Churchill over his most deadly opponents, old age and the clock. Exhaustive research has enabled David Reynolds to reconstruct the story in a compelling narrative abounding with fresh insights and evidence.

This is more than a book about a book. It is a portrait of its author and his multifarious character. During the Second World War Churchill was a patriotic public servant who drove himself to the brink of exhaustion in pursuit of victory. This was the role in which he wished to be remembered by posterity, but there were earthier aspects of his personality on which Reynolds is very illuminating. The Churchill of his pages was also a buccaneering entrepreneur with an appetite for enormous sums of money, a literary predator who exploited and appropriated other people's work, and a historical manipulator who suppressed or adapted the evidence to suit his political purposes. In the hands of Churchill's detractors this would doubtless add up to a telling indictment of a myth-making hypocrite. What Reynolds gives us a rounded and realistic picture of a great man with the defects of his qualities.

Churchill would have agreed with Dr. Johnson that "no man but a blockhead writes, except for money." He had always lived by his pen, driving hard bargains with publishers and media magnates. Reynolds shows how he exploited his growing fame *during* the war to raise extra cash from pre-war books and speeches. There was, however, a major obstacle in the way of Churchill's resumption of an authorial career after the war: penal rates of tax on high incomes. He was not prepared to pay income and surtax at a marginal rate of 19s 6d in the pound to the Inland Revenue, and it seems unlikely that he would have written *The Second World War* but for an ingenious scheme whereby he gave his papers to the Chartwell Trust, which then sold the literary rights and employed the tax-free income generated for the benefit of his children and grandchildren. Reynolds implies that Churchill received no income from the Trust, but according to the official biography he was entitled to £20,000 a year, double the salary of the Prime Minister, to cover his living and literary expenses.

In marketing the rights Churchill had no need to engage in unseemly wrangling. He relied on the hard-nosed skills of his unofficial literary agent, Emery Reves, and the friendship of Lord Camrose, the owner of the *Daily Telegraph*. Reynolds computes that the literary rights to *The Second World War*—published by Cassell in Britain and Houghton Mifflin in the United States, with serialisation in the *Telegraph* and *Life* magazine—were sold for a figure worth somewhere between eighteen million and sixty million dollars in today's money, depending on the method adopted for calculating inflation.

Churchill was a law-abiding citizen who operated within the rules, but the rules were frequently bent in his favour, and at his request. His use of government documents was a case in point. When he returned to office as First Lord of the Admiralty in September 1939 he ordered that his minutes and telegrams should be printed at regular intervals, an arrangement that continued throughout his war premiership. It was suspected with good reason in Whitehall that he intended to make use of the documents when he came to write his memoirs after the war. But were they his to dispose of? The Cabinet Secretary, Sir Edward Bridges, wanted to enforce a rule adopted in 1934 whereby ministers on leaving office were required to leave behind them all official papers. His deputy, Norman Brook, warned that Churchill would never accept this, and the War Cabinet agreed in May 1945 that ministers could take away documents they had written themselves, and would be free to publish them provided they had the approval of the government of the day.

Churchill, therefore, left office with a complete wartime set of key documents which served as the backbone of his memoirs. In theory the Attlee government could have prevented their publication but as Reynolds explains, there was never any question of this. On the contrary Norman Brook, who succeeded Bridges as Cabinet Secretary, treated Churchill's memoirs as though they were virtually an official history, popularising Britain's contribution to victory and counteracting American (and Russian?) claims to have won the war single-handedly. Churchill and his research team enjoyed the assistance of the Cabinet Office, including almost unlimited access to wartime files. In return Churchill was the most co-operative of authors, submitting drafts of the book to be vetted by the Cabinet Office, the Foreign Office and the intelligence services. The overriding consideration in Whitehall was the need to ensure that Churchill's memoirs were in harmony with the interests of Britain's Cold-War defence and foreign policies. *The Second World War* was therefore a semi-official history and, with Attlee's blessing, an exercise in post-war consensus.

To assist him in writing the book Churchill gathered together a team of researchers, who became known as "the Syndicate." The principal members were William Deakin, an Oxford historian, General Pownall, who had been Mountbatten's Chief of Staff in Burma, and Commodore Allen, a senior naval officer. Surprisingly, perhaps, the drafts and memoranda they prepared, together with materials supplied by Brook, Ismay and others, have been preserved in abundance in the Churchill papers. Having gone through the materials with a fine toothcomb Reynolds is able to show that Churchill's advisers and assistants wrote many parts of the book. The tone, structure and overall interpretation were unmistakeably Churchillian and so too were many of the set pieces and personal recollections, but it would have come as a great surprise to readers at the time to learn that the passages on the emergence of Hitler, the evacuation from Dunkirk, the rise of Japan, the Dieppe raid, the war in Burma, and numerous other topics, had been written by others. Furthermore the ghost writers soon acquired the habit of writing in the first person singular and imitating Churchill's style. Seven pages on the tensions between Churchill and Cripps over the machinery of defence policy in the autumn of 1942 were actually the work of Norman Brook. "My long experience in these matters," Brook made Churchill say, "had taught me that a Minister of Defence must work with and through responsible advisers."

In retrospect Churchill's method of organising and leading a collective project looks perfectly sensible, and Reynolds argues that it does not diminish his standing as an author. But the impact of the book has always owed a great deal to Churchill's apparent mastery of military history, and the illusion of a literary genius composing every word. Though the book still ranks as one of Churchill's most remarkable achievements, Reynolds's analysis deals another blow to the Churchill myth of the forties and fifties.

"History will say that the Right Honourable Gentleman is wrong in this matter," Churchill is alleged to have said after an argument with Baldwin in the House of Commons. "I know it will, for I shall write the history." He did indeed write the history and more to the point he got his version in first. With Roosevelt dead and Stalin keeping his secrets, he was the only one of the allied war leaders in a position to give an authoritative account of the "Grand Alliance." On the British side his only possible competitors were Eden, who lagged behind in the race, and Alanbrooke, who was spurred into action too late to halt the mighty juggernaut in its tracks. Churchill stamped his interpretation of the Second World War on the minds of a generation and even now British historians find it hard to know exactly what to make of the Churchill version. Reynolds has given us, for the first time, the technical and intellectual resources we need for a detached historical assessment.

He takes us through *The Second World War* volume by volume, explaining the circumstances in which each was written, the ways in which Churchill interpreted and manipulated the evidence, and his motives for doing so. We see the war Churchill waged, in parallel with the war as he reconstructed it, and the war as historians understand it today. Churchill, of course, was driven by a desire to vindicate himself before history. "He was trying," Reynolds writes, "to shift perceptions of himself from the man of words to the man of deeds." One of the most interesting of his discoveries is the extent to which Churchill was plagued by doubts that surfaced in early drafts but were subsequently deleted. The first of his volumes, *The Gathering Storm*, gave a highly distorted and partisan account of the 1930s which reflected the prevalence of the "guilty men" thesis, Churchill's bitterness at his exclusion from office, and the failure of Baldwin and Chamberlain's biographers to mount a robust defence of their subjects. In one of the early drafts, however, Churchill admitted his "incredible neglect" of the tank in the 1930s: "In my conscience I reproach myself for having allowed my concentration upon the Air and the Navy to have absorbed all my thought." In the first draft of his account of the Norway campaign of April 1940 he wrote: "It was a marvel—I really do not know how—I survived and maintained my position in public esteem while all the blame was thrown on poor Mr. Chamberlain." Also revealing are the wartime documents Churchill omitted from the record, though the reasons why are sometimes a puzzle. Why, for example, did he exclude his minute about the bombing of Auschwitz? And was it from a sense of guilt, or mere political expediency, that he gave so little space to the strategic bombing offensive, and deleted references to "terror bombing"?

In Command of History is a work as nuanced and complex as the text it analyses, but lucid and fascinating throughout. Nothing in the book conveys the complexities better than Reynolds's analysis of the Anglo-American dimensions, on which he writes with exceptional authority. Churchill was a fervent believer in the concept of the "special relationship" and his book was intended to demonstrate the need for closer Anglo-American co-operation in the post-war world. But Anglo-American relations had been troubled by a number of contentious issues including American hostility to the British Empire. Churchill was also under attack in the United States from writers who claimed that he had been opposed to a cross-Channel invasion and had fought hard to delay or prevent the opening of a Second Front. He was trying, therefore, to defend himself against his American critics, but he also had a case to make against Roosevelt, Truman and Eisenhower. Writing as the Cold War intensified, he sought to show that he had been more far-sighted about the Soviet threat than American policy-makers, whom he blamed for allowing the Red Army to enter Berlin, Prague and Vienna before the British and the Americans. But Churchill could not afford to offend Truman, who remained President until 1952, or his successor, Eisenhower. It was a measure of Churchill's skill in the handling of so much dynamite that he managed in *The Second World War* to assert his own claims while maintaining cordial relations with the Washington

Establishment—and marketing the book in the United States. He could only achieve this, however, by practising some economy with the truth. In particular his claims to have been a consistent supporter of a cross-Channel invasion were misleading. In October 1944, we learn, Churchill and the Chiefs of Staff came close to abandoning operation Overlord. Churchill even set out a dream-like scenario for a British strategy independent of the Americans.

It is hard not to feel some sympathy for Churchill as Reynolds, with his mastery of the sources and the historiography, deconstructs chapter after chapter with a rigorous audit of the great man's errors, omissions and spin-doctoring techniques. I had the impression at times that Churchill was always manipulating the evidence or getting it wrong. Reynolds, for example, comments that Churchill paid little attention to the eastern front, neglecting the crucial role played by the Red Army in the achievement of victory. But Churchill's main theme, following the thread of his minutes and telegrams, was the British war effort. His mistake was to expand what were essentially his war memoirs into a history of the war as a whole and to do so in a half-hearted fashion in which the eastern front—like America's war in the Pacific—was dealt with in perfunctory fashion.

Reynolds does acknowledge that *The Second World War* possessed substance as well as spin, but he could perhaps have given the substance greater emphasis. Churchill's book was Anglocentric, egocentric, and artfully constructed. Nevertheless his six volumes, published at intervals between 1948 and 1954, represented a quantum leap in historical knowledge. There was much selection and editing of the documents, but Churchill also published in complete and original form a wealth of primary source materials that would otherwise never have been available to historians until the 1970s. If Churchill commanded history, it was partly because of this extraordinarily bold act which ran clean contrary to Whitehall traditions of secrecy, and opened up his record to critical scrutiny. Churchill has often been accused of publishing his minutes and telegrams without publishing the replies. Here Reynolds does come to his aid by pointing out that Attlee discouraged Churchill from publishing documents written by other officials, especially the Chiefs of Staff.

"These six volumes," wrote J.H. Plumb in 1969, "require the most careful assessment, and one not yet made: soon, however, the scholars must get to work, and what a task they will have!" In spite of Plumb's injunction, Churchill the writer and historian has been comparatively neglected, while Churchill the statesman has been intensively researched and debated. David Reynolds has redressed the balance in a work of superb scholarship which has now received the recognition it deserves with the award of the Wolfson Prize.

REVIEW 2

THE GOOD FIGHT: BATTLE OF BRITAIN PROPAGANDA AND THE FEW

by

GARRY CAMPION

London: Palgrave Macmillan, 2010

Paperback, 358 pages. £18.99. ISBN 978-0-230-27996-4

In the seventy years since it was fought scores of books have been written about the Battle of Britain. It might have seemed impossible to produce, at this late stage, a thoroughly original contribution to the literature, but this is exactly what Garry Campion has achieved. Taking a leaf from the cultural historians, he shifts the focus from the military realities in the air to their presentation by the media on the ground. His book is an exploration of the Battle as projected to the public through the press, the radio, the cinema, books, magazines, periodicals and the work of war artists.

The Battle, he argues, was not only a military victory for the RAF, but a no less decisive victory in the propaganda war. It sustained the morale of the British through the critical period in which they fought on 'alone' against Nazi Germany, and also helped to swing American opinion in favour of sending aid to Britain. The argument hinges, of course, on definitions of the term 'propaganda'. Indelibly associated with the shameless lies and fabrications of autocratic regimes, it is no less characteristic of liberal democracies, where it often appears in more subtle guise as a carefully crafted presentation of aspects of the truth. As defined by Campion it is therefore an umbrella term covering a diversity of phenomena: 'the organised, systematic dissemination or projection of a given doctrine, information or allegations to assist, promote or injure a cause, government or movement'. In Whitehall officials shied away from the term and preferred to speak of news, information or publicity. But as Campion sees it they were propagandists all the same, magnifying the Battle and glorifying the fighter pilots in the interests of sustaining popular morale.

True, but the point is a subtle one. In the case of the Battle of Britain the dividing line between substance and spin was often blurred or invisible. Campion, who knows his military history, recognises that the RAF won a victory of great strategic importance, obstructing Hitler's invasion plans and compelling him eventually to fight a war on two fronts. The Battle therefore deserved the headlines it received and the fighter pilots were genuine heroes whose daring and courage may well have saved the nation. It was a rare case of a great historical event in which propaganda worked mainly with, rather than against, the grain of the truth.

At the level of official propaganda, the Ministry of Information played second fiddle to the Air Ministry. Adastral House (the Ministry's headquarters on Kingsway) had got by with a single press officer between the wars, but in March 1940 a Directorate of Public Relations (DPR) was established under Air Commodore Harald Peake. Divided into eleven specialised branches—PR1 dealing with film, PR2 with the press, PR3 with pamphlets, PR4 with broadcasting and so on—its staff increased from 19 in May 1940 to 37 in January 1941. Campion's end-notes bear witness to exhaustive research in the Ministry's files but no record of the day-to-day activities of the DPR survives and it is not clear how far its expansion was due to pressures of demand from the press and the BBC, and how far to empire-building on the part of Peake and his staff. Its precise role is therefore not always clear, but it was certainly active and enterprising.

Churchill immortalised the fighter pilots of the Battle of Britain in a famous tribute: 'Never in the field of human conflict was so much owed by so many to so few'. But the heroic imagery of 'the few' which appeared in newspapers and magazines was mainly the work of Air Ministry photographers. Campion, an acute observer of the visual evidence, speculates that a famous poster depicting five aircrew, of whom only two were pilots, was a deliberate attempt to align the RAF with the 'people's war': 'The poster is strongly at odds with the public school educated, Spitfire flying, derring-do junior officer perceived by many to represent the Few in the post-war years'. He is very informative, too, about the Air Ministry's insistence on photographing pilots in combat-ready attire, complete with helmets, goggles, leather gauntlets, and silk scarves to prevent chafing to the neck. But, he observes, only about 4% sported the handlebar moustache traditionally associated with pilots.

Campion credits the Air Ministry with two major propaganda coups. After every air battle they issued a communiqué giving the number of British and German aircraft shot down. In almost every case the Luftwaffe were said to have suffered greater losses than the RAF and the figures were then repeated by the press and the BBC. Not until after the war was it discovered, from the German sources, that the number of enemy aircraft destroyed had frequently been exaggerated. The RAF's figures were based on the debriefing of pilots and there is no reason to believe they were fabricated, but air battles were chaotic and confusing and errors crept in. An enemy aircraft might be reported as destroyed when it had in fact escaped, or multiple claims to a 'kill' recorded when only one aircraft had been shot down. And as Campion argues, some deception *was* involved. The Air Ministry knew that the statistics were problematic and a secret internal assessment in September concluded that the true figure was about 50% of the total claimed—but no hint of this was communicated to the public at the time. The press and the BBC stifled whatever doubts they might have had and reported the 'cricket scores' as though they were matters of fact. In the first weeks of the Battle Home Intelligence detected some scepticism among the public about the claims, but fortunately for the Air Ministry it gradually became apparent that Fighter Command was gaining the upper hand and the figures won general acceptance.

Facts were sometimes the best propaganda of all. In the south of England enemy aircraft were shot down in full view of spectators on the ground, and schoolboys collected fragments of the wreckage strewn among the fields. Campion cites a widely published cartoon of September 1940 depicting two men in a country lane. One asks for directions and the other replies: 'Go down the lane past the Messerschmidt, bear left and keep on past the two Dorniers, then turn sharp right and it's just past the first Junkers'. As yet, however, 'Battle of Britain' was a nebulous expression that referred to a series of air battles with no agreed chronology or narrative, and no authoritative assessment of its significance. It was the Air Ministry that shaped the Battle into a story with a beginning, a middle and an end, and the claim to be one of the decisive battles of world history.

The Ministry's Air Historical Branch commissioned Hilary St George Saunders, a World War One veteran, successful novelist and member of the Public Relations Directorate, to write a short history of the Battle. An Oxford historian, Albert Goodwin, was enlisted to do the basic research, but Saunders was given full access to the records, supplemented by interviews with combatants. The outcome was a 32-page, text-only pamphlet published in March 1941. 'The pamphlet's structure and headings', writes Campion, 'confirmed the Air Ministry's determination to seize the initiative, define its version of events, maximise the propaganda opportunities and enhance the reputation of the RAF.' Appearing at a time when the British were desperately short of good news, it sold a million copies, followed by an illustrated edition that sold another half million, and a Puffin edition for children. Like Churchill in his war memoirs, the Air Ministry laid hands on the title-deeds of history, and once in possession they kept a firm grip on them. When post-war historians began to research the Battle of Britain they were unable to obtain the official records, which were closed under a 50-year rule. But they were briefed and guided, and supplied with much inside information, by the Air Ministry's Historical Branch.

In spite of their flair for public relations the staff of the Air Ministry were still in some ways reluctant propagandists. They displayed no enthusiasm for documentary or feature films about the Battle. 'It is possible', Campion writes, 'that the RAF believed—unofficially—that the fighter boys enjoyed more than enough attention as it was, without the need to yet further aggravate relations between Fighter and Bomber Command.' Not until September 1941 did the RAF establish a Film Production Unit, and its coverage of the Battle of Britain was confined to an eight-minute feature produced in 1945. It was the newsreels, the Ministry of Information's Crown Film Unit, and the commercial cinema, that put the fighter pilot on the screen.

There was also an RAF tradition of hostility to cults of personality. It was the press that identified the 'air aces'—pilots credited with five or more 'kills'—and turned them into celebrities who stood out from the otherwise anonymous ranks of 'the few'. The Air Ministry also tried at first to ensure the anonymity of memoirs by fighter pilots: hence the publication of Brian Lane's *Spitfire* (1942) under the name of 'B.J. Ellan'. If they did not prevent airmen from publishing they did not encourage it either. Richard Hillary's *The Last Enemy* (1943) was the work of a pilot who happened also to be an ambitious self-publicist of great literary ability.

In his concentration on the events of 1940, Campion appears to have overlooked an instructive episode that occurred in July 1942. Richard Peck, the Assistant Chief of Air Staff in charge of publicity, wrote to Sir Archibald Sinclair, the Secretary for Air, recommending that victory in the Battle of Britain should be celebrated on 15 September, the anniversary of the greatest of the air battles over London. The Vice-Chief of Air Staff, Wilfred Freeman, commented with more than a touch of sarcasm:

> The historical precedents for self-congratulatory celebrations in the middle of a war are not very happy. Belshazzar held a banquet while the enemy were outside his gate: he lost his throne the same night.

> [...] The so-called Battle of Britain consisted of a series of successful defensive operations by Fighter Command. It is true that the RAF then saved this country from defeat, but in my view it is a misuse of words to refer to "our victory" or "our deliverance". Victories can only be won by offensive action; and deliverance must be permanent to give much cause for junketing.

This exchange of views took place during a prolonged phase of military disasters in which the Battle of Britain remained the only great victory the British could celebrate. Nevertheless Churchill in the House of Commons rejected a proposal to designate 15 September as 'Air Trafalgar Day', and the Battle was commemorated mainly by services of thanksgiving. No representative of the RAF attended the service in Westminster Abbey. Had the Battle, perhaps, already served its purpose? But if so, why was Battle of Britain Day perpetuated, with the enthusiastic support of the Air Ministry, from 1943 onwards?

The reports of Home Intelligence for the summer and autumn of 1940 tend to confirm the view that the Battle of Britain revived and sustained popular morale after the fall of France. Campion is persuasive in arguing that without the combined efforts of the Air Ministry, the press and the BBC (on which he is also very good) the public would not have appreciated the significance of the struggle or the magnitude of the victory. What remains obscure is the internal politics of the Air Ministry, where there were clearly differences of opinion over the extent to which the RAF should engage in types of propaganda that some saw as vulgar and distasteful, tensions between the interests of Fighter and Bomber Commands, and changes of policy. We are also bound to wonder how far the publicity generated by the Air Ministry was part of another propaganda war altogether: a war against the Admiralty and the War Office. The records, of course, always leave much unsaid, and mysteries that will never be resolved, but Campion's rigorous and scholarly analysis takes us as close to the truth as we are ever likely to get.

REVIEW 3

CHURCHILL: LE DICTIONNAIRE

by

ANTOINE CAPET

Paris: Perrin 2018

29€, paperback. 862 pages. ISBN 978-2262065355.

Churchill's career as a statesman was so full of dramatic events as to resemble a history of the world in the first half of the twentieth century. Add the fact that he was also a prolific author, journalist, and orator, a human being of almost infinite variety, and the subject of a vast body of literature, and we have on our hands a severe case of information overload. The official biography, a superbly researched chronicle in eight volumes, records Churchill's life in astonishing detail from day to day, but the narrative moves ponderously forward like a juggernaut, crushing historical analysis beneath its wheels. Many historians, of course, have explored particular facets of the great man's life: 'Churchill and the Dardanelles', 'Churchill and the Jews' and so on. Numerous controversies rumble on in scattered and separate fashion. All in all it is a very confusing scene, but help is at hand. Professor Capet has compiled an encyclopaedia of Churchill in which narrative and chronology, together with all the key themes, topics and controversies, have been gathered into a single volume.

Rejecting a purely alphabetical scheme, the author has organised the material into sixteen thematic sections:

I	Enfance et Scolarité
II	Famille
III	Constitution Physique et Mentale
IV	Convictions, Schémas Mentaux et Préjugés
V	Goûts et Loisirs
VI	Lieux de Résidence
VII	Churchill Officier
VIII	Carrière Politique
IX	Controverses et Querelles Politiques
X	Churchill et le Monde Extérieur
XI	Churchill Homme de Lettres
XII	Titres, Distinctions Honorifiques et Décorations
XIII	Amis et Adversaires Politiques
XIV	Autres Cercles
XV	Milieux Militaires
XVI	Lieux de Mémoire

Each section is then broken down into numerous sub-topics. The basics are here: a list of every election he contested and the votes cast, a timeline of all the allied conferences he attended in World War Two, a guide to the many decorations and distinctions he received. Most of the book, however, consists of lucid and cogent essays on every kind of topic, and concise biographies of a huge cast of characters.

As the content headings indicate, the book strikes an excellent balance between the great man's private and public lives. Professor Capet has made himself an expert on such topics as Churchill's love of animals, his clothes and his tailors, his tastes in food and drink, the villas where he liked to stay in France. Press lords, playwrights, actors and movie moguls, painters and sculptors, publishers and editors, valets and secretaries, all appear in cameo roles as cronies, courtiers and servants in the Churchill entourage. His marriage to Clementine, and the troubled lives of three of their children—Randolph, Sarah and Diana—are sensitively treated.

A Channel 4 documentary in the UK, screened in March 2018, caused a brief sensation with the claim, supported by fresh evidence in the shape of a taped interview given late in life by Churchill's former private secretary, Sir John Colville, that Churchill had an affair in the 1930s with Doris Castlerosse. This was news to most of us but Capet, who cannot have known of the Colville tape, was already aware of the alleged affair and had written an entry on Castlerosse for the *Dictionnaire*. He accepts that Churchill, who painted four portraits of her, was under the spell of her beauty, but suspects that rumours of an affair were ill-founded. He is right to be sceptical. Colville, who never met Churchill before 1939, may simply have been repeating a well-worn piece of gossip.

The lion's share of the book is rightly devoted to Churchill's public life. Capet summarises his activities in the various offices he held, and the campaigns he waged from the backbenches. From this core narrative readers can branch off to explore related topics. For Churchill's term as First Lord of the Admiralty (1911–1915), see also 'Dardanelles'. For his role as Leader of the Opposition (1945–1951), see also 'Churchill et la construction européenne'. The other great resource for readers is Capet's gallery of biographical portraits. Recognising that politics at the top was (and still is) about the rivalries and manoeuvres of a handful of leading personalities, he is an acute observer of the attitudes of men like Bonar Law or Neville Chamberlain to Churchill, and the reasons why he inspired so little trust. Until Churchill himself solved the problem by winning the premiership, successive Prime Ministers had to weigh up the trouble he would cause if he were out of the Cabinet against the trouble he would cause if he were in it. The *Dictionnaire* is excellent on his political contemporaries, but many of his top civil service advisers like Edward Troup at the Home Office or Oscar Niemeyer at the Treasury, are absent. Doubtless this is due to the fact that they were always shadowy figures in the background, but they deserve to be included.

The *Dictionnaire* is like a globe that spins around to display the many different facets of Churchill's world. In a remarkable sequence of essays in section 10, Capet traces his relationships with Ireland, India, the white Dominions, the United States, Germany, Belgium, Spain, France, Greece and the Balkans, Italy, Japan, the Netherlands, Scandinavia, Poland, Portugal, Russia, Switzerland, Czechoslovakia and Turkey. The geographical tour is followed by biographical sketches of no fewer than 64 leading imperial and foreign statesmen, including Hitler, Mussolini, Roosevelt, Stalin and de Gaulle.

In international relations Churchill claimed to be a realist acting cold-bloodedly in the national interest, but his approach to foreign affairs was always entangled with personal sentiments. Capet devotes key passages to Churchill's love affair with France, his faith in the 'special relationship' between Britain and the United States, and his sympathy with Jews and Zionism. In all three cases Churchill's policies were sometimes influenced by his sentiments, but there were often times when circumstances compelled him to override them. The consequent ambiguities in his position can be traced through Capet's entries on Roosevelt, de Gaulle, Weizmann and others.

One of the virtues of the book is the freedom it gives the reader to jump from one topic to another in any direction curiosity dictates. It is but a short step from the entry on France to the subject of his first motor car, a French vehicle with a French chauffeur, his friendship with Odette Pol-Roger, and his love of the Côte d'Azur. There is indeed a strong emphasis on his relations with France, and it is tempting to conclude that they were deeper and more intimate than his relations with the United States.

Churchill's life as a soldier, strategist and war leader receives the substantial treatment it deserves. Having written a biography of Field Marshal Montgomery, the author was well prepared to tackle the controversial question of Churchill's dealings with his generals, and his conflicts with Alanbrooke, the head of the Army and chairman of the Chiefs of Staff Committee from March 1942. In his war memoirs, Capet writes, Churchill perpetuated a legend of himself as 'un grand chef de guerre omniscient et infaillible qui avait tout prévu, tout facilité, tout organisé, et enfin tout réussi, sauf quand les piètres stratèges américains ou les malfaisants manipulateurs soviétiques avaient entravé ses plans'. The Alanbrooke diaries, published in two volumes in 1956 and 1959, revealed Churchill in an altogether different light as a hot-headed amateur strategist whose repeated demands for peripheral operations had to be stoutly resisted. In fact, as Capet observes, Churchill and Alanbrooke were agreed on the fundamentals of British strategy. And however fraught their relations might be, they managed to work together in a partnership that proved essential to the conduct of the war.

In a work of 862 pages there are likely to be factual mistakes, but I could only find two. Firstly Churchill was not, as the author claims, in the front rank of those who denounced the Hoare-Laval pact of December 1935. He was away on holiday when the crisis broke and stayed out of the country in the vain hope that Baldwin would restore him to office. Secondly Churchill did not make Attlee deputy Prime Minister in May 1940 but in February 1942. No matter. A more serious problem is the frustrating omission of source references for the many fine quotations that punctuate the text.

The final section of the book is devoted to sites of memory such as Harrow School, or the Churchill Archives Centre in Cambridge. In one respect, however, memory is conspicuous by its absence. Capet discusses the films that have been made about Churchill, but not the books that have been written about him. He examines a number of controversial episodes in Churchill's career but makes no mention of the historians involved. When John Charmley argued that Churchill should have entered into negotiations with Hitler in 1940, a terrific furore ensued, but the *Dictionnaire* passes over the affair in silence. In addition to Charmley, Martin Gilbert, Robert Rhodes James, David Reynolds and Roy Jenkins would all be worth discussing as leading figures in the historiography of Churchill.

How to sum up? In the introduction to the *Dictionnaire* Capet explains that it contains no new facts. Nor, for that matter, does it have a new or startling thesis to propose. In a broad sense Capet is in line with the prevailing school of thought among British historians, who think of Churchill as a great war leader with feet of clay, or as Attlee put it, 'half genius and half bloody fool'. The *Dictionnaire* is, however, a magnum opus and a major landmark in Churchill studies: the first comprehensive and critical guide to every aspect of his life and times. It is a prodigious feat of intellect and hard work. It emancipates readers by handing them the keys to scores of Churchillian themes and topics. It is written with meticulous attention to detail, and a mastery of the subject reflected in a sparkling stream of insights and reflections. It is deeply serious for long stretches but great fun at intervals. *C'est magnifique.*

REVIEW 4

THE END IS NIGH: BRITISH POLITICS, POWER, AND THE ROAD TO THE SECOND WORLD WAR

by

Robert Crowcroft

Oxford University Press, 2019
$34.99, 304 pages, ISBN 978-0198823698

PORTRAIT OF A BENIGN BALDWIN AND A BOGUS CHURCHILL

The history of appeasement culminated in a struggle for power between two mighty personalities: Neville Chamberlain and Winston Churchill. In 1940 Churchill was victorious, establishing his reputation as the prophet who had been right all along about Nazi Germany. Chamberlain, like almost everyone else, had been wrong. Today the picture is more complex. Churchill still has robust defenders, but his record is constantly under attack. Some historians go all or part of the way to justifying Chamberlain's actions. Robert Crowcroft brings a new and unusual kind of revisionism to bear on the debate.

In seeking to demolish Chamberlain and Churchill alike, Crowcroft argues firstly that both were self-serving politicians, and secondly that neither had the vision to save the British Empire in its hour of need.

There is no irony in Crowcroft's description of himself as a cynic. He is cynical about the history of democracy, which, he maintains, has always been a system steeped in humbug and manipulated by politicians selling bogus promises and wishful thinking. At the level of high politics, where the struggle for power was at its most intense, politicians were compulsive opportunists. They sought power for its own sake, and exploited—or fabricated—public issues in the service of personal rivalries.

BALDWIN?

In spite of this, Crowcroft's tale has a hero, albeit unlikely. Stanley Baldwin, in the author's view, was the most benign operator of the system and the architect of a tranquillising era of Conservative ascendancy. Baldwin created a reassuring ethos of moderate conservatism, conciliatory to the working class but appealing to the high-minded followers of Liberalism. Thus he tamed the forces of democracy and prevented them from degenerating into class and ideological conflict.

Alas Baldwin lost control of events. When Italy attacked Abyssinia in 1935, he courted liberal sentiment by staging a general election on a platform of upholding the principles of the League of Nations. His more serious objective was to win popular support for rearmament. But his pledge to support the League was rapidly exposed as hollow by the Hoare-Laval Pact.

Baldwin was all but swept away in the storm of outrage that followed. Although he clung to office and subsequently redeemed his reputation by skilfully handling the Abdication crisis, the age of Baldwin was over. Foreign policy was now central to the competition for power at home, enabling the government's opponents to turn popular sentiment against the dictators into a formidable political weapon.

COWLINGITE HISTORY

Crowcroft's revisionism owes much to the work of the late Maurice Cowling, the cantankerous historian whose reactionary imagination enlivened a trilogy of works on the history of British democracy, of which The Impact of Hitler was the most controversial. Cowling spoke for a dissident strand of Tory opinion in which the Second World War featured as a disaster that put an end to the social and imperial order of the interwar years, and the "Churchill myth" as a romantic fiction concealing the reality of a major British defeat.

In Cowlingite history, Churchill was an irresponsible adventurer whose gambles at the roulette wheel finally paid off when he staked a last despairing bet on Hitler. Chamberlain, meanwhile, was a sound enough conservative whose diplomacy was sabotaged by his Foreign Secretary, Lord Halifax, who sacrificed appeasement in the interests of saving the Conservatives from Labour. Unlike Cowling, whose literary style was dry and intractable, Crowcroft is a fluent narrator who conducts us along the road to war in buoyant and spirited fashion. I fear he also leads us astray.

Inside every statesman is a politician with a politician's bag of tricks. So it was with Chamberlain and Churchill. Crowcroft, however, diminishes them both by reducing their ambitions and policies to self-serving power plays. Churchill, he argues, deliberately stoked up a quarrel with Baldwin over India in order to seize control of the Conservative party. Perhaps he was trying to seize control, but he was also passionate about the issues at stake and carrying the torch handed on to him by his close friend and ally Lord Birkenhead, the Secretary for India from 1925 to 1929.

Birkenhead feared that a future Labour government would surrender the "Jewel in the Crown" to Gandhi and the Congress Party. In order to pre-empt the decision, he set up a commission under Sir John Simon with a mandate to propose a strictly limited programme of constitutional change. Churchill was happy to endorse the Simon Report but horrified when Baldwin abandoned it in favour of a declaration by the Viceroy Lord Irwin (later Lord Halifax), in favour of ultimate Dominion status for India. The bitterness of the personal quarrel between Churchill and Baldwin ought not to distract attention from the very real substance of the differences between them. Anyone who doubts the passion lurking in Churchill's breast should examine his record on India between 1940 and 1945.

THE TRUTH OF THE MATTER

Churchill was no more in favour of appeasing nationalism in Germany than nationalism in India. Crowcroft treats his demands for rearmament and collective security as transparent bids for office by a politician who was out and wanted to be in. In fact, Churchill sought office in order to make history. Who can doubt that had he been Prime Minister in September 1938, Britain would have gone to war to stop Hitler? His actions when at last he won the premiership were entirely consistent with the messages he had been delivering since 1933.

As for Chamberlain, Crowcroft claims that his initial realism was overwhelmed by an overweening vanity that led him to adopt a course of diplomatic activism when he should have had the wisdom to leave well enough alone. Britain, he asserts, had no vital interests at stake in central and eastern Europe. The UK should have allowed Hitler to pursue his quest for Lebensraum undisturbed. In this respect, he argues, both Churchill and Chamberlain were deficient in realpolitik.

It is a paradox of the 1930s that the British began to prepare for war against Germany in 1934, while the Nazis only began to prepare for war against Britain after Munich in September 1938.

Until quite late in the day. Hitler cherished the illusion that, provided he posed no threat to the Empire, the British would raise no objection to Germany's expansion in the east.

Crowcroft likewise assumes that the core national interest of Britain lay in the preservation of the Empire. The overriding national interest, however, lay elsewhere, in the preservation of the security and independence of the British as an island people a few miles off the coast of Europe. Britain was primarily a European state, a truth brutally reinforced by the rise of air power. The British military and political elite understood that the country could never be secure if an expansionist, militarising Germany dominated the Continent. A peaceful German economic hegemony, accompanied by a general reduction in armaments, would have been a very different matter and was indeed Chamberlain's ultimate objective.

Both Churchill and Chamberlain understood that Nazi Germany was a time bomb. But whereas Chamberlain imagined that it could be defused by diplomacy, Churchill believed that it could only be defused by force, or the threat of force. When the diplomacy of appeasement failed Chamberlain was compelled to accept—albeit with the profound reluctance of a man who loathed war—that no other response was possible. In the final analysis the British Empire, which was already in decline, had to be sacrificed so that Britain itself could live.

THE AUTHOR

Professor Addison, University of Edinburgh, is the author Churchill on the Home Front and Churchill: The Unexpected Hero, both of which we recommend as singular reading.

REVIEW 5

CHURCHILL, THE LIFE: AN AUTHORISED PICTORIAL BIOGRAPHY

by

MAX ARTHUR

Cassell Illustrated, 2015
£25.00, 272 pages, ISBN 978-1844038596

Churchill's life was extraordinarily rich in visual imagery. He loved the camera and the camera loved him, as did cartoonists and portrait painters. His face exhibited a range of deep emotions that others preferred to conceal behind a stiff upper lip. His eccentricities of dress and theatrical gestures were the work of a great actor who could play Falstaff one day and Henry V the next. It is no wonder that his life has always lent itself to pictorial treatment, nor that so many photographs and portraits of him have achieved iconic status over the past fifty years. Most readers of *Finest Hour* will therefore probably be familiar with the majority of pictures in Max Arthur's new compilation. He has, however, been at pains to vary the menu by including a number of hitherto unpublished pictures together with reproductions of original documents and a bonus item: specially commissioned shots of such Churchill memorabilia as his gramophone record of *HMS Pinafore*. He has also embedded the pictures, which are beautifully produced, in the text of a brief biography.

Arthur is best known as an oral historian collecting the "lost voices" of soldiers, sailors, and airmen in the two world wars. He normally writes about history "from below," with little reference to Whitehall and Westminster, and his comparative lack of interest in the nuts and bolts of politics does reveal itself from time to time. He confuses Churchill's maiden speech with his subsequent attack on the government's proposals for Army reform (56). Thomas Jones was not as he claims (160) a member of Baldwin's Cabinet. There are virtually no political cartoons here, no photograph of the Churchill War Cabinet, no glimpse of the General Election of 1945. The admirals, generals, air marshals, and chiefs of staff are almost as elusive. As a chronicle of his military and political life Martin Gilbert's *Churchill: A Photographic Portrait* (1973) is more satisfactory.

Arthur puts more of an emphasis on Churchill's life beyond Whitehall and Westminster. His family life and leisure activities feature strongly. The pictures of him with Clementine and the children convey a charming if exaggerated impression of a domesticated husband and father. His painting and bricklaying, holidays and travels, polo playing, and love of animals reveal a broad hinterland of humanity that makes him easier for most of us to relate to than the Olympian statesman. As we gaze at photos of him feeding a kangaroo at the London zoo or a deer in Richmond Park, it is easy to forget that this tender-hearted old gentleman was at about the same period contemplating a nuclear strike against Russia. Churchill's darker moods were rarely captured on camera. Nevertheless this fine portrait gallery captures one of the essential truths about Churchill, the protean character (to quote John Dryden) of "a man so various that he seemed to be not one, but all mankind's epitome."

NOTES ON CONTRIBUTORS

The **Right Honourable Gordon Brown** was Prime Minister of the United Kingdom and Leader of the Labour Party from 2007 to 2010. Prior to that he served as Chancellor of the Exchequer for ten years. He was educated at the University of Edinburgh and was Member of Parliament for Kirkaldy and Cowdenbeath for thirty-two years.

John Campbell is a freelance historian and political biographer. His first book, *Lloyd George: The Goat in the Wilderness*, published in 1977, arose out of Paul Addison 's final-year honours course on British politics between the wars and was essentially his Ph.D thesis, supervised by Paul and examined by A.J.P. Taylor. Since then he has written full-scale biographies of F.E. Smith (1983), Aneurin Bevan (*Nye Bevan and the Mirage of British Socialism*, 1987), Edward Heath (Winner of the 1994 NCR Book Award for Non-Fiction), Margaret Thatcher (*The Grocer's Daughter*, 2000, and *The Iron Lady*, 2003), and Roy Jenkins (*A Well-Rounded Life*, 2014), as well as *If Love Were All ... The Story of Frances Stevenson and David Lloyd George* (2006) and *Pistols at Dawn: Two Hundred Years of Political Rivalry from Pitt and Fox to Blair and Brown* (2009) and numerous book reviews and other articles and essays in various publications over the years.

Antoine Capet, Fellow of the Royal Historical Society, was Head of British Studies at the University of Rouen (France) until July 2014, when he became Emeritus. After submitting his Doctorat d'État on the British governing classes and social reform, 1931–1951 (published 1991), he continued to concentrate his research on Britain in and before the Second World War, more specifically on Churchill in recent years. His 862-page *Churchill, le dictionnaire* was published by Éditions Perrin, Paris, in January 2018. Professor Capet has been Editor of the 'Britain since 1914' section of the Royal Historical Society Bibliography since 2001 and he sat on the International Board of *Twentieth Century British History* (Oxford University Press) from 2002 to 2020.

David Freeman is editor of *Finest Hour*, the journal of the International Churchill Society. He teaches history at California State University, Fullerton. In addition to having published contributions by Paul Addison in *Finest Hour*, he once had the privilege of driving Addison across a wide stretch of Texas.

Richard M. Langworth, CBE, founded what became the International Churchill Society in 1968, was editor of *Finest Hour* for 34 years and has served as Senior Fellow of the Hillsdale College Churchill Project since 2014.

Kenneth O. Morgan, D.Litt. (Oxon.), Baron Morgan of Aberdyfi, was a close friend and academic colleague of Paul Addison since their time together in Oxford in the 1960s. He has been successively Senior Lecturer at Swansea University to 1966; Fellow and tutor of The Queen's College, Oxford, 1966–89; Vice-Chancellor of Aberystwyth University and Senor Vice-Chancellor of the University of Wales, 1989–95; and is now Acting Professor, King's College, London. His 35 books include studies of Britain 1918–22; *The Labour Government 1945–51; Wales 1880–1980; Labour People; The Oxford History of Britain* (new updated edition, 2020); *The People's Peace, British History since 1945* (updated 2020); and biographies of Keir Hardie, David Lloyd George, Lord [Christopher] Addison, James Callaghan and Michael Foot. He was elected Fellow of the British Academy in 1984, and made a Labour peer in 2000; he is doctor *Hon. Causa* of the University of Tours and member of the order of bards at the Welsh national eisteddfod. He is married to Professor Elizabeth Gibson-Morgan of the University of Poitiers and is Welsh-speaking.

James W. Muller is Professor of Political Science at the University of Alaska, Anchorage, and a by-fellow of Churchill College, Cambridge. He has edited Churchill's interwar books *Thoughts and Adventures and Great Contemporaries* (ISI Books, 2009 and 2012) and his early book *The River War: An Historical Account of the Reconquest of the Soudan*, 2 vols. (St. Augustine's Press, 2020). He served for some years with Paul Addison on the Board of Academic Advisers of the International Churchill Society.

Paul contributed a chapter to his edited book *Churchill as Peacemaker* (Cambridge University Press, 1997) and was featured speaker at a summer institute for teachers, funded by the US National Endowment for the Humanities, which Muller directed at Churchill College, Cambridge, and William Goodenough College, London.

Richard Overy, Fellow of the British Academy, Fellow of the Royal Historical Society, is Professor of History at the University of Exeter. He has written extensively on the Second World War, air power and British history in the age of world war. He collaborated with Paul Addison on events launched by the Second World War Centre in Edinburgh, including the conference and subsequent volume on the bombing of Dresden, and the workshop and volume on the Battle of Britain. He is currently completing a major global study of the Second World War for publication in 2021.

Roland Quinault has been Honorary Secretary of the Royal Historical Society and Reader in History at London Metropolitan University. He is currently a Senior Research Fellow at the Institute of Historical Research, University of London. He has mainly focused on the earlier career of Winston Churchill, whereas Paul initially studied Churchill's later career. He asked Paul to be the lead speaker at the Royal Historical Society conference on Winston Churchill in the Twenty-First Century, the proceedings of which were published in 2004.

Richard Toye is Professor of Modern History at the University of Exeter. He is a specialist in the history of modern Britain and is the author of numerous articles and several books, including *Rhetoric: A Very Short Introduction* (Oxford University Press, 2013) and *The Roar of the Lion: The Untold Story of Churchill's World War II Speeches* (Oxford University Press 2013). He is the editor of *Winston Churchill: Politics, Strategy and Statecraft* (Bloomsbury Academic, 2017), to which Paul Addison contributed a chapter on 'Churchill and Women'.